ISANDLWANA

D1374414

ISANDLWANA

How the Zulus Humbled the British Empire

Adrian Greaves

Pen & Sword
MILITARY

First published in Great Britain in 2011,
reprinted in 2013 and republished in this format in 2014 by
PEN & SWORD MILITARY
An imprint of
Pen & Sword Books Ltd
47 Church Street
Barnsley
South Yorkshire
S70 2AS

Copyright © Adrian Greaves, 2011, 2013, 2014

ISBN 978 1 78346 262 9

The right of Adrian Greaves to be identified as Author of
this work has been asserted by him in accordance with the
Copyright, Designs and Patents Act 1988.

A CIP catalogue record for this book is
available from the British Library

All rights reserved. No part of this book may be reproduced or transmitted in
any form or by any means, electronic or mechanical including photocopying,
recording or by any information storage and retrieval system,
without permission from the Publisher in writing.

Typeset in Palatino Light by Chic Media Ltd

Printed and bound in England
By CPI Group (UK) Ltd, Croydon, CR0 4YY

Pen & Sword Books Ltd incorporates the Imprints of Pen & Sword Aviation,
Pen & Sword Family History, Pen & Sword Maritime, Pen & Sword Military,
Pen & Sword Discovery, Wharncliffe Local History, Wharncliffe True Crime,
Wharncliffe Transport, Pen & Sword Select, Pen & Sword Military Classics,
Leo Cooper, The Praetorian Press, Remember When,
Seaforth Publishing and Frontline Publishing

For a complete list of Pen & Sword titles please contact
PEN & SWORD BOOKS LIMITED
47 Church Street, Barnsley, South Yorkshire, S70 2AS, England
E-mail: enquiries@pen-and-sword.co.uk
Website: www.pen-and-sword.co.uk

Contents

Foreword

Professor Richard Holmes

I have spent my professional career visiting battlefields, and have found that each conveys its own distinct impression. Sometimes this is frustration at haunted acres swamped by the tarmac and concrete of the 20th Century: a motorway link across the southern limit of the 1645 battlefield of Naseby, and the brook near Preston where Scots and Parliamentarians met in 1648 is choked by plastic bags, bottles and supermarket trolleys. Sometimes the site has simply been over-celebrated, and has begun to sink beneath the weight of memorials, museums and commercial outlets it has to bear: Waterloo is the prime case in point. And sometimes the place exudes an almost spectral chill that makes me profoundly uneasy; I find the charnel hills around the little French town of Verdun, scene of a dreadful battle in 1916, harder and harder to bear.

My first really clear view of the sphinx-shaped mountain of Isandlwana came from the back of a horse as I rode with half a dozen companions along the little road that crosses the Buffalo River on a new bridge alongside the drift (ford) named after the trader James Rorke. Long before I reached it, the mountain's brooding presence drew me on like a magnet. We spent the evening beneath it round a blazing fire listening to the incomparable David Rattray tell the story of what had happened there on the day of the dead moon, and as I curled up to sleep I reflected , not for the first time on that trip, on the frailty of sleeping-bag zips. I was awakened from a chilly and fitful sleep by the sound and sensation of drumming, profoundly unwelcome at that time and, above all, in that place. As I crouched and looked out of my tent I saw our horses stream past.

We spent the next hour catching them, and as I scrambled about the battlefield, stumbling, from time to time, over the low whitened cairns that cover the bones of British soldiers, I came to my own accommodation with the place. The great sphinx rode triumphantly amongst the scudding clouds in what was now clear moonlight, like the prow of a mighty ship. The men who lay beneath my feet had marched the length of South Africa in their iron-heeled boots and rough red tunics. They were no strangers to night alarms, and would have had their own brusque opinions about the brain power of horses. Some, we know, had fled, meeting death from assegai or knobkerrie as they gasped terror-stricken on what was to become known as the fugitives' trail. But the majority had looked it square in the face, through the stinking clouds of smoke from their own Martini-Henry rifles; as rifle and bayonet met shield and assegai in hand-to-hand combat, and, for the remnants of one company which charged behind its commander – Zulu oral tradition remembers an Induna (officer) with a long flashing sword – taking the bayonet to their monarch's enemies as redcoats had done for a century and a half. Their spirits now held no terrors for me. I slipped back into my sleeping bag, rearranged the saddlebag that served as a pillow, and slept dreamlessly till dawn.

On 22nd January 1879 a small British army was utterly defeated by the Zulu impies at Isandlwana: it was a battle which, as Adrian Greaves shows, caused a profound shock in a Britain unused to such disasters. Of course it was not without parallel.

In 1842 a British-Indian force, including the 44th Regiment, was cut to pieces as it retreated from Kabul; a single wounded survivor rode into Jellalabad to bring news of this signal catastrophe. And in 1880 another British-Indian force was routed by the Afghans at Maiwand, where much of the 66th Regiment perished. Other colonial powers had their share of disasters, which all too often stemmed from misunderstanding their savage opponents. However, few could equal the Italian General Baratieris' defeat by the Ethiopians at Adowa in 1896 which cost him almost half his 17,000 men. But Adrian Greaves is right to observe that there was something special about Isandlwana. In part it was the suddenness of the defeat, coming so soon after the beginning of the war: in part, too, it was the totality, with six full companies of British infantry killed to a man. And in part it reflected a fatal underestimation of the Zulus in which racism unquestionably played its part.

The chief concern of Lord Chelmsford, the British commander, was that the Zulus would not fight: he was wrong in this as in much else.

Adrian Greaves' study of the battle reflects his background as an infantry officer and senior police officer, combining a soldier's feel for the ground, which he knows well, with a detective's instinct for evidence. The latter is especially important, for some details of Isandlwana have long remained obscured, and oft-repeated myth has assumed the status of fact. The process has not been helped by contemporary distortion of the evidence to ensure that Colonel Anthony Durnford, killed while fighting bravely, shouldered the blame for the defeat. Dr Greaves uses recently-discovered material to exonerate Durnford, and to suggest that the faulty disposition at Isandlwana stemmed from Lord Chelmsford's own standing orders. Perhaps the most durable myth is that which suggests that the British lost because they ran out of ammunition. Adrian Greaves comprehensively debunks this, and in doing so gives the battle its proper balance, recognising that the single most important reason for it to take the shape it did was not British command errors (though these played their baneful part) but the enormous bravery and skill of the Zulus. No cairns or monuments marked their sacrifice until the year 2000, but, as the men who fought them that day recognised all too well, they were warriors indeed.

Richard Holmes

Acknowledgements

In preparing this book, I owe a number of people my grateful thanks for their support and willingness to supply information. I am grateful to my wife Debbie for her unfailing enthusiasm. I also owe special thanks to a number of people for their encouragement, including, during the initial drafting, David and Nicky Rattray at Fugitives' Drift Lodge for their generous hospitality and, during his life, for unrestricted access to David's extensive library. I also thank Brian Best of the VC Society and Ian Knight, Dr David Payne and Ron Lock for their advice. I also acknowledge the generosity of the Anglo Zulu War Historical Society for allowing me access to their valuable records, documents and research material, and the Royal Geographical Society and the Regimental Museums and their staffs at Brecon, Deepcut, Woolwich and Chatham for their generosity in assisting my research. Any errors and interpretations are mine alone; my research conclusions are supported by primary sources and referenced to enable others to conduct further research.

I was greatly saddened to learn of the recent death of Professor Richard Holmes, acknowledged worldwide as a brilliant historian of the Victorian military. I will be eternally grateful to him for inviting me to his home in 2000 to request me to write Isandlwana. Several years ago I was lucky enough to spend a few days with him on the battlefields of Zululand and I greatly enjoyed his company and incisive observations. He became a good friend and is sorely missed.

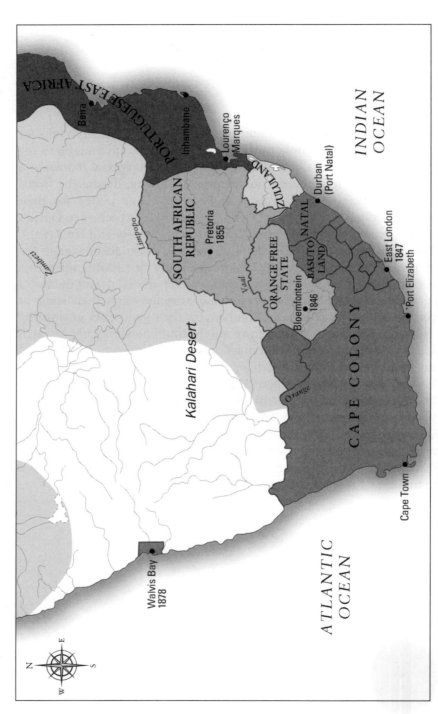

South Africa in 1878 prior to the Anglo-Zulu War

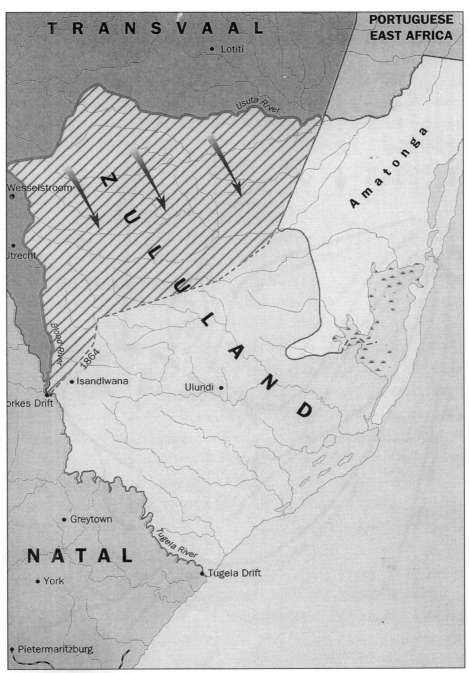

Boer encroachment into Zululand during 1877/8

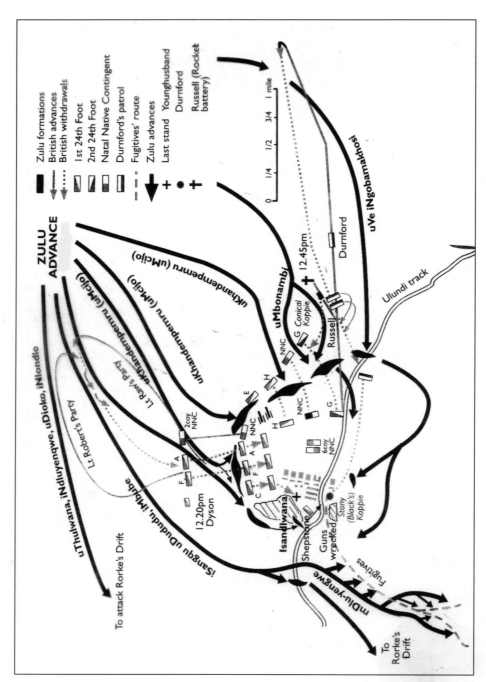

British positions and direction of Zulu attack at Isandlwana

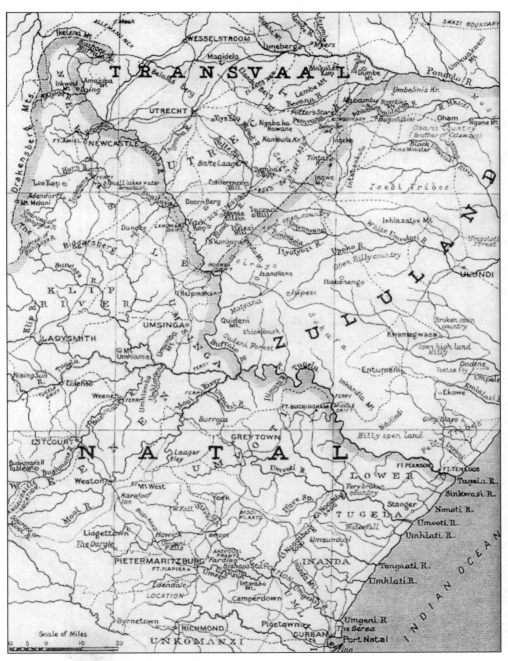

Natal, Zululand, Transvaal and the disputed area of Utrecht. (The Graphic)

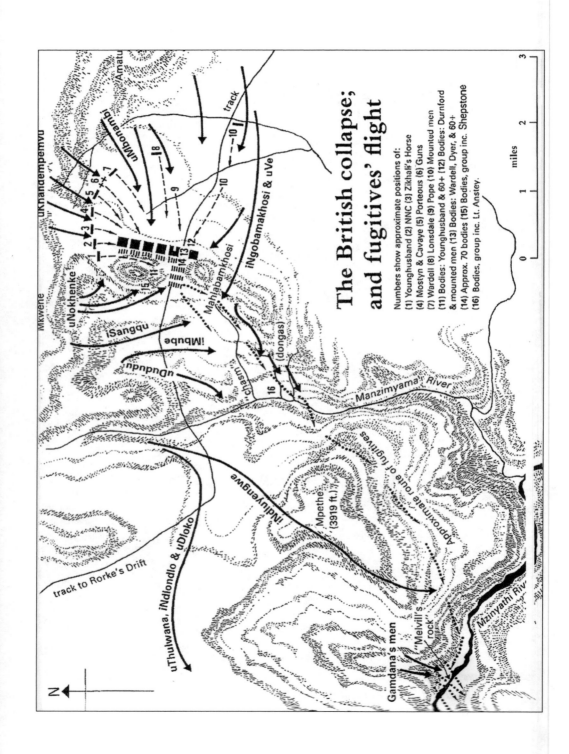

The British collapse; and fugitives' flight

Numbers show approximate positions of:
(1) Younghusband (2) NNC (3) Zikhali's Horse
(4) Mostyn & Cavaye (5) Porteous (6) Guns
(7) Wardell (8) Lonsdale (9) Pope (10) Mounted men
(11) Bodies: Younghusband & 60+ (12) Bodies: Durnford
& mounted men (13) Bodies: Wardell, Dyer, & 60+
(14) Approx. 70 bodies (15) Bodies, group inc. Shepstone
(16) Bodies, group inc. Lt. Anstey.

N

miles
0   1   2   3

Mkwene
uKhandempemvu
/Amatu
uMbonambi
track
iNgobamakhosi & uVe
uNokhenke
iSangqu
iMbube
Mahlabamkhosi
uDududu
(dongas)
chasm
Manzimyama River
track to Rorke's Drift
iNdluyengwe
Mpethe
(3919 ft.)
uThulwana, iNdlondlo & uDloko
Gamdana's men
"Melvill's rock"
Approximate route of fugitives
Mzinyathi Riv

Introduction

Disaster at Isandlwana

The terrible disaster that overwhelmed the old 24th Regiment will always be remembered, not so much as a disaster, but as an example of heroism like that of Leonidas and the three hundred Spartans who fell at the pass of Thermopylae. (1)

Between 1837 and 1901, Queen Victoria ruled the most powerful dominion in the world. During these sixty-four dynamic years, the British Empire became a realm upon which 'the sun never set', and it encompassed one fourth of the earth's land surface – arguably the richest and most powerful empire in the history of the world. During the reign of Queen Victoria, the red-jacketed British soldier was engaged in sixty-three different campaigns fighting for Queen and Country, almost one military campaign per year. Of all the conflicts, that which most seized the popular imagination proved to be the Anglo-Zulu War, partly because the war came as a complete surprise to the home government, and also because of a series of major British defeats during the first seven months of 1879. Further disaster followed with the death of the heir to the Napoleonic dynasty, the young Prince Imperial, who had volunteered to fight with the British in Zululand. Suddenly, some of Queen Victoria's over-confident regiments found themselves engaged in ferocious fighting against the most powerful and most feared of all African nations – the Zulus. The fact that the Zulus had been at peace with the British for twenty-three years, and that King Cetshwayo of the Zulus had been an ally, was ignored.

On 11 January 1879 British forces invaded Zululand; it was the beginning of a brutal campaign that was to have far-reaching repercussions. A few days later, on 22 January, the British and Zulu armies met. A ferocious battle, fought to the death of the last British soldier, took place between Zulu warriors armed primarily with spears and clubs and British soldiers equipped with modern rifles and artillery; the result was the worst defeat in the colonial history of the British army. The battle was fought at the base of a small mountain with an unusual name, Isandlwana.

ISANDLWANA

Under the command of an experienced general, Lord Chelmsford, 1,329 officers and men of the British invasion force were killed and then ritually disembowelled. Fewer than sixty whites escaped, some would say in dubious circumstances, before the Zulus arrived. Among the numerous fatalities were six fully manned companies of the famous 1st Battalion of the 24th (2nd Warwickshire) Regiment (1/24th), all destroyed to the last man. The British Army lost fifty-two officers at Isandlwana, more than it did during the three main battles of the Waterloo campaign. No battalion had ever lost so many officers in one engagement. This battle in distant Zululand was to have a numbing effect on British civilians and politicians at home, mainly because it was so inexplicable. The disaster would bring down Disraeli's government, and the defeat proved, once and for all, that neither the British Empire nor its army was invincible.

In order to understand the background to the Anglo-Zulu War, Britain's progressive foreign policy, involving confederation as a means of successfully administering her colonies, should not be overlooked. This policy is important because it directly influenced a number of complex issues that closely relate to the years immediately prior to the Anglo-Zulu War. Confederation entailed the unification of a fragmented colony, a large single territory or a collection of neighbouring territories under one central administration. With such an administration in place, a reliable and stable policy could then control economic production, and the resulting trade usually benefited Britain. Such a unified colonial area could then develop its own locally recruited military, albeit trained and supervised by British officers. This neatly solved the problem of Britain supplying and funding hugely expensive imperial garrisons in her distant colonies.

During the 1870s confederation was becoming an increasingly important factor in British foreign policy, following its successful implementation in lands as various and distant as India, Australia, the Leeward Islands and, most recently and successfully, Canada. The policy of confederation developed as a result of expensive lessons learned by Britain while administering her other colonies and lands; without imperial administration and economic policies, such responsibilities were becoming too heavy a financial burden.

With such a policy in place, most colonies flourished; they even became self-supporting and in due course generated highly profitable trade with Britain. The same system of confederation had recently been introduced

INTRODUCTION

throughout Canada under the guidance of Lord Carnarvon, then Colonial Secretary, and it is in the light of this particular success that the policy was considered, accurately or inaccurately, as the solution to the problem of uniting southern Africa's European colonies into a viable self-financing Confederation.

Other factors were also beginning to emerge which sharply focused British attention on the urgency of confederating southern Africa. In October 1867 an unexpectedly large number of diamonds were discovered at the junction of the Orange and Vaal Rivers, and the location was most inconvenient for Britain. Jurisdiction over the area was disputed between two fledgling Boer-controlled states, the Transvaal and the Orange Free State. All the while, unhindered, many thousands of prospectors headed for the district from all over the world. These hardy prospectors ignored any form of local authority, and the financial potential of further discoveries was becoming increasingly apparent from evidence that indicated the promise of even greater wealth and its associated commercial possibilities. In 1871, Britain deftly resolved the matter by annexing the whole area to the British Crown, along with the neighbouring territory of Basutoland. There was some protest from the Orange Free State administration, which nevertheless gratefully accepted £90,000 as compensation. Carnarvon then formally initiated the process of confederation by appointing Sir Bartle Frere as High Commissioner to South Africa. Lord Cadogan expressed the British parliament's view when he stated:

> Confederation will involve, we hope, self defence, which will remove the liability under which we labour of spending our blood and money upon these wretched Kaffir quarrels in South Africa. (2)

The newly-appointed High Commissioner, Sir Bartle Frere, was an experienced administrator from India whose uncompromising views on the treatment of natives who menaced imperial frontiers were well known to the Crown. Frere's Secretary of Native Affairs, Sir Theophilus Shepstone, was like-minded and favoured aggressive military intervention followed by annexation. Shepstone feared a black coalition both within and beyond southern Africa, followed by the spectre of a black uprising. He believed the most formidable of the troublesome native tribes was the Zulu kingdom ruled by King Cetshwayo. Frere and Shepstone encouraged the growing belief that King Cetshwayo's standing army of some 50,000 warriors was ready to invade the peaceful British colony of Natal. Frere and Shepstone were lucky that their views about the Zulus were shared by the Honourable Frederic Thesiger, shortly to become Lord Chelmsford following the death of his father, and recently in command of all British forces in South Africa.

The main players, political and military, believed a quick campaign would crush the savage foe; after all, the nine previous minor Cape Wars had hardly taxed the British army. When General Cunynghame handed over command to General Thesiger, he issued an order that said of the 24th Regiment:

> They have never failed to assist me; each and every duty that I have placed before them they have readily accepted and cheerfully accomplished, their excellence as marksmen bearing testimony to their good training. (3)

King Cetshwayo would quickly be obliged to understand, like all doubters before him, that Queen Victoria ruled all of Africa. In addition, the gaps in the intricate web simultaneously being woven between Briton and Boer could be mended – once the Zulu nation that threatened both communities was eradicated. The reality was very different. Ignoring the fact that the Zulus were faithful allies of the British, Chelmsford's invasion force would shortly advance with supreme confidence towards the Zulu border. Dilatoriness and lack of caution at Isandlwana were to produce the most unexpected result – the unprecedented massacre of well armed and experienced British troops.

On 22 January, under the cliffs of Isandlwana, 25,000 Zulu warriors destroyed half of Lord Chelmsford's central column, the main body of his three-pronged invasion force. (4) There was, as the title of one modern publication records, 'an awful row at home about this'. (5) Not since the sanguinary events of the Indian Mutiny in 1857 had such total and humiliating losses been reported to an incredulous British public. (6) The shock was sharper because of its total unexpectedness; for many, it was the first news that Queen Victoria's regiments were even engaged in South Africa.

Chapter 1

Conditions at Home

The sanctuary of enlistment

For those interested in the Anglo-Zulu War, the year 1879 conjures up dramatic or glorious events in South Africa and little else. Through this interest, much has been learned about the everyday life of British soldiers on campaign and the social structure of the military. Less well known are the conditions and events back home that led so many young men to enlist.

Britain in the 1870s saw widespread unemployment, poverty and endemic malnutrition. Diseases were rife, with tuberculosis, cholera, influenza, whooping cough, scarlet fever, measles, syphilis and a host of less significant infectious diseases among the major health problems of the time. By 1879 British civilian mortality rates were high, with 2.6 per cent of the population dying each year; London suffered 189 deaths from smallpox alone in January. The infant (under twelve months old) mortality rate was steady at 15.3 per cent, compared with 0.6 per cent today. Life expectancy for the working classes in Rutland and Manchester (where detailed figures were maintained) were a mere thirty-eight years and twenty-six years respectively; only the professional classes could hope to reach their mid-fifties. With surgery in its infancy, the death rate in all recorded surgical cases was nearly 50 per cent. During this age of pox and plagues, humanity remained largely powerless to prevent disease until Louis Pasteur in France and Robert Koch in Germany developed conclusive proof of the germ theory.

At home, environmental sanitation, safe water supplies, improved sewage disposal systems, pasteurisation of milk, and sanitary control of food supplies gradually resulted in the virtual disappearance of cholera and typhoid fever together with a marked reduction in diarrhoea and infant mortality. The subsequent discovery of effective vaccines would soon cause the rapid decline of such common diseases as diphtheria,

1

tetanus, whooping cough, poliomyelitis and measles. In the meantime, much of life immediately prior to 1879 was dominated by the spectre of disease.

Civilisation and syphilisation had gone hand-in-hand for five centuries, the sexually transmitted form of the disease having been imported into Spain by Columbus's sailors following their discovery of the New World and the questionable pleasures offered them by local women. The returning sailors carried the newly acquired syphilitic bacterium *Treponema pallidum* and were feted and entertained as heroes by a grateful Spanish nation. The bacteria immediately began boring into the bodies of the population, and syphilis rapidly spread across Europe to Britain. (1)

It had no regard for rank or title; royal houses infected the aristocracy while the military rapidly spread it both at home and abroad. Soldiers were, indeed, syphilis's best friends. A soldier far from home, particularly one facing possible death from an assegai or typhus, rarely bothered about sexual convention and accepted syphilis as the 'merry disease'. There was an almost total acceptance of the effects of the disease, its raging headaches, swollen joints, wart-like lesions and mouthfuls of sores and ulcers. The disease then entered a latent stage in which no outward signs or symptoms occurred, but inflammatory changes took place in the internal organs. The latent stage could last twenty to thirty years. In 75 per cent of the cases, no further symptoms appeared. When the final stage of tertiary syphilis developed, it produced hard nodules in the tissues under the skin, the mucous membranes and the internal organs. The brain and skeletal structure were frequently affected as well as the liver, kidneys and other visceral organs. Infection of the heart and major blood vessels accounted for most deaths. The widespread incidence of syphilis among the military was invariably recorded under the heading of 'other diseases'.

At the time of the Anglo-Zulu War campaign, the most ruthless killer of mankind, one in six of all deaths, was tuberculosis, more commonly referred to as 'consumption', with about 60 per cent of the population suffering its long-term effects. Tuberculosis, or *mycobacteriosis*, is as old as mankind and even today afflicts Third World countries. The germ thrives when hosts, both humans and cattle, live in squalid and overcrowded conditions and is spread by coughing and spitting, drinking contaminated milk and from contact with polluted water, grass, animal feed and soil. During the 1870s many soldiers joined the army to escape squalor and poverty at home, only to contract and then spread tuberculosis wherever they lived in the army's cramped and filthy camps; these were abundant throughout the Anglo-Zulu War.

One particular form of TB, *Scrofula*, was endemic both in the civil and military populations and was caused by sufferers spitting contaminated phlegm. In the UK scrofula was common amongst children, who frequently went barefoot and in consequence contracted the disease through the skin of their feet. This condition eventually gave rise to the familiar 'no spitting' notices that remained in public places until recent times. The only treatments at the time included surgical bloodletting, applications of phosphoric acid, ether inhalation and *digitalis* drinks. Most physicians viewed the disease with professional nihilism until Robert Koch discovered the bacillus in 1882.

Influenza was generally known at the time as 'a jolly rant', 'the new delight', 'a gentle correction' or 'the blue plague'. Because it did not disfigure the features, rot the genitals or cripple limbs, it was not generally considered to be a serious condition, especially as influenza rarely killed its victims except in the case of children or the elderly, neither of whom warranted social concern at the time. Doctors were not unduly perturbed as the condition created the *status quo* of medical perfection, of everybody ill but almost no one dying. Doctors did, however, notice that a lung from a healthy body would float in water while that of a 'flu victim would promptly sink; otherwise little medical intervention took place or was considered necessary. The several symptoms of a simple attack would have included a dry cough, sore throat, nasal obstruction and discharge from the eyes; more complex cases were characterised by chills, sudden onset of fevers, headaches, aching of muscles and joints, and occasional gastrointestinal symptoms.

Recruiting processes

All through the 1870s agriculture had been in depression, and the catastrophic harvest of 1879 caused so much damage to cereal growers that the industry never really recovered. As the Victorian essayist G.M. Young wrote, 'Never again was the landed proprietor to dominate the social fabric...The agricultural depression completed the evolution from a rural to an industrial state'. To meet the shortfall, demand for American wheat, not only in Britain but from the rest of Europe, brought prosperity to those prairie farmers who had survived years of Indian attacks, locusts, drought, fire and tornadoes. British agriculture had been in decline for some decades, and by the late 1870s only fifteen per cent of the working population were still engaged in farming. Many a growing country lad had left home to seek employment in the rapidly expanding urban areas or emigrated to the United States, Canada or Australia. There was a surge of emigration during the late 1870s, not only from Britain but also Ireland, following the worst potato harvest since the famine of 1846.

It was not only agricultural workers who were finding work hard to find. Those men employed in factories that had hitherto enjoyed a virtual monopoly in supplying products and materials to the rest of the world now found that they faced increasing competition from the United States and Germany. With the threat of sackings and lockouts, the average worker felt highly insecure. With unemployment reaching terrifying proportions, many of the unemployed and unemployable were forced, as a last resort, to enlist in the army, which offered refuge of a sort. The vast majority of recruits came from backgrounds of real squalor and wretchedness where marriage was casual and illegitimacy prevalent. Those that had survived common childhood diseases might still be suffering from bad teeth and skin disorders and have generally poor physiques. The average height of an army recruit in 1870 was 5 foot 8 inches, yet by 1879 it had dropped to an under-nourished 5 foot 4 inches. Unlike his civilian equivalent, the ordinary soldier was guaranteed to eat regularly, if not well. The meat served in the army was infamous for its poor quality. Throughout the British army in the late 1870s, boiled meat was called 'Harriet Lane' after a woman hacked to death by Henry Wainwright, a notorious murderer. Compressed biscuit, known as 'hard tack' because it was difficult to bite, was another staple food. On the march, soldiers frequently placed the biscuit in their armpits to soften it. There was a lack of vegetables, while fruit was generally regarded with suspicion.

In 1870 Parliament passed an Education Act that enabled the poor to have an elementary education, and the rise in literacy during the 1870s resulted in a small number of soldiers writing home about life on campaign. Army life closely reflected civilian society, with the officers drawn from the upper classes and having little or no contact with the working-class, non-commissioned ranks. Soldiers' letters are unique sources as they are the only indicators of what the average soldier was experiencing or thinking. A working-class civilian was less likely to put his thoughts on paper whereas a soldier, far away on campaign and able to write, would do just that.

Recruiting processes – the Queen's shilling

During the reign of Queen Victoria, Britain's army never needed conscription to fill the ranks. Civilian life was sufficiently unattractive to ensure a steady flow of recruits, and most were both hungry and jobless by the time they took the shilling – acceptance of which was considered to be a legally binding contract. Recruiting sergeants knew only too well where to look for an easy source of recruits – public houses and taverns where unemployed young men drowned their sorrows or sought camaraderie. The Cardwell reforms of the early 1870s had attempted to remove the worst excesses of the recruiting sergeants, and any recruit who could prove he had been deceived into enlisting could, theoretically, be released from duty. The recruiters, though, were skilled in the art of regaling such men with accounts of the delights of foreign service and frequently ignored the rules, especially those relating to plying potential recruits with drink.

Recruits were normally 'sworn in' before a magistrate within twenty-four hours. Those who had signed on while under the influence of alcohol could escape their responsibility by paying £1 – failing which, the recruits were medically examined before being led off to join an understrength regiment or to drafts being sent overseas. They would not necessarily join their local regiment, although by the late 1870s an increasing proportion was recruited specifically for local brigades. Such recruits came from a cross section of the working class; the one common factor was their poverty. They could not immediately expect their quality of life to improve; they would invariably get the worst of everything, the least comfortable bed, the smallest amount of food, and they would have to defer to their veteran colleagues, something which often entailed 'lending' them new kit and having to perform mundane and dirty jobs.

Many joined the army to escape unsatisfactory marriages or relationships, often enlisting under a false name. It is known that one Anglo-Zulu War Victoria Cross winner joined the army for this reason: Private 1395 John Fielding VC of the 2/24th won his medal at Rorke's Drift under the alias of Williams. Within a few months of his sudden enlistment, a certain Miss Murphy gave birth to a daughter, Annie. On the soldier's return to the UK, now with the Victoria Cross, he sought out the young lady and promptly married her. Sadly, their daughter died in her early twenties; later, a few lines appeared in the *South Wales Argus*: 'Death of Miss Fielding. Great sympathy is felt on all hands with Private John Williams (Fielding) of Rorke's Drift fame, who has just lost his eldest daughter after a long and painful illness'.

A soldier's pay was poor; from the single daily shilling various deductions were made which ensured continued poverty. Any money left over was usually spent on drink (beer was 3d a quart), or on the prostitutes who frequented garrison taverns. A soldier could have an element of his pay deducted and paid to his wife or family, although a soldier's widow could expect no help other than charity. It was not until 1881 that any form of widow's pension became payable, even for soldiers killed on active service. By the outbreak of the Anglo-Zulu War, many of the soldiers were short-service recruits with a liability for just six years' active service.

Those who were to serve in the war would have little or no idea of the overall plan or why they were fighting. They would live on rumour and hearsay, and no official attempt would be made to keep the men informed. Their ambition would be to survive, to stay dry and as comfortable as conditions would permit, to establish a supply of alcohol and generally endeavour to keep out of trouble. They would soon learn that their well-being depended on keeping a low profile, as flogging was still widespread throughout the British army even for minor infringements of discipline. The practice had been outlawed in peacetime but remained lawful on active service; indeed, no fewer than 545 soldiers would be flogged during the Anglo-Zulu War.

The British officer class
Officers were drawn from the wealthy landowning class and were generally taller and enjoyed better health. Physical defects counted for little as long as the officer was a gentleman. Sir Garnet Wolseley and General Frederick Roberts had but two eyes between them. The latter was only 5 foot 3 inches tall and would have been rejected if he had tried to enlist as a private. Gonville Bromhead (Rorke's Drift) and Walter Kitchener (Lord Kitchener's brother) were almost completely deaf. Other eminent officers of the period were missing various limbs, something that spelled the end of service for other ranks.

The Cardwell reforms had recently abolished the practice of officers purchasing commissions, yet most of the officers who fought and died in the Anglo-Zulu War had purchased their commissions prior to the reforms. Even so, British army officers of the period invariably came from the upper class, simply because they needed independent means to meet their mess expenses and social liabilities. Even Lord Chelmsford, the British military commander in South Africa during the Anglo-Zulu War, had originally applied to serve in India; he had found the cost of social entertaining in the UK a great strain on his personal resources. Whereas soldiers were generally despised by society, officers were highly regarded, and this was reflected in their daily pay: one shilling for a soldier but 5s 3d for a newly-appointed second lieutenant.

Commissions from the ranks were virtually unknown due to this wide social divide, but, as a result of his endeavours at Rorke's Drift, Colour Sergeant Bourne was awarded the Distinguished Conduct Medal and offered a commission, a rare honour in Queen Victoria's army. (2) Aware of the financial implications to someone without private means, Bourne initially declined the commission. He was, however, eventually granted a Quartermaster's commission in 1890 with the rank of Honorary Lieutenant. He retired as a Lieutenant Colonel.

During peacetime, officers could expect up to six months' leave each year; only the Battalion Adjutant and his Instructor of Musketry had any contact with other ranks on a regular basis. Emphasis was placed on officers' fitness, loyalty, team spirit and physical bravery. Most enjoyed sport, particularly hunting, and many relished the prospect of going to Africa for the opportunity of hunting big game as well as the native foe. For many officers, especially those from the Royal Engineers and Royal Artillery, promotion could be very slow in peacetime; they therefore welcomed the opportunity of conflict, where brevet or field promotions could be gained. Such promotions were invariably confirmed by the War Office and thus became permanent.

Colonial officers and NCOs

The total number of colonial units who took part in the Anglo-Zulu War was less than fifty, and most were made up of only a dozen or so men. The NNC (Natal Native Contingent) was the largest, numbering several thousand, although it was something of an afterthought as far as the

British were concerned. Both Lord Chelmsford and his political superior, the High Commissioner to South Africa, Sir Henry Bartle Frere, had entered the war in the belief that the Zulus would pose no real military threat. They had expected to defeat the Zulu army quickly and easily, and then march on to intimidate republican elements in the Transvaal. Indeed, Frere had gambled that he could out-manoeuvre the opposition of the Colonial Office in London to the war by provoking and bringing hostilities to a successful conclusion before the home government had time to object. Such an approach made it difficult for Chelmsford to accumulate the resources necessary for the campaign; indeed, he received minimal regular reinforcements before the war began. Faced with the difficulties of operating across a huge tract of rough unexplored country, and needing to drive the Zulus into a corner and make them fight, Chelmsford admitted the inevitable and authorised the raising of a black levy from Natal's African population.

General Orders authorising the raising of the Natal Native Contingent were published on 23 November 1878. The war began on 11 January 1879, allowing six weeks to raise, organise, officer, equip and train the contingent. Moreover, while the rank and file seemed generally to have responded enthusiastically to the call, there was a shortage of white officers. While a number were appointed from regular officers who had volunteered for special service, most were appointed from colonial volunteers. Where possible, senior ranks were filled with men who had both experience in the British army – a number of battalion commandants had once been officers in British regiments – and had served under Lord Chelmsford in the recent Cape Frontier War. There were not enough of such men to go round, neither was it possible to fill all the posts from white volunteers in Natal. Many captains and lieutenants of the NNC were recruited from the settler gentry and adventurers on the Eastern Cape Frontier. While a few spoke some African language – usually Xhosa or the Mpondo dialect – few spoke any Zulu. Moreover, because the Contingent was such a last-minute affair, most of the better-quality volunteers in Natal had already found posts, and the white NCOs of the NNC were recruited largely from the ranks of the recently-disbanded irregular units on the Frontier, many of whom drank away their pay in frontier canteens, or from unemployed labourers. The NCOs were, by all accounts, a rough lot.

The effects of this on the NNC were disastrous. Given the mixed origins of the other ranks, it had always been considered important that the commanders took pains to treat them well and instil a sense of *esprit de corps*. Yet the Contingent would be pitched into the war before the men had come to know, or learned to trust, their officers. Many, indeed, complained of being bullied by their officers and NCOs, who issued incomprehensible orders, then used their fists to enforce them. The Africans found European drill confusing, and only the most imaginative commanders made any attempt to harness their traditional military outlook. So far from using African terms of respect when addressing their headmen – as they were urged to do – many officers referred to them with utter contempt. Furthermore, early good intentions to stimulate the morale of the corps by issuing uniforms and firearms were abandoned for reasons of economy. Only one in ten – usually the designated black NCOs – were issued with firearms; the rest of the men carried their traditional weapons. Although some commandants attempted to procure old military uniforms from the government stores, most native troops were distinguished by nothing more than red rags worn around their heads.

Colonial officers had no authority over troops commanded by a British officer. A classic example of this inverted hierarchy occurred at Rorke's Drift, where Captain Stephenson of the NNC worked under both Lieutenants Chard and Bromhead. This was fortunate, since Stephenson deserted the mission station as the Zulus attacked.

The attitude of the British officer towards his colonial colleague can be summed up in a remark by Captain Edward Essex, 75th Regiment, who said simply of the NNC at Isandlwana: "I did not notice the latter much, save that they blazed away at an absurd rate". (3)

Joining the 24th (2nd Warwickshire) Regiment of Foot

Unusually, both battalions of this famous regiment were destined to serve together in the Anglo-Zulu War. The battle-experienced 1st Battalion and one company of the 2nd Battalion would jointly bear the brunt of the massive Zulu attack at Isandlwana and, with the exception of five regimental officers, all would be killed there.

The origins of the 24th Regiment date back to 8 March 1689, when Colonel Sir Edward Dering of Pluckley, known as the 'Black Devil of Kent', was instructed by a proclamation of King William to raise one of ten 'Regiments of Foot' to fight in Ireland against the Jacobites. The occasion is recorded on a memorial stone in Pluckley church that commemorates the event. In 1703 the regiment began its collection of battle honours under the colonelcy of John Churchill, Duke of Marlborough, with deeds at Ramillies, Blenheim, Malplaquet and Oudenarde being recorded on the regiment's colour. In 1751 it became known as the 24th Regiment of Foot. In those days, there were few permanent training depots, and most regiments recruited soldiers from their immediate locality. The Jacobite rebellion in Scotland in the 1740s and the disturbances in Ireland in the 1790s and 1830s created a need for more soldiers, and the growth of large cities provided the majority of recruits for the British army.

After their return from the American War of Independence, the 24th Regiment of Foot was based in Warwickshire. On 31 August 1782 a Royal Warrant conferred county titles on all regiments not already possessed of special designations such as 'The Queen's' or 'The King's Own'. The 24th Regiment was accordingly given the title '2nd Warwickshire' and ordered to send a recruiting party to Tamworth, as it was intended that regiments should cultivate a recruiting connection with the counties whose names they took. No special link with the County Militia was established, nor were any depots or permanent recruiting centres set up. At the same time, the 6th Regiment of Foot, a separate regiment, was given the title '1st Warwickshire'. They subsequently became the Royal Warwickshire Regiment (1891), the Royal Warwickshire Fusiliers (1963) and the Regiment of Fusiliers (1968). The 24th Regiment was never part of the 6th Regiment of Foot.

In 1873, as a direct result of the Cardwell reforms, Brecon in Wales became the regimental depot of the 24th; thereafter, recruits were still enlisted from across English and Irish counties, with those from counties bordering Wales going to the local 2nd Battalion. The 1st Battalion, though, had seen continuous service in various Mediterranean garrisons for the eight years prior to arriving in South Africa on 4 February 1875. At that time, the 1st Battalion's link with Brecon was virtually non-existent. The 24th had no special depots for recruiting; had it tried recruiting in Wales, or specifically in Brecon, it would have encountered a logistical problem since Wales was sparsely populated until the expansion of the coal, iron and steel industries in the late nineteenth century. For example, until 1880

Brecon had a static population of just 5,000 people over a wide rural area, with only 2,551 males of all ages, so the number of fit men of recruiting age was therefore very small.

In view of the subsequent change in designation of the 24th to the South Wales Borderers in 1881, it is worth considering the actual representation of Welshmen then serving in the two battalions at Isandlwana and Rorke's Drift. With regard to the 1/24th lost at Isandlwana, there was virtually no connection with Wales, as the battalion had neither served in the UK since 1867 nor ever recruited from Wales. Indeed, when the news of the loss of the 1/24th reached Britain, the *Daily News* commented, 'Death had prematurely visited hundreds of peaceful and happy homes in England', a comment which sadly ignored the high proportion of Irishmen serving in both battalions.

The 2/24th certainly had a small proportion of Welshmen (born in, or living in Wales when recruited) serving in its ranks. The composition of B Company 2/24th when they defended Rorke's Drift gives an indication of the spread:

1st Battalion

England: 1 from Staffordshire
Scotland: 1 from Midlothian
Ireland: 1 from Dublin
Other: 1 from Peshawar, India (of British parents)

2nd Battalion

England (47)
1 each from: Cheshire, Gloucestershire, Leicestershire,
Nottinghamshire, Surrey, Sussex, Worcestershire, Yorkshire
2 each from: Kent, Middlesex
3 each from: Herefordshire, Warwickshire
4 from Somerset
9 from Lancashire
11 from London
5 from Monmouthshire (Monmouthshire was English in 1879. This
county became Welsh in 1976 following boundary changes.)

Ireland (13)
1 each from: Antrim and Limerick

2 each from: Clare, Cork, Kilkenny, Tipperary
3 from Dublin

Wales (5)
1 each from: Breconshire and Pembrokeshire
3 from Glamorgan

Other (1)
(France – of British parents). See Appendix A for an examination of this subject.

On 1 February 1878, the 2nd Battalion (2/24th), with 24 officers and 849 other ranks, sailed from Chatham in Kent for South Africa in HM troopship *Himalaya*. They were scheduled reinforcements for the British force being assembled in South Africa.

By the outbreak of the Anglo-Zulu War, the total strength of the British army was still only 186,000, compared with the Prussian army of 2.2 million.

Chapter 2

The Adversaries

The Zulu people before 1835

It remains true today that the origins of the Bantu tribe, from the ancient *abaNtu,* are unknown, but reasoned supposition suggests that they entered Africa from the Middle East as long ago as 8,000 BC. As their lives were always centred on cattle, they led a nomadic life and in due course spread south and then laterally across central Africa, eventually reaching the west coast. They then retraced their route and progressed south-east around the wastes of the Kalahari Desert; one Bantu tribe, the Nguni, settled extensively in the area known today as Natal, probably between 1500 and 1700 AD. This left the bulk of the Bantu, the predominately Xhosa tribe, steadily moving south while, unknowingly and only 500 miles away, the Boers were busy founding their first colony in the area known today as Cape Town. It is ironic that a migration of such magnitude should have failed to reach the Cape and that Europeans should fill that vacuum at exactly the same point in time.

By the end of the seventeenth century the Nguni tribe probably amounted to no more than three or four thousand people living under the vague and aged chieftaincy of Jobe. An insignificant and little known fringe group of between one and two hundred people lived near the coast on the banks of the White Mfolozi River. Their chief, Malandela, had a son named Zulu, meaning 'of heaven', who eventually succeeded him and under whose chieftaincy the small group thrived. Two brothers followed him, Mageba and Punga, who then gave way to Senzangakona at the time the Xhosa first came into conflict with the Boers at the Great Fish River. During this embryonic stage of their development, the group adopted the title 'Zulu' and had grown in size to well over one thousand. Senzangakona had many wives but, not being satisfied with them, secretly dallied with the daughter of a neighbouring eLangeni chief. Marriage to the unfortunate pregnant girl, Nandi, was impossible because she was not a Zulu.

After Nandi gave birth to a son, the eLangeni banished the disgraced Nandi and her child, which morally forced Senzangakona to appoint Nandi as his unofficial third wife, and she was readmitted to her tribe. Senzangakona refused to recognise his son so, in defiance, Nandi named him Shaka after a common intestinal beetle.

By 1802, the eLangeni could no longer tolerate Nandi and her family and banished them into destitution at a time when the whole land was suffering widespread famine. Nandi fled to the Qwabe clan, where she had once given birth to a son by a Qwabe warrior named Gendeyana. Under Gendeyana's guidance, Shaka developed into such an excellent warrior that Senzangakona sought the return of this fine young combatant – whether to develop his skills or to murder him is unclear. Nandi's suspicions led her to move her family to yet another clan in order to protect Shaka from his father. Shaka's reputation increased, and legend records both his fearlessness when hunting wild animals and his great prowess with the spear. At the age of twenty-four, Shaka was called to join King Dingiswayo's regiment of 'national service' warriors. During the next five years he closely studied the king's strategy of establishing control over other tribes by the use of brutal and aggressive tactics, a policy frequently but incorrectly attributed first to Shaka.

Under Dingiswayo, Shaka rose through the ranks until he led the IziCwa regiment, and it was here that he taught his warriors the close combat for which they became famous. As proof of his stamina and fitness Shaka always went barefoot, considering sandals to be an impediment. He ordered the ineffective throwing spears to be melted down and recast as the long, sharp, flat-bladed assegai or ikwa – the onomatopoeic term taken from the sucking sound of the blade being withdrawn from a body. Shaka was frustrated with conventional spears which when thrown were lost to the enemy, or when used during close combat tended to snap at the shaft. He ordered his regiment's traditional weighty shields to be cut down and made stronger, so that in close combat the new shield could be hooked under that of an opponent and when twisted sideways would expose the opponent's body to the deadly ikwa thrust.

Shaka was in his early thirties when his ruthless reign began. Opponents and dissenters were mercilessly executed, as were warriors who did not reach the exacting physical standards required for a Zulu impi, the fighting unit, usually of regimental strength. Shaka embraced all the techniques he had learnt during his years with the IziCwa: he perfected the ikwa stabbing spear and developed the impondo zankhomo (see Fig.2 on p. 23), the feared encircling technique known as the 'horns of the buffalo', whereby an enemy was encircled by the fast running flanks of each horn until completely surrounded. The main Zulu body would then engage and slaughter the surrounded enemy, using the close-combat techniques of shield and stabbing assegai. Shaka drilled his Zulus remorselessly until he had a highly trained impi numbering no more than three hundred warriors. The first major test of this small regiment was a confrontation with his neighbours, the belligerent Buthelezi clan. Shaka ordered his regiment to advance with their shields 'edge on' to give the illusion of minimal numbers. His 'horns' rapidly encircled the Buthelezi, whose vocal dependants were watching from a nearby hillside. Shaka then gave the order for shields to be turned to face the deceived Buthelezi, revealing the true numbers of his men. His disciplined regiment drove into the terrified Buthelezi warriors, quickly slaughtering them before the distraught onlookers.

By 1818 Shaka's impi had grown to more than two thousand warriors, and his sphere of influence was steadily increasing while other Bantu tribes engaged in totally destructive warfare against each other.

In early 1824 an event occurred which was to bring radical change to the Zulus. Shaka had heard of the handful of white men living at Port Natal, and to satisfy his curiosity sent them an invitation to visit his kraal at kwaBulawayo (the place of he who kills). The visiting party consisted of Lieutenant Francis Farewell RN, Henry Fynn, the British resident in Zululand, four hardy pioneers, John Cane, Henry Ogle, Joseph Powell and Thomas Halstead, and they carried a large number of gifts. The party arrived in July and was awed by the size of the royal homestead. It measured at least three miles in circumference and housed the royal huts, the royal cattle pen containing seven thousand pure white cattle, and two thousand domestic huts. Shaka, who was protected by twelve thousand of his best warriors, greeted the party. After various displays and feasts, Farewell and Fynn finally met Shaka, and during one of their meetings they sought and were granted trading rights for the Farewell Trading Company. The party returned to Port Natal, but without Fynn who remained at Shaka's request

– not as a hostage, but to enable Shaka to learn more of the white men. Fynn was residing at the royal kraal when an attempt was made on Shaka's life. He was stabbed through the left arm and ribs by an unknown assailant and lay at death's door for a week. During this time, Fynn cleaned and bandaged the wound and generally watched over Shaka, who quickly recovered. Shaka believed that members of the distant Qwabe tribe had made the attempt; accordingly, two impis were dispatched which captured the Qwabe cattle and destroyed their kraals. The settlers' position was assured, and Shaka allegedly signed an agreement granting Farewell nearly four thousand square miles of land around Port Natal.

During 1826 Farewell and Fynn accompanied Shaka's army of over forty thousand warriors on an expedition against the Ndwandwe clan. The result was a total slaughter of the Ndwandwe; an event that distressed even Farewell and Fynn, though Shaka was delighted with the sixty thousand captured cattle. Shaka's disregard for human life was difficult for the Europeans to comprehend; a dozen executions a day was normal. When Shaka suspected that some of his younger warriors were visiting the girls of the isiGodlo he had two hundred youngsters summarily executed. The young women of the isiGodlo have often been misrepresented as forming a chief's harem; they were certainly a ready source of wives and concubines but were principally young women presented to a chief or king as a tribute – for him to dispose of in marriage in return for a high lobola or bride price.

Shaka's rule was total until 1827 when his mother Nandi suddenly died. Shaka's grief was so intense that he required every Zulu to experience his loss. At a gathering of some twenty thousand souls within the kraal, enforced wailing and summary executions commenced and continued for more than a day, until well over one thousand of the multitude lay dead. Shaka then decreed that during the next twelve months no crops could be grown, children were not to be conceived, or milk drunk – all on pain of death. These proscriptions continued for three months until Shaka tired of mourning, whereupon some normality returned. Shaka's wanton brutality has invariably been attributed to his allegedly repressed sexuality. This is another myth; too many contemporary Zulu accounts refer to newborn babies among Shaka's isiGodlo being put to death or smuggled away. Contrary Zulu legends, perhaps dubious, suggest Shaka had a long and faithful relationship with his sister's friend, Pampata, who supported Shaka until his death. (1)

The damage and carnage of the mourning period was such that Shaka's half brothers, Dingane and Mhlangana, agreed that Shaka must die. They waited until the army was away on campaign, then stabbed Shaka to death during a meeting with his senior indunas, the sub-chiefs. His body was unceremoniously buried in a pit, weighted down with stones. Many years later, the site was purchased by a farmer, and today Shaka's grave lies somewhere under Cooper Street in the small town of Stanger, north of Durban.

Dingane seized control but lacked Shaka's reputation, and almost immediately stirrings of rebellion began emanating from tribes who had suffered the excesses of the late king. Dingane was in dire peril, as the Zulu army was still absent on campaign against the Shangane tribe and the only regiment remaining at the royal kraal had previously been loyal to Shaka. Dingane and Mhlangana surrounded themselves with trusted warriors and awaited the return of the army. Several weeks went by, and the hitherto close relationship between the two brothers deteriorated. Dingane received a warning from a trusted spy that Mhlangana was plotting his death. That night Dingane was injured by a spear thrown under cover of darkness; and though wounded he immediately retaliated by having Mhlangana murdered. Within days the exhausted and anxious army returned in expectation of Shaka's wrath, only to be relieved when Dingane welcomed them back, fed them and then authorised their leave. Dingane thus ensured their loyalty and, being unchallenged, assumed the mantle of king. Curiously, the title 'king' appears to have evolved from a spontaneous gesture by Lieutenant Farewell during an early meeting with Shaka. In awe of the Zulu, Farewell took a smear of grease from the wheel hub of one of his cannons and ceremonially anointed Shaka on the forehead – after which ceremony he was referred to as 'the king'. Dingane, at no more than thirty years of age, settled into a life of luxury and security. He enjoyed singing and dancing and clearly had artistic inclinations. Unlike Shaka, Dingane was gluttonous and spent most of his time in his harem or reviewing parades of warriors and cattle. He reduced the size of the Zulu army, and Shaka's previous policy of random butchery ceased, though miscreants were still summarily executed.

In the spring of 1834 a relatively unknown incident occurred which helps explain Dingane's subsequent suspicion and treatment of white settlers. A Zulu impi returning from a minor campaign came across a small party of half-caste hunters from the Cape. Thinking the impi was about to attack them, the hunters fired several shots and within minutes were annihilated by the Zulus for their mistake. News trickled back to the settlement at Port Natal, where the Boer settlers incorrectly presumed that the impi had attacked their own hunting party who were, by sheer coincidence, in the same area but had not been involved and were unaware of the incident. The settlers retaliated by mounting a small expedition which ambushed the impi, taking the Zulus by surprise and killing scores.

The settlers returned to Port Natal fully expecting a major Zulu attack; curiously, Dingane did not retaliate. It was during this period of heightened tension that Piet Retief, leader of the trekking Boers who sought to escape British rule in the Cape, visited Port Natal while on his way to Dingane to seek settlement rights for his followers. His small party easily doubled the port's population, and it is evident that the residents welcomed the possibility of a Boer settlement in the same vicinity. To Dingane it was becoming evident that white settlement now posed a serious threat to his rule. Piet Retief was certainly unaware of the incident and of its consequences for his visit to Dingane, both for the Boers and subsequently for the Zulu nation. Retief set out to visit Dingane to seek permission to settle, but Dingane had Retief and his party killed. Shortly afterwards, Dingane was killed by his own people, and his younger half-brother Mpande succeeded.

In 1845 Britain seized the opportunity to annex the whole of Natal into Cape Colony, including Boer-held territory. Reluctantly, the Boer Volksraad (parliament) acquiesced. The Boers had overreached themselves and in provoking the British lost sovereignty over lands won by great sacrifice. Settlers continued arriving from Europe, but the biggest change since the Boers' crossing of the Drakensberg came with the dredging and channelling of the mouth of Durban harbour. As a result of this single engineering undertaking Durban rapidly prospered as the influence of Pietermaritzburg declined. During the European upheaval in Natal, the Zulus under their new king Mpande had withdrawn to the north of the Buffalo and Tugela rivers. By now, the Zulus were under political and territorial pressure from Europeans based at Portuguese-controlled

THE ADVERSARIES

Delagoa Bay, from British-dominated Natal and by voortrekkers (Boer pioneers) north of the Tugela and Mzinyathi rivers.

Mpande ruled the Zulu nation fairly but firmly according to Zulu custom during the relatively peaceful years that followed. It was a period of consolidation after the internecine wars of 1838 and 1840, and the Zulus were also recovering from the economic impoverishment caused by white settlers' encroachment. Mpande turned his attention to the isiGodlo and feasting, until he became too obese to walk. His activities in the isiGodlo produced nearly thirty sons. The firstborn was named Cetshwayo, who was followed shortly by a brother named Mbulazi. Under Zulu custom, the heir to the throne was the firstborn male of the head wife, but Mpande never nominated such a wife. Mpande was fully aware that the question of succession would be complex; he postponed the matter by sending the two sons and their mothers to villages separated by some fifty miles. As Mpande aged, schisms developed within the Zulu nation, and gradually the subservient chiefs and clans graduated to either Cetshwayo or Mbulazi. The two brother princes were now in their early twenties and led the uThulwana and amaShishi regiments respectively, though neither had any actual combat experience. Cetshwayo was a traditionalist and hankered after the regal days of Shaka, whereas Mbulazi was more inclined to intellectual matters, though equally devious and powerful; in the year 1856 both sought to become king.

As usual, resolution came through bloody conflict, perhaps the worst seen or recorded in African history. Near Ndondakusuka hill, Cetshwayo mustered twenty thousand warriors, the uSuthu, and pitted them against Mbulazi's army of thirty thousand, the iziGqoza, which included many women and old men. The confrontation took place on the banks of an insignificant stream, the Thambo, which fed into the Tugela River. The battle lasted no more than an hour, and Mbulazi's army was heavily defeated. In customary Zulu fashion, Cetshwayo gave orders for their total slaughter, and only a handful of survivors escaped. Cetshwayo was later praised in song for his victory, as being the victor who "Caused people to swim against their will, for he made men swim when they were old". (2)

Following the battle, Cetshwayo ordered the murder of several of his own brothers and half-brothers who could have challenged him for the kingship. Within weeks he was pronounced heir to Mpande and immediately took over the rule of the Zulu nation, leaving Mpande as a mere figurehead. Cetshwayo had observed the underlying tension between the British in Natal and the Transvaal Boers and knew this placed him in a position of considerable strength. He now had full control of Zululand, and in order to strengthen his grip further he courted the friendship of the British, whereupon Theophilus Shepstone, Secretary for Native Affairs, went to Mpande and suggested that, in the name of Queen Victoria, Cetshwayo be appointed heir apparent. Mpande accepted on behalf of the Zulus, though Cetshwayo was aware that his future now depended, to a degree, on British support. Mpande died in 1872 after thirty relatively peaceful years on the Zulu throne, a reign marred only by his two sons' recent battle by the Tugela. Mpande was the only Zulu king to die of natural causes.

Cetshwayo thus became king while in his mid-forties and immediately sought British confirmation of his position. Shepstone readily agreed, and in a sham ceremony on 1 September 1873, Cetshwayo was crowned king of the Zulu nation – in the name of Queen Victoria. He established his royal homestead at Ondini near the present-day Ulundi. Cetshwayo, perhaps the most intelligent of all the Zulu kings, now ruled a united nation. His army was at its strongest and the Zulus had a most powerful friend, Queen Victoria – and no apparent enemies.

With his military position secure, Cetshwayo began to strengthen his economic and political control. Since Shaka, young men had been obliged to serve in the army as a means of binding the nation together. The units or amabutho were the king's active service troops and in peacetime gave service at the king's command as tax officials or by undertaking policing duties. Apart from drawing young men into an amabutho for military and work purposes, this also served to accustom warriors to identifying the Zulu king as their leader, regardless of their origins. However, where young men came from an outlying area or one which had only recently been absorbed into the Zulu nation, they were allocated menial work and were known as amalala (menials), amanhlwenga (destitutes) or iziendane (unusual hairstyles).

These warriors remained in their regimental amabutho until the king authorised their 'marriage'; this was another misunderstood concept that has often led to confusion. Zulu marriage has invariably been interpreted through European eyes with Freudian overtones of repressed sexuality, and confused with European values. To a Zulu, marriage was the most significant event of his life: it gave him the right to take a number of wives; he was free to establish his personal kraal; and he could own land for his cattle and crops. The king controlled marriage as a means of keeping his young men under arms and out of the economic structure of Zululand. Had every warrior been permitted to establish his own kraal at will, the effect on Zulu society, including both production and reproduction, would have produced economic instability. Concomitantly, by delaying the time when Zulu women could marry, the pressure of population growth could be strictly controlled and the Zulu birthrate maintained in line with economic capability.

Meanwhile, the British became occupied with minor conflicts elsewhere in southern Africa, mostly brought about by native resistance over land occupied by white settlers. Land became scarce and, in time, there was little available to offer those still en route to Natal. Severe drought throughout 1876 and 1877 made matters worse, and Britain, through its High Commissioner Sir Bartle Frere, encouraged the solution of 'Confederation'. By combining all the territories in South Africa, Britain could control both resources and policy through a system of central and regional government. To this end, Shepstone had already annexed the Transvaal on the pretext of saving the Boers from their own bankrupt economy and to discourage the Zulus from raiding Boer farms in disputed areas of Zululand.

The British knew full well that Zululand must be included in any Confederation, principally because Zululand still possessed sufficient available land for settlement and an untapped source of labour. There remained one problem: the Zulus' autocratic king and his army of forty thousand warriors would never agree to an effective surrender and dissolution of Zululand merely to facilitate British economic development. Government officials in Natal initiated rumours of a bloodthirsty and defiant Zulu army plotting to invade Natal, and hysteria among the white settlers was fanned until conversation and newspaper reports spoke of little else. Occasional Zulu incursions against isolated Boer farmers increased, as did numbers of Bantu migrants illicitly settling in Zululand – simply because cattle were the single currency applicable to all races, and as the settlers' wealth increased, so they sought additional grazing land. Retaliatory raids encouraged European speculation that war against the Zulus was inevitable, though Cetshwayo appeared to be unaware of this subversive undercurrent. But for the Zulus the writing was clearly on the wall.

By the time the Anglo-Zulu War commenced, successive Zulu kings had efficiently controlled the development of Zulu social organisation and ensured a comparatively healthy and prosperous population. Anthony Trollope travelled through southern Africa and parts of Zululand during 1877 just as European hysteria was mounting, yet he viewed the Zulus as perceptive and living in sympathy with their time and environment. He wrote, 'I have no fears myself that Natal will be overrun by hostile Zulus, but much fear that Zululand should be overrun by hostile Britons'. (3)

Zulu tactics

Prior to Shaka, inter-tribal warfare was not very destructive – defeated tribes lived to fight again. Shaka's new battle tactics were totally different and completely ruthless. This was demonstrated when Shaka mobilised his highly trained and efficient force against the neighbouring Buthelezi tribe. Both sides adopted the traditional abuse-hurling confrontation known as *giya* that usually took the form of a shouting match between the two sides separated by a gap of about forty yards. *Giya* usually lasted about two hours, before the two sides separated and returned to their respective home areas.

Fig. 1
Tactics before Shaka
Traditional *giya* formation

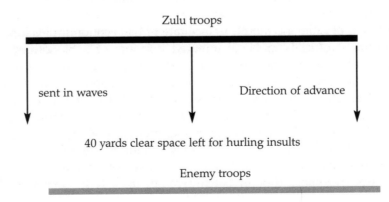

Zulu troops

sent in waves   Direction of advance

40 yards clear space left for hurling insults

Enemy troops

Fig. 2
Shaka's battle tactics
The 'horns of the buffalo', *impondo zankhomo*

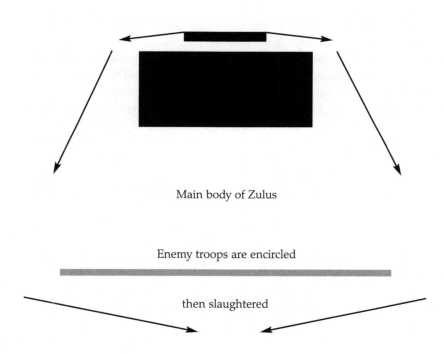

Main body of Zulus

Enemy troops are encircled

then slaughtered

The Zulus thereafter used the invincible *impondo zankhomo* not only for inter-tribal warfare but also when hunting. These tactics had stood the test of time since Shaka; the British invading force was about to experience them for the first time.

Zulu weapons
The Zulus' tough leather shields were the most visible part of their warriors' armoury. Shields were always made by specialist shield-makers who would begin the construction by cutting a large oval from a cowhide, leaving the hair on the outer face. The colour of the hide was important. In

the time of Shaka, the combination of colour and patches was carefully monitored, the differences between each regiment's colour being detailed and specific; the whiter the shield, the more senior its owner. By the 1870s the practice was less strictly observed, although married regiments carried predominantly white or red shields, while those of unmarried regiments were black, or black with white markings. The full war shield was the *isiHlangu*, which was intended to cover the warrior from his eyes to his ankles, and thus varied in size from one warrior to another. The largest shields of this type were as much as five feet long and two feet six inches wide. During the civil war of the 1850s Cetshwayo introduced a smaller variant called the *umbhumbhulosu*. Three feet six inches long and two feet wide, it was considered lighter and easier to use. In the 1870s both shields were carried, even within the same regiment, although the *umbhumbhulosu* may have been more popular with younger and more adventurous warriors. The shields were strengthened by a single vertical stick fastened to the back by a double row of hide strips threaded through slits carefully cut in the shield; it was held by a small handle. The bottom and top of the stick both protruded, the former sharpened to a point and the latter decorated with a strip of fur. All shields were the property of the king rather than the individual; they were kept in special raised stores, out of the way of ants and rodents.

Zulu weapons of aggression consisted of both traditional Zulu spears and obsolete European rifles. Shaka had introduced the famous Zulu stabbing spear or assegai into his army at the start of his career; this short spear had a blade some eighteen inches long and two and a half inches wide at its widest point, set into a wooden shaft two feet six inches long. He drilled his soldiers in shock tactics that involved a mass charge and close-quarter fighting, thrusting the stabbing spear underarm into the belly of the opponent. There were also a number of different types of throwing spear common in 1879, most of which had a blade of about five or six inches, with the iron shank visible for several inches before being set into a long shaft made of various easily-worked but strong woods, for example *iPahla* (Brachylaena discolor), *iLalanyati* (Grewia occidentalis), *iMindza* (Halleria lucida) and *unHlwakele* (Cyclostemon argustus).

The manufacture of assegai stabbing spears was a highly skilled craft, entrusted to particular clans such as the Mbonambi and the Cube. The iron ore was collected at surface deposits and smelted in a clay forge with the

24

aid of goatskin bellows. The blade was hammered into shape, tempered with fat and sharpened on a stone, before being set into a short wooden shaft. It was glued with strong vegetable glues and bound with wet cane fibre. A tube of hide, cut from a calf's tail, was rolled over the join and allowed to shrink. At its best, such a weapon was tough, sharp and well designed for its purpose. However, there is a suggestion that by 1879 the importation of iron implements from white traders had led to a decline in the indigenous iron industry. Certainly there are a number of stories of blades bending or buckling in use.

Warriors were responsible for their own weapons, but the King initially received the spears in bulk from those clans that made them, distributing them to warriors who had distinguished themselves. Most warriors carried clubs or knobkerries, the *iWisa*, which were simple polished sticks with a heavy bulbous head. Zulu boys carried them for everyday protection, and their possession at all times became second nature. A number of axes were used; these were often ornamental and were imported from tribes to the north.

By the time of the British invasion, the Zulu army possessed firearms in large numbers. A trusted English trader, John Dunn, had imported them in quantity for Cetshwayo. During the 1870s as many as 20,000 guns entered southern Africa through Mozambique alone, most of them intended for the Zulu market. The majority of these firearms were obsolete military muskets, dumped on the unsophisticated 'native market'. More modern types were available, particularly the percussion Enfield, and a number of chiefs had collections of quality sporting guns. Individuals like Prince Dabulamanzi and Chief Sihayo of Rorke's Drift were recognised as good shots, but most Zulus were untrained and highly inaccurate; numerous accounts of Anglo-Zulu War battles note both the indiscriminate use of their firepower and its general inaccuracy. After Isandlwana, large numbers of Martini-Henry rifles fell into Zulu hands. King Cetshwayo attempted to collect these at Ulundi to distribute them more evenly, but most warriors retained their own booty, claiming they had personally killed the man from whom they took it. Cetshwayo pragmatically allowed warriors to keep the rifles; many would shortly be used against the British.

Chapter 3

Preparations for War

The system of government in the Zulu country is so bad
that any improvement was hopeless – we should, if necessary,
be justified in deposing Cetshwayo.
Sir Henry Bulwer (*The Zulu War*)

The annexation of the Transvaal

Since the Boers first crossed the Drakensberg Mountains in 1836, their settlements had continued to spread progressively towards the heart of Zululand, itself protected by a natural boundary, the Tugela River. This temporarily deterred further encroachment by the Boers. By the mid-1870s Boer settlers had again begun surreptitiously moving into Zululand, and these incursions were opposed with increasing vigour. One such area of heightened tension was an unofficial extension of the Boers' Transvaal into Zulu territory between the Buffalo and Blood rivers immediately north of Rorke's Drift, named after James Rorke, born in 1821 and the son of an Irish settler. He later married, settled near Durban and in 1849 moved near to the Buffalo River, where he purchased a remote farm. Rorke lived in harmony with the local Zulus and even began trading with them. Over the years, the trading post became known to the Zulus as *KwaJimi* (*Kwa* meaning 'of', as in *KwaJimi, KwaZulu* etc.). Rorke died in 1874, and a Swedish missionary, Otto Witt, purchased the farm. Witt named the low rocky hill behind the solitary house *Oskarsberg* after his Swedish king.

It was evident to the British, Boers and Zulus alike that the relationship between Boers and Zulus was seriously deteriorating and that decisive action needed to be taken with increasing urgency if peace was to be preserved. The Zulu king Cetshwayo had traditionally regarded the encroaching Boers as his enemy and treated them with great suspicion, whereas he regarded the British as his true friends.

At the same time, the British became aware of potentially massive riches from newly discovered diamond and gold fields. Notwithstanding that these two new sources of wealth were situated in areas not directly under British control (diamonds in the virtually uninhabited Griqualand West and gold in the Boer Transvaal), Britain nevertheless resolved the territorial problem in typically high-handed colonial fashion. To gain the diamond fields, the British administrators simply redrew the border and adjusted their maps to bring the diamond fields of Kimberley under direct British control. The newly discovered gold fields in the Transvaal were not so easy to obtain, being under the control of the regional Boer administration. The British solved the problem by simply annexing the Transvaal . They did this with considerable subterfuge.

During April 1877 a serious confrontation between the Zulus and Boers began to develop as a result of trekkers moving onto land unanimously recognised to be Zulu territory. Cetshwayo decided to resolve the problem by massing his army, amounting to over thirty thousand warriors, at strategic crossing points along the Transvaal border. Before Cetshwayo could give the order for a full-scale Zulu attack, two events occurred simultaneously, either by coincidence or as a result of astute British diplomatic design. Firstly, the Secretary for Native Affairs, Sir Theophilus Shepstone, ordered Cetshwayo to withdraw his army. Cetshwayo reluctantly complied but sent a strong letter warning Shepstone that he had intended driving the Boers 'beyond the Vaal River'. (1) Secondly, on the very same day, 12 April 1877, Shepstone actually attended a secret meeting with the Boers, with the sole intention of persuading them to surrender the Transvaal to British authority. He gave them two reasons to do so: firstly, that the Transvaal government was actually bankrupt; it had debts of £156,883 against a Treasury balance of £1. Secondly, he played on the Boers' belief that the Zulus were about to attack. The Zulus believe to this day that Shepstone encouraged Cetshwayo to mass his army on the Transvaal border in order to coerce the Boers into submission.

An agreement was quickly reached by which Shepstone then and there annexed the Transvaal to the Crown. The secretary to the mission, Melmoth Osbourne, read the declaration to the assembled Boers. Appearing to suffer a bout of chronic anxiety in the middle of the declaration, he began to tremble and his voice failed. Shepstone's twenty-year-old clerk, H. Rider Haggard, later to win fame as the author of *King Solomon's Mines* and other tales of African adventure, had to continue reading the script.

The turning point in the history of the relationship between the British and the Zulu kingdom was the annexation of the Transvaal. Previously, the British had largely supported Zulu claims against their own rivals, the Boers; but as soon as they had assumed control of the Boer republic, they repudiated their support for the Zulus and demanded that King Cetshwayo should abandon his claim to the 'disputed territory'. His reluctance to do so was interpreted by the British as unwarranted aggression. Cetshwayo had initially welcomed the British annexation of the Transvaal, as he believed it would protect Zululand from further Boer attention. Cetshwayo had even told Shepstone, 'I am glad to know the Transvaal is English ground; perhaps now there may be rest'. (2)

By annexing the Transvaal Britain had inadvertently assumed responsibility for the perpetual Boer-Zulu strife. Boer citizens, previously viewed as 'foreigners', became *de facto* British subjects who promptly demanded that the British must resolve their territorial disputes with the Zulus. Britain immediately faced the choice of conflict with either Boers or Zulus; they allied themselves with the Boers. The British High Commissioner to South Africa, Sir Henry Bartle Frere, soon became convinced that the independence of the Zulu kingdom posed a threat to his policies. By breaking up the Zulu kingdom, Frere hoped not only to intimidate potential future opponents but also to demonstrate British strength.

Matters came to a head during early 1878, when a number of Boer and displaced native settlers joined those already illicitly farming a particularly sensitive Zulu area, which was generally becoming known as the 'disputed territory', directly to the north of Rorke's Drift.

In the British tradition of apparent compromise, Frere deferred the problem by reluctantly constituting an independent Boundary Commission; this was at the persistent request of the Governor of Natal, Sir Henry Bulwer, a longstanding friend of the Zulu people. The Commission was instructed to adjudicate on title to the disputed territory. Cetshwayo was consulted and he agreed to abide by the Commission's decision on condition he could nominate three senior chiefs, *indunas*, to participate in its deliberations. The Commission's principal members were three highly respected officials: Michael Gallwey, a barrister who had become the Attorney General of Natal in 1857 at the age of thirty-one, Lieutenant Colonel Anthony Durnford RE, who had served in South Africa for many years and knew the area and the Zulus thoroughly, and John

Shepstone, brother and deputy of the Secretary for Native Affairs. The Boers sent Piet Uys, a farmer who had lost relatives to Dingane's impis, together with Adrian Rudolph, the Boer Landdrost (3) of Utrecht and Henrique Shepstone who served on his father's staff in Pretoria.

The Commission sat for nearly five weeks, during which time they considered voluminous verbal and written representations. Gallwey utilised all his legal training to evaluate the material impartially, a task made especially difficult because several unsigned Boer documents proved to be outrageously fraudulent and to contain many worthless claims put forward as evidence. In fact, the picture became a confused tangle of spurious claims and counter-claims. Boundaries defined on paper simply could not be traced on the ground. There were many contradictions not only in the documents but also in the testimony of witnesses. Gallwey concentrated the Commission's attention on two main issues: who owned the land prior to the dispute, and whether land under dispute had been properly purchased or ceded.

No boundary line had ever been agreed between the Zulus and Boers, and for many years the local Zulu chiefs had repeatedly implored the British Governor in Natal for advice and help in dealing with incidents involving aggressive, land-hungry Boers. It had long been Boer policy, if policy it may be called, to force the Zulus gradually to retreat further and further from their rich pasturelands. Hitherto, little notice had been taken of their petitions. The Boundary Commissioners concluded that:

> No cession of territory was ever made by the Zulu people, and that even had such a cession been made by either Panda or Cetywayo [sic] it would have been null and void, unless confirmed by the voice of the nation according to the custom of the Zulus. (4)

The right given to the Boers was, the Commissioners maintained, simply a grazing right, and any such right was conferred only in respect of land within the Utrecht district, west of the Blood River. The Commissioners held that the Boers never acquired, and the Zulus never lost, dominion over the disputed territory, that it was still properly a portion of Zululand and, furthermore, the developing Boer settlement at Utrecht must also be surrendered. The Boundary Commission eventually delivered their unexpected verdict in July 1878 to an astonished Sir Bartle Frere, who determinedly sought to coerce the Commissioners to amend their findings, without success.

On 4 June Durnford wrote home that the report of the Commission was nearly ready 'and will please no one except perhaps Cetewayo [sic]'. Durnford drafted the report, which was completed on 20 June 1878. The Commissioners were not permitted to divulge the result to anybody until the High Commissioner had decided to make it public. However, Durnford could not resist hinting to his family at the satisfactory conclusion the Commission had reached. He wrote on 24 June 1878, 'I think our views will be maintained – at least I hope so. You see we have gone in for fair play'.

On 28 July an incident occurred which Frere used to agitate widespread anti-Zulu sentiment. Two sons of Sihayo, a local but important chief, crossed the river border to restrain two of their father's absconding wives on suspicion of their adultery. The terrified women were duly apprehended and marched back across the border at Rorke's Drift, only to be clubbed to death in accordance with established Zulu custom. Throughout Natal the incident received officially orchestrated publicity out of all proportion to the event, in order to further inflame public antagonism against Cetshwayo. Shepstone had initiated this policy of subversion in a report to Lord Carnarvon dated 11 December 1877 in which he wrote, 'The sooner the root of the evil, which I consider the Zulu power and military organisation, is dealt with, the easier our task will be'. Even the pro-Zulu Bulwer was forced to agree that the danger of collision with the Zulus was growing and he wrote to Frere that, 'the system of government in the Zulu country is so bad that any improvement was hopeless – we should, if necessary, be justified in deposing Cetshwayo'.

Rebuffed by Durnford and the Boundary Commission, Frere knew that publication of the Commission's findings could unleash powerful forces against Britain. Native nations would believe their campaign against encroaching European settlement was vindicated, and the furious Boers faced the prospect of surrendering their land and farms in Zululand. Frere knew the Boers could well retaliate against Britain by resorting to military action against British-controlled Natal – which, in turn, might provoke additional antagonism from a number of the Boers' European allies, especially Holland and Germany. This possible complication would be most inconvenient, as Britain was also becoming seriously engaged in war in Afghanistan, and relations with Russia were consequently deteriorating.

To Frere, the invasion of Zululand remained the single option; after all,

British victory was a certainty. A Zulu defeat would facilitate British progress to the north, and Confederation could then proceed. It would also placate the Boers, and such a display of British military force would certainly impress any African leader who might have contemplated making a stand against British expansion. Invasion would also overturn the Zulu king by eradicating his military potential and unshackle a valuable source of labour for British and Boer commercial activities. Frere ordered his General Commanding British Forces in South Africa, Sir Frederic Thesiger (shortly to become Lord Chelmsford), to proceed to Natal and secretly prepare his forces for an immediate and brief war against the Zulus. For the previous ten years Chelmsford had been concerned with administration, as Adjutant General in India. A pedantic figure, he would have well understood the theory of British army tactics underlying every military operation undertaken anywhere in the Empire. These tactics involved meticulous planning, rather like contemplating a game of chess, but nevertheless stuck to rigid rules and used equipment totally unsuitable outside of Europe. This attitude would inevitably lead Chelmsford's invading army to defeat. His army would wear red jackets in temperatures of 35°C, use tactics better suited to the previous century and ignore intelligence reports of his enemy's intentions and movements. This gave King Cetshwayo and his commanders the advantage of perfect knowledge of British positions in Zululand's difficult terrain, provide them with easy and accurate intelligence of British action and inaction, and enable Zulu subterfuge and decoys to mislead Chelmsford.

While they were blissfully ignorant of such implications, there were important personal considerations for both Frere and Chelmsford: success for Frere would embellish his already glittering career, and for Chelmsford an early defeat of the Zulu army would be popular and ensure him a heroic return to England. Meanwhile, Frere pondered the Boundary Commission's findings and decided that inactivity was the best, albeit temporary, solution.

Frere gained more time by forwarding the report to Hicks Beach, the new Colonial Secretary in London (who had succeeded Lord Carnarvon). He also requested additional Imperial troops, ostensibly to protect Natal and the Boer families still within the disputed area. Frere knew full well that Hicks Beach's official reply would take several months to reach him, by which time the Zulus would be defeated.

On 9 October an incident occurred which precipitated action by Frere. A local chief, Mbelini, led his warriors through the Pongola Valley in the area under dispute, attacking immigrant Boers and natives and stealing their cattle. Frere was already in the process of devising an ultimatum that he and his advisers knew would be impossible for Cetshwayo to accept. It would also negate the Boundary Commission's report and justify war against the Zulus. The raid by Mbelini formed the basis of the first item in the draft ultimatum.

The Ultimatum

On 11 December 1878 Zulu representatives were summoned to the site of an enormous shady fig tree on the Natal bank of the Tugela River to learn the result of the Boundary Commission's deliberations. Today, the stump of the tree, a national monument, languishes underneath a motorway bridge. John Shepstone represented the British officials, while Cetshwayo sent three of his senior *indunas* together with eleven chieftains and their retainers to report back the findings.

John Shepstone was an insensitive choice for several reasons. He was the brother and deputy of the Secretary for Native Affairs, Sir Theophilus Shepstone. He was actually working for the Boers at the time of the Commission, and whilst it could be argued that he could therefore represent the Boers, he caused confusion among the Zulus by announcing the findings on behalf of the British. He was also infamous among the Zulus for having once led a party that tracked down, shot and wounded a wanted Zulu, Chief Matyana. Matyana escaped and John Shepstone lost both his captive and his reputation.

Writing was unknown to the Zulus, who were nevertheless accomplished at memorising even lengthy speeches; this probably accounts for the number of senior Zulu representatives who would have to corroborate each other's account when they reported back to Cetshwayo. At the first meeting, the findings of the Boundary Commission were announced, though couched in heavily veiled terms designed to cause the Zulus confusion. Mr Fynney, Border Agent, carefully translated these to the Zulu deputies. The meeting adjourned for a roast beef lunch and reassembled in the afternoon, when the ultimatum was read and translated, sentence by sentence, again by Mr Fynney, and was listened to by the deputies with the utmost attention but with increasing indications of concern and apprehension. The astonished Zulus then anxiously set off to report the terms of the ultimatum to their king; Cetshwayo had a reputation for executing messengers who bore bad news, and therefore, understandably, his emissaries tarried. A white resident, John Dunn, duly learned of the ultimatum and sent his own messenger to Cetshwayo with advance warning.

The main requirements of the ultimatum were two-fold:

1. Conditions to be fully met within twenty days
a. The surrender to the British of the Swazi Chief, Mbelini (for cattle raiding).
b. The surrender of Chief Sihayo's two sons (for crossing the river border into Natal, abducting and then murdering two of Sihayo's adulterous wives) plus a fine of 500 cattle.
c. A fine of 100 cattle for having molested two British surveyors, Deighton and Smith, at a border crossing.

2. Conditions to be fully met within thirty days
a. A number of prominent Zulus were to be surrendered for trial (no names were specified).
b. Summary executions were forbidden.
c. The Zulu army was to disband.
d. The Zulu military system was to be abandoned.
e. Every Zulu was to be free to marry.
f. Missionaries were to be re-admitted to Zululand without let or hindrance.
g. A British resident official was to oversee Zulu affairs.
h. Any dispute involving a European was to be dealt with under British jurisdiction.

In the meantime, the British invasion force was already advancing on three fronts towards the border of Zululand in total confidence that Cetshwayo could not comply with the British ultimatum. Hicks Beach's reply finally reached Frere and it was, as Frere anticipated, an indication that the British government was indifferent to southern Africa. It contained little more than a request that caution must be exercised. The reply read:

Her Majesty's Government are not prepared to comply with a request for reinforcement of troops. All the information that has hitherto reached them with respect to the position of affairs in Zululand appears to justify a confident hope that by the exercise of prudence and by meeting the Zulus in a spirit of forbearance and reasonable compromise it will be possible to avert the very serious evil of a war with Cetshwayo. (5)

Frere interpreted Hicks Beach's reply as implying authority to initiate a local war; once this had started, he was fully aware that the British government would be powerless to stop him. It took at least ten weeks for a message to travel to London and back; his exploitation of the delay, on the grounds of the tension and urgency he had created, was blatant.

At Frere's request, Colonel Henry Evelyn Wood VC, commanding British forces in the north of Natal, sought a meeting with the Transvaal Boers with the express intention of gaining their support in the forthcoming war. The Boers had previously informed Wood that, in the event of war with the Zulus, 800 mounted Boers would volunteer to fight under Wood's command. Arriving for the meeting, Wood learned that few volunteers would actually come forward. One Boer leader pointed out that the British were too few to invade Zululand, to which Wood replied:

Where we soldiers are ordered to go, we go. If you remain behind, and we are victorious – as please God we shall be – you will regret not having helped towards the securing of the quiet enjoyment of your property. If we fail for want of your help, the Zulus will over-run your farms. (6)

Three days later the Boers discovered that the Boundary Commission had already found against them. Realising the deception, the Boers became even more antagonistic and accordingly withheld their support – with the exception of isolated individuals, most notably Piet Uys, whose father and brother had been killed by the Zulus. The British now prepared for war against the Zulus, their former allies.

British preparations for war
The 1st Battalion, 24th (Warwickshire) Regiment had been stationed in the Cape since January 1875. The 2nd Battalion, with 24 officers and 849 other ranks, arrived in South Africa on 28 February 1878 and shortly afterwards

commenced their duties at King William's Town. Both battalions were then engaged in quelling small pockets of rebellion throughout the Cape area. Their final military operation took place on the plateau west of Buffalo Poort, which they attacked on 8 May. Meanwhile, news of a Boer insurrection at Kimberley reached Natal; Colonel Richard Glyn was ordered to take the 1/24th to quell the dissent, and he did so by marching his men the 650 miles to Kimberley, only to discover a Boer change of heart. Glyn promptly marched his men back to the Cape; one positive aspect of the long march was the toughening of the regiment in preparation for the arduous campaign looming in Natal.

Both battalions then regrouped at Ibeka before returning to King William's Town. Officially orchestrated rumours were beginning to spread throughout Natal that King Cetshwayo was threatening to invade, so the 2nd Battalion was directed to Pietermaritzburg where they assembled on 6 August. The 1st Battalion was not long in following the 2nd; it had been back at King William's Town about a month when C and D Companies, under Brevet Lieutenant Colonel Henry Pulleine, were also ordered to Pietermaritzburg.

During the recent operations against the Galekas and other native tribes, neither battalion had sustained significant casualties. Only two officers, Captains Frederick Carrington and Frederick Godwin-Austen, were wounded, one man was killed and a few wounded – though the losses from disease were higher: eighteen men of the 1st Battalion and twenty-one of the 2nd. On the other hand, the work certainly had been strenuous, and both battalions had earned much praise for their cheerfulness in facing hardships and discomforts and for their good conduct and discipline in the field. General Thesiger (later Lord Chelmsford) spoke in the highest terms of both battalions, emphasising how well the younger soldiers, of whom the 2nd Battalion was in large measure composed, had come through this severe ordeal of hard work in the face of difficult conditions.

Their achievement was of no slight importance. It was well to have destroyed the menace of the unsubdued native tribes on the eastern frontier and thus to be free from serious anxieties in that quarter before a far greater danger had to be tackled. The award of the CB to Colonel Glyn and Lieutenant Colonel Degacher, of the CMG to Captain Paton, and of Brevet Majorities to Captains Upcher and Carrington was not only a recognition of their good work but of the services of the 24th. Sir Arthur Cunynghame, in congratulating the Colonel, described it as 'your excellent regiment'.

Chelmsford's main fighting force was to consist of two battalions of the 24th and the 90th and a single battalion of the 3rd, 4th, 13th and 99th regiments, with a battalion of the 80th held in reserve at Luneburg – a total of nearly 9,000 professional British soldiers. To this force were added irregular units based on the quasi-military Natal police, together with frontier guards and local defence groups with grand names such as the Natal Hussars, Royal Native Carbineers and Royal Durban Rangers.

Logistics and supplies

Despite the disasters of the Crimean War, caused in part by insufficient supplies, there was still no established system of transport within the British army of 1879. Lord Chelmsford's invasion force included an estimated total of 16,000 fighting men (including native auxiliaries), 985 waggons and 60 mule carts, over 10,000 oxen, 870 horses and 450 mules. The force carried enough ammunition to eliminate the Zulu population of 200,000 many times over. The overall task of the invasion was relatively simple when compared with the job of supplying this force with food and water for men and animals. There were extensive stockpiles of tins of bully beef, 200lb bags of locally grown corn and wooden crates of tough army biscuits. Sufficient tentage consisting of Bell tents (named after their inventor, not the bell shape) had to be transported, one for every twelve men, together with mobile bakeries, engineering equipment, ammunition and medical supplies. The list of supplies was virtually endless and included much other valuable equipment (soon to fall into Zulu hands), including items such as axes, blankets, kettles, lanterns, shovels, tools, lifting jacks, stretchers, ropes and waterproof sheets. The stores also had to include such incidentals as sufficient supplies of grease for the mens' boots, and spare flannel shirts. Chelmsford's staff calculated that the total weight of these stores would amount to nearly two thousand tons.

The task fell to the existing Commissary, General Strickland, with a staff of less than twenty officers and men, to commence the organisation of supplies for the whole invasion force. Following the first of a number of scathing observations by Major John Crealock of Chelmsford's staff, that the commissariat and storage system had utterly broken down, these officers were soon supplemented by regular commissariat officers sent from the UK, including Lieutenant Horace Smith-Dorrien, who was later to escape from Isandlwana. Due to their inexperience, these commissariat officers were very vulnerable to a variety of fraudulent deals, and the British suffered considerable financial losses. Horses and cattle were sold to the military at highly inflated prices and, in some cases, were not even delivered. The most successful fraud, perhaps just a sharp business practice, was the widespread practice of wily civilian contractors purchasing, at knockdown prices, Zulu cattle seized by the British troops during skirmishes; these were then immediately resold to the army caterers as fresh meat at twenty times the price.

Having assembled sufficient stores, the establishment of an effective transport system was the next problem. All assembled stores had to be scaled down according to the size and purpose of the unit. The scale of transport was also meticulously prepared down to company level so that, remarkably, each company was mobile yet totally self sufficient. This was a huge logistical undertaking. The total number of waggons per infantry battalion amounted to seventeen, including one HQ waggon; a battery of artillery was allocated ten waggons and a squadron of mounted infantry had four. The overall responsibility for transport fell on the appointed Transport Officer, one per invading column, assisted by a sub-conductor for every ten waggons.

It is likely that the marching soldier was more concerned with the availability of his daily rations and the bottled beer acquired from travelling salesmen. His official daily entitlement was a minimum of 1lb of fresh meat, 1½ lb of fresh bread or its equivalent in biscuits, plus fresh vegetables and fruit or lime juice and sugar in lieu. Rum was available, but only if authorised by the accompanying medical officer. The soldiers' uniforms were well worn by the time of the invasion, and the only replacements readily available were shirts and steel-shod boots. Even so, a soldier was required to appear before a Board of three officers in order to obtain a replacement pair of boots. Soldiers knew how to care for their boots by keeping them well greased; they also combated fungal foot infections by regularly washing out their boots with urine.

Chelmsford quickly realised that the invasion force would be slow-moving and therefore vulnerable to attack by the fast-moving Zulus. He knew only too well that victory depended on the Zulus attacking prepared positions where they would face awesome firepower. He accordingly gave priority to the implementation of regulations relating to ammunition. Each artillery battery of two guns carried 68 rounds, together with 12 rockets, and additional reserves were to be readily available in accompanying carts and waggons. Rifle ammunition was calculated at 270 rounds per soldier, 70 in the possession of each man and 200 rounds in clearly identifiable ammunition waggons. All column commanders had received written instructions that 'a commanding officer would incur a heavy responsibility should required supplies fail to arrive in time, through any want of foresight and arrangement on his part'. (7)

By the time of the invasion, Chelmsford had succeeded in an almost impossible task. He had assembled sufficient supplies and transport to sustain his campaign. Unusually for the period, he had also carefully informed his officers of the nature of the campaign and of the strengths of the enemy.

British firepower

In 1879 the Martini-Henry rifle was the backbone of British infantry firepower, the product of a fiercely fought Prize Competition between the rifle manufacturers of Europe, first held in 1867. Amongst the short list of competitors were a M. Frederich Chevalier de Martini of Frauenfeld, Switzerland and Mr Alexander Henry of Edinburgh. After lengthy trials in which none of the competing weapons was truly outstanding, the prize of £600 was awarded to Mr Henry. The competition, from the point of view of finding an acceptable breech-loading rifle for the British army, was officially regarded as a failure. Because of the rigid conditions imposed by the Prize Committee, many promising designs were not considered. It was decided to continue the trials but to standardise the calibre and size of the bullets.

During the subsequent trials it emerged that Henry's barrel and Martini's action were superior to all others, and it was decided that they should combine into one rifle. From this hybrid was born one of the most enduring of British arms.

After several modifications, the Martini-Henry Mark II, as carried in the Zulu War, had the following specifications: it was 4' 1½" in length and weighed 9lbs. It fired a black-powder, 0.45 calibre, centre-fire Boxer cartridge in a flat trajectory, which gave it considerable stopping power.(8)

The weapon's accuracy can be attributed to Henry's rifled seven-groove polygon barrel, while Martini's distinctive enclosed all-steel breech gave it robustness and protection. The hammerless action was simple compared with the complexities of muzzle loading. The breechblock was hinged at the rear and opened when the lever behind the trigger guard was lowered. An ejector would throw out the expended round and a fresh cartridge was laid on top of the grooved block, thumbed into the chamber and the lever raised. This action also automatically cocked the weapon, and a tear-shaped indicator on the right showed that the gun was cocked. The rifle was sighted up to a theoretical 1,000 yards, but the average sighting for volley firing was 600 yards; in calm conditions on a rifle range, a well-trained infantryman was capable of firing twelve rounds per minute; most soldiers could manage to fire five rounds. Soldiers knew that the barrel would become unbearably hot with use, so they bound their weapons with individually made leather protectors – as can be seen in Plate 13 of Lieutenant Lloyd's *On Active Service* (Chapman & Hall, 1890). As with all rifles of this period, the stock and fore-end were fashioned from European walnut. The rifle was soon followed by carbine equivalents for the Cavalry and Artillery. (9)

The 1853-pattern equi-angular bayonet with three hollow ground faces had long been the standard issue. With so many already in service, it was decided to have them bushed to fit the Martini-Henry. In 1876 the specially designed socket bayonet, which looked similar to its predecessor, was 4½" longer at 21½". Fitted to the end of a Martini-Henry, it gave its handler an imposing reach and was most effective against native foes. Another bayonet designed especially for the Martini-Henry by Lord Elcho was known as the Pattern Sword Bayonet. This was also carried in the Zulu War and eventually took the place of the socket bayonet.

The Martini-Henry was subjected to more trials during 1873 when it was issued to the 4th and 46th Regiments and the 60th Rifles. Some of their findings found echoes in 1879: 'Barrels heat with quick firing . . . may prove a serious drawback to rapidity of fire. A barrel cannot be touched after five or six rounds on some occasions. A leather shield attached to the fore-end may be found a necessary addition'. (10) The Inspector-General of Musketry wrote in his report:

I can only account for the inferior shooting of the 4th and 46th Regiments with the Martini-Henry rifle by the fact of the recoil being so great; the men in most instances fire with less confidence,

39

and consequently at a great disadvantage; the shortness of the stock also frequently causes a smart blow on the cheek, particularly at the short distances and this naturally increases the chances of bad shooting. (11)

Although some modifications and improvements were made, the barrels still grew hot with rapid fire and the kick remained fearsome. This was less to do with the weapon itself but rather with the black-powder propellant. After a few rounds the barrel became fouled with residue, which reduced the bore slightly. This was enough, however, to produce greater backward force when fired, causing the gun to kick fiercely. Bruised shoulders and cheeks, torn firing fingers and bloody noses were often the result, and much of the poor marksmanship observed during the Zulu War was certainly attributable to flinching by young recruits at the moment of firing.

The overheating of the barrel was caused by the same source, and only frequent cleaning could reduce the problem. The suggestion of leather shields, which had been recommended at the trials, was shelved for later consideration. Soldiers subsequently followed the Boer example of stitching wet rawhide around the fore-end and allowing it to dry and shrink to form some protection.

The Boxer cartridges caused additional problems. As the barrels heated, so the cartridges were prone to 'cook' and prematurely discharge the rounds. The thin rolled brass became soft and stuck to the chamber, while the ejectors tore off the iron rim. The soldier then had to remove the empty case with a knife or try to knock it out with the cleaning rod. The cartridge was also found wanting in other respects. If carried for any length of time in an ammunition pouch, rounds became deformed, causing the bullets to loosen and to shed black powder. They were also prone to dampness.

Colonel Buller VC wrote a memo after the Zulu War in which he was heavily critical of the Boxer cartridge compared with the Snider:

My men carried their service ammunition in bandolier belts. This did very well for the Sniders, but the Martini-Henry ammunition is more delicate. It becomes unserviceable far more rapidly than the Snider
i.   By becoming bent in the front of the swell.
ii. By getting bruised more easily.
iii. The bullet is far more apt to drop out.

iv. It is far more liable to get damp. This I consider very important. I found that Snider cartridges hardly ever became unserviceable from this cause, but a good shower of rain would spoil at least one-third of the ammunition (Martini-Henry) exposed to it. I could not account for this to my satisfaction, though I made many experiments. The result was always the same; Snider remained good, Martini-Henry carried in the same bandolier became damp. (12)

Major General Newdigate also wrote to the War Office: 'Numerous complaints were made about the ball-bags; the weight of the cartridges makes the bags open, and when the men double the cartridges fall out'. (13) Shoulder-to-shoulder firing created its own perils; a volley would produce thick acrid smoke that stung the eyes and parched the throat. A pause was required to allow the smoke to disperse before another volley could be fired. Lieutenant Edward Wilkinson of the 3rd Battalion, 60th Rifles wrote:

We followed suit, firing volleys by sections in order to prevent the smoke obscuring the enemy, and we had repeatedly to cease fire to allow the smoke to clear off, as some young aspirants out of hand paid little attention to section firing. One lesson we learnt in our fight was, that with the Martini-Henry, men must fire by word of command either by individuals, or at most, by sections: independent firing means in firing in twenty seconds, firing at nothing; and only helped our daring opponents to get close up under cover of our smoke. Officers had to be everywhere, and to expose themselves to regulate the fire within bounds, and I feel sure that for the future, only volleys by sections will be fired. (14)

Private George Mossop (at the battle of Hlobane) also alluded to the problem in his celebrated book *Running the Gauntlet*. He wrote about the matter following the battle at Kambula:

The camp to be defended was large, we had lost a lot of men on Hlobane mountain the previous day. We were armed with Martini-Henry rifles charged with black powder, and each shot belched out a cloud of smoke; it became so dense that we were almost choked by it – and simply fired blindly into it. There was one continuous roar from cannon, rifles and the voices of men on both sides shouting. The smoke blotted out all view. It made every man feel that all he could do was to shoot immediately in front of him – and not concern himself with what was taking place elsewhere.

Nevertheless, the Martini-Henry was a real man-stopper. The soft lead slug flattened on impact, causing massive tissue damage. Even if not hit in a vital organ, the victim would almost certainly die of trauma. There is evidence, however, that the Zulus were sometimes able to lessen the impact. This is supported in various letters about the Zulu War that mention the Zulus bravely advancing under sustained volley fire. At Gingindlovu, the British volleys commenced when the Zulus reached the 800-yard markers, yet the Zulus were still able to get to within a few yards of the British lines. There are several reasons for this, including the facts that the Zulus were in vast numbers and many soldiers fired inaccurately or too high. However, Captain Edmund Wyatt-Edgell of the 17th Lancers noted that after the battle there were few Zulu bodies further than 300 yards from the British line. 'At 300 yards a thin boundary of black bodies and white shields might be traced; at 200 yards and 100 yards from our lines their walls of dead were more thick.' (15)

When advancing on the scattered companies of the 24th at Isandlwana, many Zulus held their shields at an angle in order to deflect the bullets. This tactic certainly appears to have had some success at ranges beyond 300 yards and may well have accounted for the Zulu warriors' belief that their ritual indoctrination of immunity against British rifle fire was, indeed, effective.

Rifles and ammunition taken by the Zulus after their victory at Isandlwana were subsequently used against the British, and if the Zulus had mastered the use of the rifle's leaf sight there would have been many more British casualties. By the end of the war, during which time the Martini-Henry had been subjected to sustained heavy rain, mud, dust and rough handling, it had emerged as a solid and reliable arm. It was acknowledged, however, that there were now superior weapons in service with other armies. During the Zulu War, the average cost to the government of each Martini-Henry rifle, including bayonet and cleaning kit, was £14 1s 8d.

Artillery at Isandlwana

The Royal Artillery, under the command of Major Stuart Smith RA, had two 7-pound rifled muzzle-loading guns at Isandlwana. These were originally designed for mountain warfare and were considered to be ideal weapons for Zululand. They were towed by three horses and were highly manoeuvrable, although prone to overturning on rocky ground. These guns could fire their explosive shells to a maximum range of 3,000 yards, whereas the shrapnel rounds or case-shot were used at close range.

The Royal Artillery was also equipped with Congreve rockets, whose efficacy was dubious. The rockets could not be accurately aimed and, theoretically, their main purpose was to alarm native troops by the screaming sound created by the rockets in flight.

British strategy and tactics in Zululand

Once Sir Bartle Frere had committed Lord Chelmsford to an offensive campaign against Zululand, five independent columns were prepared and assembled ready for the invasion on 11 January 1879. Chelmsford then reduced this number to three: Colonel Charles Pearson's Coastal Column (1st) consisting of 1,800 Europeans and 2,000 natives; Colonel Richard Glyn's Central Column (3rd) with 1,600 Europeans and 2,500 natives; and the Northern Column (4th) commanded by Colonel Evelyn Wood VC, with 1,700 Europeans and 300 natives. The remaining two columns were given other tasks: Colonel Anthony Durnford's column (2nd) was to act as a rearguard on the Natal border to prevent a Zulu incursion and had a theoretical strength of 3,000 natives. In reality, its effective strength amounted to 500, of which half were the elite and very loyal (to Durnford) Natal Native Horse and a small Rocket Battery commanded by Major Francis Russell RA. The remaining 5th column, with 1,400 Europeans and 400 natives under Colonel Hugh Rowlands VC, was to police the north near Luneburg and maintain a defensive watch on the malcontent and increasingly rebellious Transvaal Boers. Lord Chelmsford's strategy of invading Zululand with three independent columns was devised to discourage the Zulus from outflanking any one column or, more seriously, retaliating against a defenceless Natal before he could inflict defeat on the main Zulu force. The British invasion was to be spearheaded by the 24th (2nd Warwickshire) Regiment; both battalions were enthusiastic at the prospect of leading operations against the Zulus. (16)

Chelmsford's invasion date in early January 1879 was chosen deliberately, as the spring rains were late, thus delaying the Zulu harvest, and on advice from his staff he presumed the Zulus would be unprepared for a lengthy campaign during the intensive harvest period. From January until early April the rivers forming the Natal boundary with Zululand were expected to be in full flood and would thus provide a natural defence against a retaliatory Zulu counter-attack on a defenceless Natal. Chelmsford also relied on natural grazing for the invasion force's numerous oxen and horses, which precluded invading during the later grassless, dry season.

Due to the rocky terrain of Zululand and the ponderous progress of ox-drawn supply waggons, the British invasion force would be very slow-moving. Ordinarily, such serious transport deficiencies would have been a serious handicap, but Chelmsford turned this slow progress to his tactical advantage. A measured advance towards the Zulu capital of Ulundi permitted both adequate reconnaissance of uncharted Zululand and progressive destruction of Zulu crops and villages as his invasion force advanced, actions which were deliberately calculated to provoke the Zulus into attacking his prepared troops or entrenched positions.

British use of intelligence

For the senior British officers invading Zululand, the main point of military intelligence was to learn the Zulus' intentions and predict their tactics. Henry Curling (see *The Curling Letters of the Zulu War*, Greaves & Best, Pen & Sword Books, 2004) wrote that the advance into Zululand was handicapped by a lack of accurate maps. Chelmsford was, technically, invading Zululand blindly and so had to rely on local information for his intelligence. Much of this intelligence came from local officials, men such as John Robson and Henry Fynn, both local magistrates, who were familiar with the countryside and Zulu ways.

As late as 6 January, Robson's string of agents was reporting regular patrols of well-armed Zulus along the Buffalo River who appeared to be eager for a fight. Right up to the time of the British making camp at Isandlwana, daily reports were reaching Chelmsford that indicated massive concentrations of Zulu warriors between Ulundi and Isandlwana. Having already made up his mind, however, the supremely confident Chelmsford did not want to be bothered with the facts – he treated the reports with indifference and ignored them. The same mindset would afflict Colonel Pulleine, to whom the defence of Isandlwana would fall on 22 January.

British tactics

Lord Chelmsford confidently anticipated the swift and total defeat of the Zulu army. His officers and their troops were all experienced in African native warfare, and their main fear was that the Zulus would not fight. Chelmsford knew the Zulus had lived peacefully for the previous twenty-three years though they were highly disciplined as a nation. He had nevertheless been very strongly warned by a number of Boer leaders experienced in Zulu affairs that he faced a powerful and tactically astute adversary. Within days of the invasion, the very first skirmish at Sihayo's homestead met with only a token resistance by its Zulu occupants, as most of Sihayo's warriors were already attending King Cetshwayo. This insignificant victory clearly strengthened Chelmsford's haughty and over-confident attitude.

The standard battle tactic employed by the British in South Africa was good reconnaissance followed by ruthless skirmishing. In rough country, both the infantry and mounted troops would advance to meet the enemy, the infantry breaking up any established groups by volley fire and the mounted troops harassing them in flight. In the unlikely event that the Zulus appeared in any number, the British were trained to form a square or entrench their position, thus drawing the Zulus into the range of their overwhelming firepower. Well-aimed rifle volleys from calm and experienced troops supported by rockets, artillery and, later in the campaign, Gatling guns, would, in Chelmsford's view, ensure the invincibility of the invasion force. Once a Zulu attack on such a well-defended position faltered, the cavalry would leave the protection of the entrenched position to harass and then rout the attackers.

Immediately prior to the invasion, Lord Chelmsford issued a circular to his officers pointing out certain notable Zulu characteristics. He wrote that the Zulus were 'masters of the ambuscade and other ruses', and that 'in going through bush, remember that natives will often lie down to let you pass and then rise to fire on you'. Perhaps the wisest section related to ambushes: 'A common ruse with the natives is to hide a large force in the bush and then show a few solitary individuals to invite an attack. When the troops enter the bush in pursuit of the latter the hidden men rise and attack them'. (17) It was this fundamental advice that the British would frequently and spectacularly ignore – to their cost.

Zulu strategy

Faced with the inevitable British invasion of Zululand, King Cetshwayo's overall strategy was either to trap or inflict a decisive preliminary defeat on the British invaders. At the time of the British invasion, Cetshwayo's army was well trained but totally inexperienced in actual warfare. Knowing the British possessed overwhelming firepower, Cetshwayo decided against the traditional Zulu mass frontal attack, preferring the use of siege tactics. He reasoned that, once trapped or starved into submission, the invaders would be forced to withdraw to Natal rather than face a humiliating defeat on the battlefield. He accordingly instructed his commanders to bypass the invading columns and isolate them from their supply lines.

The Zulu king was also a shrewd diplomat. Cetshwayo knew that once the British invasion force was trapped he could seriously embarrass Britain internationally and even force her invading army commanders to sue for peace. Unfortunately for Cetshwayo, his field commanders were autonomous and were either unable or unwilling to follow the King's orders. After the Zulu success at Isandlwana, Natal was utterly helpless to defend itself; the British invasion force was in part defeated and partly surrounded, yet Cetshwayo did not capitalise on his victory. Had he ordered his army into Natal, the consequences for the population of Natal and the subsequent history of southern Africa would have been difficult to imagine.

Zulu tactics

The Zulus historically favoured a dawn attack but were prepared to fight at any time. Prior to an attack, the Zulus would be indoctrinated by *sangomas* (witchdoctors), and the use of cannabis and other narcotics as stimulants was widespread. Senior Zulus, usually from a remote vantage point, always controlled military operations, although one of their number would be ready for dispatch into the battle to rally or take command if an assault faltered, as was to happen at Isandlwana.

Zulu tactics were based on the encircling movement of massed ranks of warriors, the 'horns of the buffalo' or *impondo zankhomo* (see Fig. 2, p. 23). At Isandlwana, the encircling horns consisted of the younger fitter men, with the body or chest made up of the more seasoned warriors who would bear the brunt of a frontal attack. The tactic was most successful when the two horns completed the encirclement of the enemy, and relied in part on the main body remaining out of sight until the horns met; the main body would then close in to slaughter the surrounded enemy. Features of the attack were speed and precision. Popular myth records the Zulus moving into the attack in mass formation. However, the reality was an attack in open skirmishing lines, although at Isandlwana these lines of warriors were more than half a mile deep. Certainly, from a distance, such a large force carrying shields would have appeared very densely packed. The force would advance at a steady jogging pace and complete the final attack at a run. Once amongst the enemy, their short stabbing *assegai* was most effective. Although the Zulus rarely used firearms with any effect, by 1878 they already possessed an estimated 20,000 serviceable firearms and 500 modern breech-loading rifles. (18) A sizeable reserve of warriors was always kept behind the main body to bolster any weakness which developed during an attack, and on several occasions the reserves were kept out of sight of the action to mislead the enemy as to their strength and to ensure the reserve remained calm until required. Such a tactic would succeed brilliantly against the British at Isandlwana.

By the end of September 1878 Cetshwayo was fully aware that events were rapidly moving beyond his control, and from his royal homestead on the rolling Mahlabatini Plain, the site of modern day Ulundi, he mobilised the Zulu army to assemble before him. He also ordered animal hunts to be held along the border with Natal, and the hunters were instructed to ensure that Shepstone's spies observed them. By the time the ultimatum reached Cetshwayo, most of the *amabutho* were already gathered and the ritual preparations for war began. Notwithstanding soothing reassurances from Shepstone, Cetshwayo was not to be caught off balance and shrewdly decided to wait and watch. He sent a number of senior emissaries to implore British restraint, but on presentation of their credentials they were arrested and imprisoned.

Even when the British threatened Cetshwayo with an impossible ultimatum and massed troops along the border with Zululand, Cetshwayo still withheld the order for his army to attack, in the hope that his final request to delay the implementation of the ultimatum would be accepted. Anticipating rejection, he finally gave his *indunas* their orders for a specific attack on Chelmsford's central column, though with certain restrictions – they must not attack any fortified or static position. There exists a post-war account by Mehlokazulu, Chief Sihayo's son and heir, a respected subchief in his own right, who was present at Ulundi when King Cetshwayo gave his chiefs their orders to attack the British invaders. Mehlokazulu's second interrogation report reads:

> He [referring to Cetshwayo] then gave Tsingwayo orders to use his own discretion and attack the English wherever he thought proper [indicating clearly that Ntsingwayo was at liberty to attack as and when he thought fit] and if he beat them he was to cross the Buffalo River and advance on Pietermaritzburg, devastating the whole country and to return with the spoil. (19)

This report is supported by the account of a post-war discussion between Mr J. Gibson, a magistrate in Zululand, and King Cetshwayo's brother, Chief Undabuko, confirming there was no suggestion that to cross the border would have contravened the King's orders. According to Undabuko:

> seeing that portion of the army which had not been engaged cross the border, [he] called to members of his own regiment, the Mbonambi, to join them but they declined on the ground that it was necessary to return to the field of battle to attend to their wounded. (20)

During the lull in fighting at Isandlwana, Muziwento recounted that his men were exhorted to fight by the call of their commander:

> Never did the king give you the command 'Lie down upon the ground'. His next words were:'Go, and toss them to Maritzburg'. (21)

Cetshwayo knew exactly where the British were massing their forces and correctly gauged their objective.. Chelmsford's tactic of using three columns to approach and surround Ulundi was a direct copy, probably unwittingly, of the Zulu *impondo zankhomo* tactic. Cetshwayo would certainly have noticed the irony, and his understanding of the intricacies of the technique is perhaps one reason why the Zulu army was able to inflict such a stunning defeat on the British at Isandlwana. Because Chelmsford was accompanying the centre column, Cetshwayo correctly singled it out as being the most dangerous force.

On 17 January the Zulu army formed up to undergo ritual purification against evil influences during the coming conflict. That same day they began leaving their base on the Mahlabatini Plain to face the invaders, and the trail they left in the grass was to remain visible for many months. Their destination was a gorge just five miles from a huge, dominating rock outcrop known locally as Isandlwana. As the British soldiers of the 24th approached Isandlwana they immediately compared its lion-like crest to their regimental badge.

The time for peaceful negotiation had passed; both sides were ready for war. The Zulu nation had been at peace for twenty-three years, and no British settler or traveller had ever been harmed by them.

Chapter 4

The Days Before

Never has such a disaster happened to the English Army.
Trooper Richard Stevens, Natal Mounted Police (1)

By the time Lord Chelmsford embarked upon his invasion of Zululand, the Zulus had yet to secure their enduring reputation for tactical skill and ferocious bravery. Their record against white men was undistinguished; their only previous encounter was in 1836, when they suffered defeat at the hands of a relatively small party of Boer trekkers at the Battle of Blood River, a defeat highly exaggerated by Boer history.

As early as July 1878 Chelmsford had written, 'I shall strive to be in a position to show them [the Zulus] how hopelessly inferior they are to us in fighting power'. (2) Indeed, Chelmsford's overriding concern was that the Zulus would not fight. 'I am inclined to think', he wrote, 'that the first experience of the power of the Martini-Henrys will be such a surprise to the Zulus that they will not be formidable after the first effort'. (3) Even as late as 8 January 1879, Chelmsford demonstrated this concern when he wrote, 'All the reports which reach me tend to show that the Zulus intend, if possible, to make raids into Natal when the several columns move forward'.

Unexpectedly, Chelmsford was faced with the threat of mutiny by his previously loyal colonial troops. He had unthinkingly given command of the Natal Mounted Police and all the Natal volunteer units to Brevet Major John Russell of the Mounted Infantry, ignoring their own commandant, Major Dartnell. Chelmsford had previously decreed that all commanders were to be Imperial officers and had given an instruction to this effect in para. 144 of his 'Regulations for Field Forces in South Africa'. The effect of this regulation was to debar any colonial officer, regardless of his rank, from having command over Imperial troops. The severely disgruntled colonials paraded at Helpmekaar and took a vote on the matter; they unanimously decided that they would not enter Zululand under the command of an unknown British officer, especially when they respected Major Dartnell's proven experience in native warfare. Chelmsford was forced to compromise, and promoted Dartnell to the rank of Lieutenant Colonel and appointed him to his own staff, which gave him authority over Russell. The decision was grudgingly accepted by the colonials, who then obeyed their orders and moved down to Rorke's Drift.

The British force invaded Zululand on 11 January 1879. The centre (3rd Column) crossed the Buffalo at Rorke's Drift into Zululand, the troops making their way over at different points. Lieutenant Harford kept a meticulous diary of events and he wrote on that day:

> The Artillery and the 24th Regiment went over by degrees in the pontoon, a little above the main Drift, known as Rorke's Drift after the Dutchman Jim Rorke, whose house and farm buildings were occupied by us as a Fort, after being entrenched. I was ordered to find a crossing for the 2nd/3rd Natal Native Contingent, higher up the river. The fog was so dense one could barely see anything a yard in front, but at last, after hugging the bank very closely for about half a mile or more, we came to a spot that looked worth a trial. So I put my pony at it and got across all right, the bed of the river being nice and hard; but the water came up to the saddle flaps, and there was a nasty bank to scramble up on the opposite side. However, that did not matter, it was good enough.
>
> Then followed a truly unforgettable scene, first of the Natives crossing over and then of the impressive ceremony when the Regiment had formed up again on the other side and were addressed by old Ingabangi, the witch doctor. In order to scare away any crocodiles that might be lurking in the vicinity, the leading Company formed a double chain right across the River, leaving a pathway between for the remainder to pass through. The men forming the chain clasped hands, and the moment they entered the water they started to hum a kind of war-chant, which was taken up by every Company as they passed over. The sound that this produced was like a gigantic swarm of bees buzzing about us, and sufficient to scare crocodiles or anything else, away. Altogether, it was both a curious and grand sight. (4)

The mounted troops cautiously rode their horses through the swirling waters, using the submerged flat rocks of the original traders' crossing point. Once across, they spread out in a wide semicircle in anticipation of a Zulu attack. All they saw were three startled Zulu boys tending their cattle. The mounted troopers held their defensive position while the infantry were slowly ferried across the river. The native forces had been assembled downstream of the main crossing point and were cajoled by their officers into the fast-flowing, muddy river. They began the crossing in their customary style by linking arms and entering the water in a 'V' formation, those in the point of the 'V' being pushed across by those in the rear. When the front ranks reached the far bank, they then pulled their colleagues over; the native contingent lost several men in the crossing but, as their officers did not know how many natives they commanded, little concern was shown.

Once across, the force spread out in a defensive formation until the mounted patrols confirmed the absence of Zulu defenders. A few hundred yards from the crossing point a new campsite was prepared, and by noon the slow process of bringing stores and waggons across from Rorke's Drift was well under way. It is unlikely that during the crossing any of the troops would have noticed the prominent rocky outcrop of Isandlwana that dominated the skyline some eight miles away. It is equally unlikely that they would have known its name, but it was a name their relatives would shortly become familiar with; the Zulus called it *Isandula*.

The following day, 12 January, British troops commenced actual hostilities against a small Zulu clan living just two miles inside the Zululand border under the chieftaincy of Sihayo ka Xongo. The area was virtually deserted as most of Sihayo's warriors were already at Ulundi preparing for war. The few Zulu warriors left at the homestead fired some inaccurate shots at the approaching British then fled, which reinforced the troops' perception that their enemy would not fight. This minor skirmish, and the torture of captured Zulus for information, were to have disastrous consequences for the few survivors of Isandlwana. The captured Zulus kept secret the fact that a great force of 25,000 warriors, accompanied by another 10,000 reserves and camp followers, was closing with the unsuspecting British. During the skirmish Harford distinguished himself by fearlessly leading his men across a rocky hillside in pursuit of fleeing Zulus. His bravery was witnessed by Chelmsford, who afterwards complimented Harford and informed him he would be 'rewarded' for his action. Ever the gentleman, Harford replied that it was unnecessary;

Chelmsford accepted Harford's polite response, but the fact that no decoration was forthcoming seriously rankled with Harford for the rest of his life. He kept a diary during his service in Zululand, and his account of the attack on Sihayo's homestead gives a strong indication of why Chelmsford thought any battle with the Zulus would be an easy victory for his forces:

> Reveille sounded very early, about 3 a.m. the next morning, and we marched to attack Sihayo's kraal, up the Bashee valley, through thick bush. It was most unpleasant going, for above us, on our right, were hills with the usual cavernous rocks encircling them a little below their crests. It was evident that the warriors we had heard singing their war-chant the day before were ensconced in these caves, for the instant the troops got within range a continuous popping went on from these places. The crack, crack, crack of their guns and rifles echoed and re-echoed among the hills in the still morning air and made it impossible to detect exactly where the shots were coming from. Now and again a Zulu was seen in the open, and on one such occasion I saw the man taking deliberate aim at Colonel Glyn who was standing in an open patch above me. Shouting as loud as I could, I told him to get out of the way before the shot was fired.
>
> Colonel Glyn was in command of the troops, and Lord Chelmsford took up a position with his staff on the opposite side of the valley, to watch operations. Colonel Degacher commanded the 2/24th Regiment, and Major Black our Contingent, as Lonsdale was still in hospital. We started skirmishing through the bush, Major Black leading the 1st Battalion N.N.C. under Commandant Hamilton-Browne, and I following in support with the 2nd Battalion under Commandant Cooper. Before many minutes, bullets were whizzing about in all directions, and one of our Natives, who was close by my side, got a bullet in the thigh, breaking the bone. A short distance further on, seeing two NCOs sheltering behind a rock instead of leading their men, I went to drive them on; and had just got them away when 'ping' came a bullet and cut away a branch just at the spot where my head was a second before. This was luck!
>
> As we got further into the bush all sorts of obstacles, such as

rocky ground, ravines, and especially thick masses of creepers, prevented any sort of formation being properly kept, in consequence of which the firing line and supports soon got mingled together. Nevertheless, the men were kept well in hand. Before very long I could hear Major Black's shrill voice in broad Scotch urging his men on, and, making my way up to him with supports, I found that he and Commandant Hamilton-Browne were in a hot corner close to some caves, with hand-to-hand fighting going on. When I was within about twenty or thirty yards of the place, one of their men fell almost at my feet with a terrible assegai wound, which had nearly cut him in half, right down the back. The poor fellow was not dead, and although I could see it was only a matter of minutes my feelings almost led me to try to put him out of his misery with my revolver. But I abstained. I went on to the ridge of the spur of the hill in front of me as fast as I could, with some men, to see what was on the other side and to assist on Major Black's flank.

Eventually, on reaching the foot of a ledge of rocks, where they curved in a horseshoe bend overhanging a deep valley, a somewhat grim sight presented itself. Confronting me across the bend was a large, open-mouthed cave, apparently capable of holding a good number of men, and hanging below it were several dead Zulus, caught in the monkey-rope creepers and bits of bush. They had evidently been shot and had either fallen out, or been thrown out, by their comrades when killed. Later on, I learned that a Company of the 24th Regiment had been firing at this particular cave for some time, and had been ordered to cease firing on it when our men came up. It was an uncommonly awkward place to get at, as it meant climbing over nothing but huge rocks and in many places having to work one's way like a crab, besides which a loss of foothold might have landed one in the valley below. However, there was not much time to think, and I determined to make an attempt, so, sending some men to work round below; I took a European NCO who was close at hand, and told him to follow me. Clambering at once over a big piece of rock, I got rather a rude shock on finding a Zulu sitting in a squatting position behind another rock, almost at my elbow. His head showed above the rock, and his wide-open eyes glared at me; but I soon discovered that he was dead.

Scarcely had I left this apparition behind than a live Zulu . . . suddenly jumped up from his hiding place and, putting the muzzle of his rifle within a couple of feet of my face, pulled the trigger. But the cap snapped, whereupon he dropped his rifle and made off over the rocks for the cave, as hard as he could go. Providence had again come to my aid, and away I went after him, emptying my revolver at him as we scrambled up. Out of my six shots only one hit him, but not mortally. I stopped for a second to reload, but finding the wretched thing stuck I threw it down into the valley below, at the same time turning round and shouting to the NCO, who I thought was following me, to let me have his revolver. But he remained behind, where I had left him at the start, and all he did was to call out, as loud as he could, 'Captain Harford is killed!' However, I soon put this right by shouting down, 'No, he is not, he is very much alive!'

All this was a matter of seconds, and after pronouncing my blessings pretty freely on the Corporal, followed up my quarry, who by this time was standing in the mouth of the cave. Speaking to him in Kaffir, I called upon him to surrender, explaining that I had no intention to harm him in any way and would see to it that he was not ill treated by anyone. He then squatted down in submission. Before getting up into the cave myself, not caring to run my head into a noose thoughtlessly, I demanded to know if there was anyone else inside and was assured that there was no one, and as all was quiet, although I must say I had some slight misgivings, I clambered in.

Close to the entrance lay a wounded man with his feet towards me. Although unable to rise, he clutched hold of an assegai that was by his side, but I told him at once to drop it, that I was going to do him no harm, and questioned him as to who was with him in the cave. He stoutly denied that there were any others there. By this time I was getting accustomed to the darkness, and saw several likely-looking boltholes and kept on repeating that I knew there were others somewhere in hiding and that they were telling me lies. At the same time adding, in a tone loud enough to be heard by anyone near the place, that if they would come out I would promise on oath that no harm should be done to them and that I would accompany them myself to the General . . . who would see that they were well treated.

In a short time this had the desired effect, and presently a head appeared from a hole, and as the object crept out I kept careful watch for any sort of weapon that might emerge with it; another and then another crawled out from the same spot. All were unarmed, and squatted down close to me. I then wanted to know where the others were, but they swore that there was no one else. As this seemed to be the case, I moved off with my four prisoners, leaving the badly wounded man in the cave. We soon made our way down the valley to where the General and his staff were, and I was met by Major Clery, the Adjutant-General, who greeted me with, 'Well, Harford, I congratulate you on your capture, the General and I have been watching your gallantry for some time.' Then he told me that a section of the 24th Regiment had been firing into the cave half the morning, owing to the sniping that had been going on from it, and when Lonsdale's men were seen to be approaching, orders had been sent to them to cease fire. Having handed over my prisoners and telling the Adjutant-General the promise I had made them, and after seeing the man that I had myself wounded was placed in the ambulance waggon for conveyance to hospital, I went off again.

On getting back to the Contingent, one of the men walked up to me and with the usual salutation of 'Inkosi' gravely handed me my sword, spurs and courier bag, all of which had been torn off me in walking through the bush, as well as the discarded revolver. Never was I more thankful than to get these things back, especially the courier bag which had been a parting gift from my Captain, Captain Moir, when I left Chatham and contained my field glasses, knife, fork and spoon, as well as other valuable odds and ends. It would have been almost impossible to have found them again, even if a search party had been sent out, but luckily this Good Samaritan had followed carefully in my tracks and picked up the things as they were dropped. Curious to say, in the excitement of the moment I never felt anything going.

Now that the Cavalry, Mounted Police and 24th Regiment had gone on to Sihayo's kraal, one or two companies of the Contingent were sent off to capture some cattle, and after a short rest and a meal the whole force returned to camp, drenched to the skin in a thunderstorm. After a day's rest to clean arms and dry clothing, camp was moved forward to the Bashee Valley, not far from the scene of our operations two days before, and here we remained for the next four or five days, the 24th and ourselves working hard at making and repairing roads for our advance to Isandlwana on the 20th.

Following the skirmish at Sihayo's homestead, the subject of captured Zulu cattle caused much discontent among column troops who all expected a fair share of the plunder. Evidently, the cattle captured at Sihayo's and in the surrounding area had been sold cheaply to contractors, and word of this spread quickly through the column.

The *Natal Witness* correspondent at Rorke's Drift sensed the widespread disquiet among the troops and sent the following report on the subject, published on 22 January:

> The captured cattle, than which a finer lot I have rarely seen, a large portion being oxen fit for the butcher, and milk cows with calves, were absolutely sold to the contractor by the prize committee, who consisted (I believe) of two captains in the N.N.C. – though it does not much matter who they were – for the sum of £2 a head, the goats for 2s 6d and the sheep for 6s a head. There will be very considerable discontent among all ranks if the bulk of our prize money goes to enrich contractors.

After destroying Sihayo's homestead, the invasion force made a temporary camp halfway between Rorke's Drift and Isandlwana to enable the Royal Engineers to repair the waggon track that ran through two swampy areas along the invasion route. Lieutenant MacDowell RE had been brought from Rorke's Drift to supervise the repairs, there being no further need for an officer at the ponts (rafts on which to cross the river). The following morning Chelmsford, accompanied by his staff and escorted by fifty mounted infantry, made a reconnaissance along the roadway leading towards Isandlwana. The morning was fine and dry, and until the heat became great – which it very soon did – the ride was a pleasant one. The first part of the ride was over the section of road that had been lately undergoing repairs. The soil was of a dark alluvial nature, and so soft that the wheels of a waggon would stick fast in it. The worst places had to be filled up with stones, and deep trenches had to be cut on each side of the track to permit drainage. Nearby Zulu huts were found to be most useful; they were pulled down and the wattles and supports of which they were composed were spread over the roadway.

The invasion column was ordered to the camp site at Isandlwana, but there were considerable misgivings on the part of officers of experience, including Major Dartnell, with regard to the selection of this site, owing principally to the broken and wooded country in its immediate rear which offered ample cover for a large force of the enemy to concentrate unseen and attack suddenly. To an officer of the Natal Mounted Police who had suggested to one of Chelmsford's staff officers that the British camp might be attacked from the rear, Chelmsford retorted, 'Tell the police officer my troops will do all the attacking'.(5)

That morning, several natives came into the camp with a warning for Chelmsford that Cetshwayo intended to decoy the British; when they had been lured into the bush, the Zulu army would make for Natal. The same report arrived from Chelmsford's own local adviser, Mr Fanin. Chelmsford dismissed all these warnings; he believed the drifts were adequately covered and resolved to push on deeper into Zululand without delay. The *Natal Witness* reporter with the Carbineers submitted the following dispatch to his newspaper on 18 January; it was published on 23 January:

We have already had three different patrols into the enemy's quarters. Rumour had it that there were thousands near to us: but, though we hunted up hill and down dale, 'saw we never none.' It is impossible to know what to believe. The Zulus must assuredly be somewhere, but wherever we go, we only come across deserted huts. It is evident that a large number of the people have taken to flight, but whether they have done so through fear of us, or of their own 'noble savage' defenders, I cannot undertake to say. As a change, however, on the last occasion we came across a Zulu, whom we took prisoner. On questioning him as to why there were so few men about, he said that they were quite scared away at the manner in which we had taken their mountain fortress [Sihayo's] from them – as they had not ever dreamt that we should venture up it. This amount of fear does not look very much like the wonderful prowess of the Zulus, of which we heard so much in Natal. I imagine they are much like other natives – very great at bragging, but easily depressed and panic-stricken by any sudden reverse.

By 21 January most of the British invading force had arrived at Isandlwana. The location was ideal: there was an ample supply of both water and wood for cooking, the position was elevated, with a sheer rock face to its rear, and therefore easy to defend. It looked down and across the open plain towards the Zulu capital at Ulundi, so that any approaching Zulu force would be observed for several miles before it could form up for an attack. The camp consisted of some 750 tents neatly erected according to strict military regulations, company by company, street by street, over an area nearly one mile square. There were troop tents and numerous headquarters and administration tents, together with hospital and messing tents; within hours, the area was transformed into a thriving, bustling tent town. The Bell tents each provided cramped accommodation for sixteen private soldiers sleeping in a circle with their feet towards the single centre-pole. Sergeants and above fared better, mostly enjoying a tent to themselves. Each tent, including the space around it which accommodated the ropes and pegs, occupied 1,440 square feet – thus thirty tents to the acre, more or less.

The regulations for laying out and erection of tents saw the British army at its ritualistic best:

The NCOs in charge of squads will be extended 16 paces from the left by Officers Commanding Companies in prolongation of their arms and turned to the right . . . The senior Major will dress the NCOs of the first row of tents, along the front of the column, so that they will stand exactly on the line marked out as the front of the camp and the Captain of each Company will, from them, dress the NCOs of his squads who whilst being so dressed will stand to attention. After being dressed, No 7 of each squad will drive a peg in-between the heels of his NCO, who will, after turning about, take 18 paces to the front where another peg will be driven in a similar manner.

There was a similar ritual in the striking of camp, and in the events which were to follow at Isandlwana such time-consuming drill must be remembered:

On the order being given to strike tents, all ropes except the corner ones, will be quickly undone and hanked up close to the flies; walls will be unlaced and packed into bags.

The corner ropes will then be loosened and the tents dropped on the bugle sound 'G', Nos 1, 2, 3, 4, 9 and 10 will remove poles, bank corner ropes, fold up flies and lace them carefully up in the hold-alls, while Nos 5, 6, 7 and 8 take out pegs, count them, and pack them in the peg bag.

Each unit's waggons were parked behind their own tents; those required for resupply were left in the adjacent waggon park ready to return to Rorke's Drift. Foot patrols were posted to the front of the camp, while mounted patrols were detailed to the surrounding hills.

During the afternoon of 21 January, Chelmsford dispatched Major John Dartnell, with a sizeable reconnaissance force consisting of sixteen companies of the Natal Native Contingent (NNC) together with most of the Natal Mounted Police and half the Natal Mounted Volunteers, into the distant hills near Isipezi, the site of the next British camp. Unconfirmed reports were indicating that large numbers of Zulus were approaching from the direction of the Zulu capital at Ulundi, fifty miles away. It was to be a precautionary patrol, and Dartnell had strict orders to reconnoitre the area and return later that day. Major Clery later wrote in a note to Colonel Harman on 17 February:

> He (Chelmsford) gave orders to their commandant of the natives to take his two battalions out at daybreak the following morning to work through some ravines ten miles off, and he also gave orders to the commandant of the volunteers to go in the same direction and cooperate. The orders to both these commandants were given personally by the general himself, and this was absolutely necessary in this case as neither Colonel Glyn nor myself knew in the least where they were being sent to, or what they were being sent for. (6)

Authors and researchers have persistently accepted earlier beliefs that Dartnell's column spent the day in the vicinity of the Magogo Valley, ten miles to the south-east of Isandlwana camp. The fact is, the Magogo Valley is not on the route between Ulundi and Isandlwana, and there is no evidence from the participants to confirm that this was where they were. It was at Isipezi hill, twelve miles due east, on the direct route from which the Zulu army was expected, that Dartnell's column fruitlessly sought the deliberately elusive Zulus. There is one utterly reliable report that confirms Isipezi as the area where Dartnell's column was engaged; the account is from Lieutenant Charles Harford, who at about midday called a halt for a meal and some rest. He wrote:

> Most of us, and especially the Europeans who were on foot, were very nearly dead beat. At the head of the valley the two Battalions got together again, somewhere between 4 and 5 p.m. and went on to the Isipezi hill, Lonsdale riding off to see Major Dartnell, who was with the Mounted Police a mile or so to our left.
>
> The sun was full setting as we reached the top of the Isipezi, and as we got to the ridge the natives, with their sharp eyes, at once spotted a lot of Zulus on the opposite hill, across a very steep and rugged valley about 800 or 900 yards off in a straight line. The men were ordered to keep well out of sight below the hill, and from behind some rocks Hamilton-Browne, Cooper and I watched the Zulus stealthily moving about, their outline being well defined against the clear evening sky. Before long Major Dartnell joined us with his mounted men; they also had seen the enemy and had found them to be occupying a very strong position, and as it was still daylight he called for volunteers to go over and try to draw the Zulus out in order to see what sort of force confronted us.
>
> Instantly a number of men jumped on their horses and were off, with orders on no account to engage the enemy but simply draw him out and then gallop back. The manoeuvre was most successful; scarcely had our men crossed the valley and got up to within some 800 yards of their position than a regular swarm of Zulus, which we estimated to be over 1,000 men, swept down upon them in their horn formation and tried to surround them. Our men got back as hard as they could; no shots were fired and the Zulus returned back over their hill again. A council of war was now held, and Major Dartnell decided that the troops should bivouac on the spot, a message being sent to the General at once by Lieutenant Walsh (Somerset Light Infantry), with his three mounted infantrymen to explain our position and asking for reinforcements and food. It was very evident that we were opposite a very large impi, if not the whole Zulu army. (7)

The journalist Charles Norris-Newman later reported that, 'Lieutenant

Harford again distinguished himself by going in alone under a nasty crevice, shooting two men and capturing another.' (8)

One of Dartnell's commanders, Hamilton-Browne, interrogated under torture two young Zulus who were caught making their way home. They both confirmed that the Zulu army was approaching the nearby Isipezi Hill. No Zulu army could be seen, so two companies were returned to Isandlwana with captured Zulu cattle and delivered the report extracted from the Zulu youths. Later in the day Dartnell saw large groups of Zulus, amounting to several hundreds of warriors, moving from the direction of Isipezi; Dartnell declined to give chase, but in the excitement a young soldier, Trooper Parsons, accidentally fired his revolver. It was a costly mistake on the part of the young man, since Dartnell immediately sent him back to Isandlwana, where he was killed in the battle the following day. By dusk, Dartnell had been unable to determine what the Zulus were doing and decided to spend the night out in the hills to await events the following day.

Meanwhile, Isandlwana camp was not prepared for a Zulu attack, depite Colonel Glyn's proposal to form a defensive position or *laager* in the traditional Boer manner. Laagering, entrenching, the spreading of broken glass and other routine defensive measures were not considered necessary by Chelmsford, even though experienced Boers had personally warned him to laager each camp. Just prior to the invasion, Chelmsford had given his commanders specific orders requiring British positions in Zululand to be laagered or entrenched at night. Chelmsford's total belief in his force, together with his disdain for any native adversary, probably caused him to overrule his own written orders to entrench or fortify the camp. Certainly, the ground was rocky and hard; digging would have been impossible, but a solid defensive embankment of rocks could have been constructed within a few hours. Chelmsford was probably swayed by the knowledge that some of his transport waggons had yet to arrive at the camp and further supplies remained to be collected from the supply depot at Rorke's Drift. Chelmsford was also impatient to move the force to the next campsite at Isipezi Hill, only twelve miles away across the plain. After all, Isandlwana was merely a staging post, and in the hazy distance Isipezi Hill appeared tantalisingly close. Four days earlier, Lieutenant Colonel John Russell and his Mounted Infantry had reconnoitred the site and no Zulus had been seen. Chelmsford was certainly complacent about defending the camp, and his experienced junior officers demurred at their peril.

The Dunbar and Mansell incidents

On 14 January Major William Dunbar of the 2/24th was detailed to take his company and some native troops to the Ibashe Valley, between Rorke's Drift and Isandlwana. Dunbar's men were to repair the old waggon road and make a depot for firewood. He was ordered to pitch his tents beneath a rock outcrop close to Sihayo's homestead and among heavy thorn bushes with no field of fire. Dunbar did his best to clear the ground but was obliged to mount strong guards every night, recruited from men who had been working hard all day. On the 16th, Lord Chelmsford, Colonel Glyn, their respective staff officers and an escort rode up to inspect the work. Dunbar made his fears known to Chelmsford and asked for permission to move his camp to the other side of the stream. In the discussion that followed, Chelmsford's senior staff officer, Lieutenant Colonel John Crealock, seems to have lost his temper and remarked impatiently, 'If Major Dunbar is afraid to stay there, we could send someone who was not.' (9)

Dunbar, a big and imposing man, walked off in a rage and resigned his commission; it was several hours before Chelmsford could persuade him to withdraw the resignation. Until his promotion in 1874, Dunbar had been the senior captain of the 1/24th and possessed the most distinguished war record of any officer in the two battalions. The embarrassment caused to both Chelmsford and Glyn (whose mutual relationship was already difficult) and to all the officers of the 24th should not be underestimated.

At Isandlwana camp on the 21st, according to the *Historical Records of the 24th Regiment,* 'A field officer of the 2/24th being on duty with the pickets expressed strong misgivings to the staff officer who was showing him the line to occupy, pointing out that the broken ground was no protection and that there was no picket in the rear'. 'Well Sir' was the reply, 'if you are nervous we will put a picket of the pioneers there'. The field officer was evidently Dunbar. On the same day, Lieutenant Teignmouth Melvill remarked to this same field officer, 'I know what you are thinking by your face, Sir, you are abusing this camp and you are quite right'! (10)

On the very same day, Inspector George Mansell of the Natal Mounted Police had placed lookouts along the ridge of the Nqutu Plateau, one mile from and overlooking Isandlwana. They were placed to give the British maximum warning of any Zulus approaching the camp across the broad plateau. Major Clery, a professor of tactics and the senior staff officer of the 1/24th, later withdrew the lookouts on the grounds that they served no useful purpose. He also mocked Mansell for his prudence, and Mansell grudgingly accepted Clery's judgement. There can be little doubt that following Mansell's and Dunbar's humiliating experiences and Melvill's cautious expression of doubts, other battle-experienced junior officers would have been reluctant to challenge or query any order from their General or his staff. In fact, Mansell's assessment of the likely location of the Zulu army was correct; they would hide in the nearby valleys on the Nqutu Plateau, not in the Ngwebeni Valley.

When interviewed after the war by the British, and describing the position the Zulus would occupy the night before the attack, King Cetshwayo stated unequivocally that they were at Nqutu. The account of the interview records the king's statement as follows:

> During the same night that followed upon the day on which my troops took up their encampment at the Ingudu [Nqutu] Hill. (11)

This statement is supported by Lieutenant Anstey's base map 'Country Around Isandlwana', which shows a range of hills rising from the Nqutu Plateau. Anstey marked this range as the Nqutu Range. The Ngwebeni Valley cannot be defined as part of the Nqutu range as it is a further two miles east of the last hill in the range. King Cetshwayo's statement and Anstey's map explain the location of the Zulu army prior to its attack on Isandlwana. In any event, the Zulu army was now within striking distance of the unsuspecting British camp.

The Zulu trap is sprung

Back at Isandlwana camp, 21 January had developed into a frustrating day for Lord Chelmsford. It was made worse by a local Zulu chief, Gamdana, arriving at the camp. Gamdana had considered defecting to the British but was still wavering. As a sop to Chelmsford, Gamdana correctly reported that the Zulu army was approaching Isipezi Hill, but he and his information were dismissed. Rebuffed by Chelmsford, Gamdana was able to assess the strength and layout of the British camp, an accusation that would later be levelled against Chelmsford by some of his own staff officers. That afternoon, Dartnell's report having reached Chelmsford, Dartnell was sent orders to attack the Zulus the following day, and supplies of food were sent out from the camp to sustain the NNC.

Later that afternoon, Chelmsford decided to accompany a reconnaissance party to the top of the Nqutu Plateau. One of the officers leading the patrol, Lieutenant Milne RN, later wrote:

> On reaching the summit of the highest hill I counted fourteen Zulu horsemen watching us at a distance of about four miles; they ultimately disappeared over a slight rise. There were two vedettes at the spot from where I saw these horsemen; they said they had seen these men several times during the day, and had reported the fact. From this point the ground was nearly level; there were slight rises, however, every now and again, which would prevent our seeing any men who did not wish it. (12)

Neither Chelmsford nor his accompanying officers realised the significance of so many mounted Zulus; only senior Zulu chiefs rode horses. From their vantage point high on the Nqutu Plateau, these chiefs were reconnoitering the British position around Isandlwana. Throughout that night the Zulu army consolidated its position on the Nqutu Plateau and their scouts were sent to observe the British; on one occasion they came so close that they conversed with an NNC picquet on Magaga hill, less than two miles from the main camp. The Hon. Standish Vereker later confirmed this. (13)

Later that evening, Chelmsford received a message that indicated Dartnell, commanding the reconnaissance force now bivouacked on and around the Isipezi hills, was still awaiting orders for the following day. In particular, he wanted to know whether or not he could attack the advancing Zulus. Chelmsford replied that Dartnell was to use his discretion and was at liberty to attack. After dark, hundreds of campfires could be seen in the surrounding hills which alarmed the NNC. Naturally Dartnell presumed he had found, or been found by, the Zulu army, and his mainly native force were growing restless with fear. An incident then occurred that led to their disbandment at Rorke's Drift a few days later. Many accounts discuss the growing unreliability of the NNC from this night onwards. The true reason conflicts with the published account of Norris-Newman, whose incorrect version of events was based on hearsay, since he had abandoned the NNC position at the sound of a shot. This irritated Harford, who wrote of Norris Newman's account:

Rubbish! This is what happened. It was now getting dark, and a rare business it was. The Natives showed unmistakable signs of being in a mortal funk, and all wanted to clump together in one spot. At last, however, we strung them out like a thread of beads, each man squatting and touching his neighbour, and behind each section a European NCO and a superior native were ordered to keep up a continual patrol to see that they kept awake and didn't stir from their position. The captains and other company officers then exercised further control over their own men. In this manner more than a mile of outposts were strung out, almost encircling the bivouac. By this time the Zulus had lighted fires all along their position and kept them going throughout the night, and from this fact we felt pretty certain that we would be attacked in the morning. There was very little fear of a real attack during the night, as night fighting was not the Zulu method.

Having satisfied myself that the outposts were working, and after taking special note of different features, such as bushes, rocks, etc. to guide me on my visits during the night, I got back to the bivouac. Then, hitching my pony on to the others, went to report to Lonsdale whom I found sitting chatting with some of the officers and Newman Noggs [Norris-Newman].

Intending to make a round of the outposts again in about an hour's time, I plumped myself down to snatch a rest and a short sleep, but had scarcely closed my eyes when bang went a shot from somewhere in the outpost line, and in a second the whole square rose up. Hearing the noise the men were making, rattling their shields and fumbling about for their things, I rushed up and speaking to them in their own language ordered them to keep quiet and lie down. Their own company officers, too, did all they could to establish calm, but it was of no avail. The whole lot made a clean bolt of it and came bounding over us like frightened animals, making their way down the hillside behind us. In this terrific stampede of some 4,000 men the wretched ponies were swept along in a solid mass, kicking and struggling, with several Europeans hanging on to try and stop them. As these passed me, on looking round I caught a glimpse of both Lonsdale and Noggs turning a somersault as a lot of natives bounded over them. Poor

Noggs, who highly resented such treatment, spent the rest of the night with the Mounted Police, having, as he afterwards told me, "had enough of the Contingent".

Amid all this confusion, someone managed to get my pony free and brought him to me, for which I was more than thankful as the situation was serious and I was now able to go in pursuit of the runaways who, at the pace they were going and the rate at which Kaffirs can travel, might soon be out of reach. Luckily, however, I found them almost at the foot of the hill, squatting in various-sized clumps, and addressing them in anything but Parliamentary language, hounded them back to the bivouac.

Further on, I was more successful and found Lt Thompson with his company intact, and as we met I asked him what on earth had happened at the outpost, and told him all that had taken place at the bivouac. He solved the problem by telling me that an NCO of one of his sections, who should have been patrolling in company with a Native, had sat down and fallen asleep, then suddenly waking up and seeing, as he thought, a Zulu coming towards him, fired at him. He said, "It's no use your going any further, as directly the shot was fired the remainder of the outpost went. There is no one now on my front."

However, I thought it best to go and see for myself, but only found that he was quite right. Everyone but his company had vanished. A nice state of things, had we been really attacked! (14)

It took Harford and his colleagues the rest of the night to restore order. Later the same night at about 1.30 am, Chelmsford received a further message from Major Dartnell requesting the immediate support of two or three companies of regular infantry. The urgent message contained the awaited news that a strong Zulu force had been seen a few hours earlier that day and, more importantly, that captured Zulus confirmed the imminent arrival of the Zulu army. On the strength of Dartnell's report, Chelmsford presumed the main Zulu army of some 25,000 warriors had been located. After a brief consultation with his staff officers he decide to split his invasion force, and at about 3 am he set out with Colonel Glyn and a force of 2,500 men, including the 2/24th Regiment and four of the six guns of the Royal Artillery; Chelmsford left only two guns 'in case the enemy should have the temerity to attack the camp during his absence' (as Lieutenant Curling put it in a letter to his mother).

As 'G' Company of the 2/24th had been employed on night guard-duty, they remained at Isandlwana to rest and then help with the camp move.

Chelmsford was aware that Colonel Durnford RE and his mainly mounted column were still camped only six miles away at Rorke's Drift. As a precaution, he instructed Major Clery, his staff officer attached to the 24th Regiment, to order Durnford to move up from Rorke's Drift – but to where? Clery later stated that his order to Durnford was very specific; he claimed he ordered Durnford to 'take command of it', referring to the Isandlwana camp. The actual order was ambiguous and proved Clery was not telling the truth:

> 22nd, Wednesday, 2 am
> You are to march to this camp at once with all the force you have with you of No.2 Column. Major Bengough's battalion is to move to Rorke's Drift as ordered yesterday. 2/24th, Artillery and mounted men with the General and Colonel Glyn move off at once to attack a Zulu force about 10 miles distant.
> J.N.C.
> If Bengough's battalion has crossed the River at Eland's Kraal it is to move up here. (15)

It is not surprising that the officer left in command of Isandlwana camp, Lieutenant Colonel Henry Pulleine of the 1/24th Regiment, should have felt secure. His camp was manned by 1,700 men armed with two 7-pound artillery guns and reserves of nearly one million rounds of Martini-Henry rifle ammunition. Nevertheless, the soldiers were uneasy. The reports arriving at the camp during the day were well known to the troops: the Zulu army was approaching. Pulleine was clearly confident; at forty-one years old, he had been in the army for over twenty years but had never seen action. Furthermore, he had only rejoined his regiment five days earlier, after holding various administrative positions in Durban and Pietermaritzburg. His orders for the day were straightforward – to defend and prepare the camp for departure. If he knew of the intelligence reports' significance, he ignored it.

Chapter 5

Decoy and Defeat

Do the staff think we are going to meet an army of schoolgirls?
Why in the name of all that is holy do we not laager?
Captain Duncombe to Commandant Hamilton Browne
(*A Lost Legionary in South Africa*)

Even before dawn, news from his scouts was reaching Chief Ntshingwayo commanding the Zulu army that Dartnell's column was some twelve miles from Isandlwana and still spread out among the hills between Isipezi and Mangeni. Of even greater importance were the Zulu scouts' reports that during the night another large column had departed the British camp and was at that very moment marching to support Dartnell's scattered force. Chelmsford's decision had halved the size of the Isandlwana camp's defenders; the Zulu decoy had succeeded beyond Ntshingwayo's expectations.

One can only imagine Ntshingwayo's astonishment when, before dawn on the 22nd, Chelmsford led five companies of the 2/24th, four guns and most of the remaining mounted men to rendezvous with Dartnell at the base of the bare shoulder of Hlazakazi, some ten miles beyond the camp, thus dividing his forces still further. The Zulu commanders soon realised that the camp was almost entirely deprived of its most formidable weapon, the mounted troops, and half of its infantry and artillery. No wonder that a group of Zulu chiefs was moved to say, after the battle, 'You gave us the battle that day . . . for you dispersed your army in small parties all over the country'. (1)

In camp at Isandlwana

During that night at Isandlwana, Pulleine and the men of the 1/24th had heard Chelmsford's column march out of camp. Pulleine, in compliance with Chelmsford's orders to defend the camp, then dispatched the infantry to form a line extending for almost a mile approximately 1,000 yards to the left front of the camp. Further positions were taken up at dawn by several companies of the Natal Native Contingent; these covered the base and shoulder of the Nqutu Plateau to the north of the camp, while a mounted patrol watched the top of the plateau itself.

Pulleine and his officers were totally unaware of their looming predicament; their camp was now highly vulnerable to the unseen massed Zulu army hidden on their flank only five miles distant. The British were now unwittingly spread over a vast area, from Rorke's Drift to Isipezi and from the Ngwebeni Valley to Mangeni; they were in the wrong place and covering an unmanageable 200 square miles.

In camp, normal activities proceeded in a soldierly fashion; the bugle call for breakfast was sounded at 7 am – but then a number of disquieting events occurred. Unexpectedly, a group of Zulus was observed on the rim of the plateau overlooking the camp about a mile to the north. Unknown to Pulleine and the British, this group watching them consisted of a number of senior chiefs completing their pre-battle reconnaissance. The Zulu commander, Ntshingwayo, now fully appreciated that the British were in unwitting disarray; his decoys were still confusing both Dartnell and Chelmsford ten miles to the east beyond the camp, while at the same time the remaining Zulu forces were fast approaching from Isipezi and would soon join the main advance on Isandlwana camp.

At 7.30 am Lieutenant Vereker brought Pulleine the very first report from the plateau, confirming that a patrol had observed a large force of Zulus advancing towards the camp. Lieutenant Hillier, Lonsdale's NNC, wrote:

> At half past seven a.m. Lt. Veriker [sic] of the NNC who was on picquet duty with Captain Barry rode into camp and reported to Colonel Pulleine that the Zulus were advancing on the camp in large numbers. (2)

This early report corroborated a number of eye-witness reports received by Pulleine that, regardless of British scouts and outposts on the plateau, Zulus were already deploying and advancing towards the camp. Within minutes, a large body of Zulus were seen on the hills to the front left of camp, so Pulleine ordered the artillery out on to the front line.

A mixture of uncertainty and excitement was now spreading throughout the camp at Isandlwana. The bugler sounded the 'Stand To', the camp breakfast was abandoned and the troops collected themselves to meet the foe. Within the hour, another patrol reported large bodies of Zulus moving north-west across the plateau; groups of Zulus were again seen on the plateau ridge overlooking the camp. The intermittent sound of distant firing was heard, but due to its re-echoing among the hills it was impossible to pinpoint its exact location. The Zulus watching the camp then disappeared. At this stage, Pulleine had no idea what was happening; he knew the Zulus should not have been on the plateau to the north since they were supposed to be in the east being engaged by Chelmsford's attacking force.

Trooper Barker of the Natal Carbineers, one of the colonials earlier sent out at 4 am to patrol the Nqutu Plateau, later wrote of events that occurred about 7 am:

> Hawkins, my bosom friend, and myself were posted on a hill to the extreme front, quite six miles from the camp, and arrived on the hill about sunrise. After being posted about a quarter of an hour we noticed a lot of mounted men in the distance and on their coming nearer we saw that they were trying to surround us . . . we discovered they were Zulus. We retired to Lieut. Scott [at Conical Hill] about two miles nearer the camp and informed him of what we had seen, and he decided to come back with us but before we had gone far we saw Zulus on the hill we had just left and others advancing from the left flank near where two other videttes [sic], Whitelaw and another had been obliged to retire from. Whitelaw reported a large army advancing, 'thousands' I remember him distinctly saying . . . this would be about eight a.m. He returned with a message to Lieut. Scott that we were to watch the enemy carefully and send back reports of their movements. Shortly afterwards, numbers of Zulus being seen on all the hills to the left and front, Trooper Swift and another were sent back to report. The Zulus then remained on the hills, and about two hundred of them advanced to within three hundred yards of us, but on our advancing they retired out of sight, and a few of us went up this hill where the Zulus had disappeared, and on a farther hill, at about six hundred yards' distance, we saw a large army sitting down. We returned to Lieut. Scott, who was then about three miles from camp, and reported back what we had seen. Hawkins and I were then sent back to camp to report a large army to the left front of camp. (3)

With the message delivered to a camp staff officer (Lieutenant Coghill), Barker and Hawkins returned to Lieutenant Scott's position and saw 'masses of Zulus on all the hills'. (4) It was just before 7.30 am when Whitelaw galloped back to the camp and reported this same sighting to Lieutenant Coghill, who sent him back with orders to monitor the advancing Zulus – still unseen from Isandlwana camp. Lieutenant Ardendorff, an Afrikaner of Scandinavian descent, was also dispatched to try to get a detailed report from the scouts, but soon returned in such a state that his report about the enemy, in broken English, was incoherent.

Such accounts confirm that for at least an hour Zulus had been seen both on the ridge from the camp and by scouts on the plateau, moving deliberately and in considerable numbers towards the camp. The Zulu advance on Isandlwana was clearly well coordinated. Pulleine was obviously confused by the accounts and could not comprehend the possibility that the Zulus were now massing no more than four miles from his position; he sent a second more urgent report to Chelmsford:

8.5 a.m. Staff Officer – report just come in that the Zulus are advancing in force from the left front of the camp. H.B. Pulleine.

In the midst of this uncertainty, Lieutenant Chard arrived at the camp from Rorke's Drift to ascertain his orders and find some breakfast. There being no orders, he took breakfast and saw through binoculars the gathering Zulus watching the camp from the plateau ridge. The Zulus began to move towards the western end of the ridge, which made Chard believe they might make for Rorke's Drift. He then set off to return to his men, who were manning the river ponts at Rorke's Drift. On his way back he met Colonel Durnford and appraised him of the situation. Durnford was making his way from Rorke's Drift to Isandlwana and, on hearing Chard's account, set off with 500 mounted troops for the camp, with orders for his main column to follow at best speed.

Curling noted events as they unfurled that morning:

About 7.30 a.m . . . a large body of Zulus being seen on the hills to the left front of the camp, we were ordered to turn out at once, and were formed up in front of the 2nd Battalion 24th Regiment camp, where we remained until 11 o'clock when we returned to camp with orders to remain harnessed and ready to turn out at a minute's notice. The Zulus did not come up within range and we did not come into action. The infantry also remained in column of coys [companies]. Col. Durnford arrived about 10 a.m. with Basutos and the rocket battery; he left about 11 o'clock with these troops, in the direction of the hills where we had seen the enemy. (5)

Out on the plain with Chelmsford

As dawn spread across the plain, Chelmsford and over half the strength of the Centre Column had passed the Hlazakazi hills and were well on their way towards joining up with Dartnell in the region of the Magogo hills. Chelmsford was fully anticipating engaging the main Zulu army. Instead he was to confront an elusive enemy decoy that would repeatedly appear and disappear among the surrounding hills, drawing Chelmsford's force into a thankless chase that would separate and exhaust his weary men as the unbearably hot day wore on. Now ten miles beyond the imperilled camp, Chelmsford was becoming thoroughly irritated by the confusing reports reaching him of Zulus advancing and then retreating. Lieutenant Milne later wrote two accounts to his superior, Commodore Sullivan RN:

1. We rode on quickly and at 6 a.m. had arrived at the ground taken up by Major Dartnell. The enemy had retired from their former position and was not in sight. No patrols had been sent out by Major Dartnell, so in what direction they had gone was unknown.

2. No doubt the force we were after on Wednesday [the 22nd] was a blind as we could never get near them, they kept edging away drawing us further from the camp. (6)

Lieutenant Mainwaring wrote, after the battle:

The mounted infantry reported the Zulus to be retiring from hill-top to hill-top, and it must have been their plan to draw us away from the camp.

At 8.30 am Chelmsford realised that he was not about to engage the main Zulu army, and breakfasted with his staff officers near Magogo hill. He ordered Commandant George Hamilton-Browne of the 3rd Natal Native Contingent to report to him. (7) The order Hamilton-Browne received is recorded in his book published over thirty years later:

Commandant Browne, I want you to return at once to camp [with your men] and assist Colonel Pulleine to strike camp and come on here. (8)

Hamilton-Browne then met Colonel Glyn and he later recalled their interesting conversation:

Colonel Glyn rode over to me and drawing me aside said, "In God's name Maorie, what are you doing here?" I answered him with a question, "In God's name Sir what are you doing here?" He shook his head and replied, "I am not in command". And fine old soldier as he was, I could see he was much disturbed. (9)

Hamilton-Browne's men had ten miles to march back to Isandlwana, which, over rough terrain and in the heat of summer, would take three to four hours.

The *Natal Witness* later commented on the Zulu deception:

Although they showed themselves in very considerable form [numbers] along all the hill tops, they kept retiring according to what, as after events taught us, must have been their conceived plan. The general, however, did not, of course, at this time, imagine that the Zulus were carrying out a concerted scheme, but thought they were probably falling back on their supports . . . It was the opinion of all those who understand the natives and their method of fighting that this small body of Zulus who paraded themselves so openly had certainly an army behind them which was only awaiting the proper moment to come into action. (10)

The ever prescient newspaper reporter accompanying Chelmsford, Norris-Newman, wrote in his book *In Zululand with the British* (1880):

The idea did not seem to have occurred to anyone that the enemy were carrying out a pre-constructed plan.

The battle for Isandlwana
Back at Isandlwana, Pulleine was still contemplating the various reports of Zulus advancing on the camp, but little could be heard and nothing could be seen of the Zulus due to the location of Pulleine's headquarters tent. Furthermore, Pulleine had not realised that, in order to cover the extensive dead ground before the camp, his front-line troops had crept forward out

of sight over the lip of the plain, which would shortly leave him 'battlefield-blind'.

During a formal archaeological survey of the Isandlwana battlefield in the summer of 2000 by Glasgow University and the South African authorities, it was discovered that the British front line was 200 yards further from the camp than had previously been supposed, a discovery based on the quantity of spent ammunition cases and ammunition box straps found along the new position. This position confirms that the front line was completely out of sight of both Pulleine and the main camp and was covering the dead ground to its front. No such evidence had been found where the line had previously been thought to be situated.

Pulleine organised the remaining six NNC companies still in the camp to be ready and await orders. At about 10.30 am Colonel Durnford arrived at the camp with 500 mounted men of the No. 2 Column. Durnford was a Royal Engineers officer with many years' experience in South Africa; his orders from Chelmsford, received early that morning, were ambiguous:

> You are to march to this camp at once with all the force you have with you of No.2 Column. Major Bengough's battalion is to move to Rorke's Drift as ordered yesterday. 2/24th, Artillery and mounted men with the General and Colonel Glyn move off at once to attack a Zulu force about 10 miles distant. (11)

Much comment has been made by historians that Durnford was senior in service to Pulleine. Their presumption is that command of the camp naturally devolved upon Durnford, thus relieving Pulleine of overall responsibility, for which Pulleine would have been grateful. The facts are different: Durnford was never ordered to 'take command of the camp', he was the Commander of the second column and no orders were given to merge the two columns. Durnford nevertheless met with Pulleine in his headquarters tent to discuss the sightings of the Zulus, and a brief discussion ensued after which Durnford detailed patrols of his men to ride to the plateau and ascertain what was happening. One patrol was lead by Captain Shepstone of the NNH. Lieutenant Cochrane accompanied Durnford and on arrival at Isandlwana he wrote that a number of Zulus had been seen since an early hour on the top of the adjacent hills, and that an attack was expected. (See Appendix B for Cochrane's full account). Having received a note from another patrol that Zulus were moving east (indeed, according to Lieutenant Curling's evidence to the Court of Inquiry, they could now be seen from the camp), Durnford concluded that a large enemy force was deploying along the plateau, possibly to drive a wedge between Chelmsford's force and Isandlwana camp. Pulleine no doubt accepted Durnford's calm analysis with some relief and gave the order for his men to 'Stand Down' but to keep on their accoutrements. Preparations then went ahead for the camp move. Durnford took his force to intercept this Zulu threat, departing the camp at, according to Curling, about 11 am.

Out on the firing line, Lieutenant Charlie Pope 2/24th somehow managed to scribble a diary line. Pope, by direct personal observation, provided confirmatory evidence that a large Zulu force had been sighted. Furthermore, the deployment was taking place prior to Durnford's arrival. This report is a valuable, and completely uncorrupted corroboration. It reads:

> Alarm 3 Columns Zulus and mounted men on hill E. Turn Out 7,000 (!!!) more E.N.E., 4000 of whom went around Lion's Kop. (Isandlwana Hill) Durnford's Basutos arrive and pursue. (12)

Meanwhile, leading his patrols eastwards along the top of the plateau, Shepstone could see scattered Zulu impis, probably the Zulu advance guard. Lieutenant Charlie Raw was one of Shepstone's officers; when Raw's Basuto riders came across the Zulu army, the Zulus had already advanced some two miles from the Ngwebeni Valley. Historically, Raw has been credited with finding the Zulu army sitting quietly in the Ngwebeni Valley, but this is story tellers' mythology and cannot be correct, unless all the other observations of massing Zulus are untrue. If these other observations are correct, the Zulus had been advancing towards Isandlwana for at least two hours before Raw, commanding two troops of the NNH, even arrived at Isandlwana camp with Durnford.

Raw departed Isandlwana camp at about 11 am. Once on the plateau, Raw and his men came across a herd of cattle which they followed over rising ground. From here they had seen the Zulu army about a mile off, advancing in line and extending towards its left. Raw's report is unambiguous in the description of the contact area and distance; it is not the Ngwebeni Valley. Raw's report, interestingly ignored by the official enquiry, reads:

> We left the camp proceeding over the hills [Nqutu Plateau], Captain George Shepstone going with us. The enemy in small groups

retiring before us for some time, drawing us on for four or five miles from the camp where they turned and fell upon us, the whole army showing itself from behind a hill in front of where they had evidently been waiting. (13)

After the war, it took a professional Victorian historian, Professor Coupland, to deduce what Raw saw. He wrote:

The Basutos [Raw's mounted men] climbed the plateau and spread out over it. No Zulu were seen at first, only a herd of cattle. The Basutos rode on to round it up. Presently they came to the brink of a valley, and saw, about a mile off, what they had never dreamed of seeing. Thousands of Zulu were gathered there. Most of them were sitting on the ground, taking their ease. One body was moving westwards, probably taking up position to encircle the north flank of the camp at the appointed time. (14)

From an examination of available military maps, the valley was between Ithusi and Mabaso hills, and not that of the Ngwebeni stream. Mr Hamar, the commissariat officer riding with Shepstone, later wrote:

After going some little way, we tried to capture some cattle. They disappeared over a ridge and on coming up, we saw the Zulus, like ants in front of us, in perfect order and as quiet as mice, and stretched across in an even line. We estimated those we saw at 12,000. (15)

Shepstone rode to warn Pulleine and reported that the advancing Zulus had been sighted some three miles away. To experienced officers who had served in the previous Cape skirmishes, large forces of natives were not necessarily considered to be dangerous, but the Zulu numbers had alarmed Shepstone. Captain Gardner arrived moments before Shepstone and delivered a note from Chelmsford ordering the camp to be struck. Pulleine dithered, so Shepstone interjected, 'I am not alarmist, Sir, but the Zulus are in such black masses over there, such long black lines, that you will have to give us all the assistance you can. They are now fast driving our men this way.' (16)

Pulleine's dilemma worsened. Should he continue with Chelmsford's order to strike the camp, or call in his distant extended line to form a defensive position? After all, there were sufficient waggons in the camp to form a barricade. Norris-Newman estimated there were some 125 or more waggons available, and the men now busy packing up the camp could be ordered into the firing line. If the Zulu force proved to be only skirmishers, the initiation of normal defensive precautions, which involving dropping the tents to provide the camp defenders with a clear field of fire, would mean many hours of subsequent work to re-pack the tents in the precise manner required by Army Regulations. Pulleine was fully aware that there were still 350 tents to be struck before the camp could be moved; it was going to be a major task, as Army Regulations required one NCO and ten men to stow each tent. Pulleine knew that if he made the wrong decision he would become the laughing stock of the army. Lieutenant Henry Curling RA survived the battle, and his recently discovered letters confirm that many of Pulleine's men were not deployed on the front line as has previously been believed, but were engaged in packing the tents. He wrote:

> At 7.30 I got the message to turn out at once and we got ready in about 10 minutes forming up by the 1/24th on their parade ground. The companies were very weak, no more than 50 in each and there were only 6 of them in all. We congratulated ourselves on the chance of our being attacked and hoped that our small numbers might induce the Zulus to come on. I suppose that not more than half the men left in the camp took part in its defence as it was not considered necessary and they were left in as cooks etc.

Pulleine's blind and loyal obedience to Chelmsford's last order to 'break camp' may have been the reason why so many soldiers continued to pack the camp even as the Zulus approached. To Pulleine, the risk of humiliation if he was proved wrong was possibly greater than the risk of defeat. He metaphorically 'put his head in the sand' and dithered. He ordered the 'Fall In' to be sounded and sent 'F' Company 1/24th under Captain Mostyn to support Lieutenant Cavaye. Not wishing to disobey Chelmsford's order to pack the camp, he sent a note to Major Clery for Chelmsford:

> Heavy firing near to camp. Cannot move camp at present.

Captain Gardner added the following message:

> Heavy firing near left of camp. Shepstone has come in for reinforcements and reports that the Basutos (Shepstone's men) are

falling back. Whole camp turned out and fighting about one mile to left flank.

At 11.30 am Pulleine sent his final message to Lieutenant Cavaye, whose men Pulleine thought might get cut off from the camp by the rapidly advancing Zulus. It reads:

Cavaye,
Zulus are advancing on your right in force. Retire on camp in order.
E Coy [company] will support your left. H.N. Pulleine. 11.30 am.

Durnford had not long departed when heavy firing was heard coming from the spur leading from the camp to the plateau; two companies of the 24th commanded by Lieutenants Cavaye and Mostyn and a company of the NNC had been positioned there earlier that morning. The two companies were firing at a large body of Zulus moving off the plateau out of sight of the camp behind Isandlwana. The Zulus were about 800 yards from the troops, and due to the ineffectiveness of their fire the Zulus ignored the British. This large body of Zulus turned out to be the right horn, whose intention was to seal the only route of escape from Isandlwana back to Rorke's Drift.

Lieutenant Dyson had been sent to the furthest point on the spur some 500 yards beyond his nearest support. Although isolated, his men had a good view across the valley to the Nqutu Plateau. Once the Zulus appeared in force, he and his men must have realised that their exposed position was in dire peril; although trapped, they continued to pour fire into the approaching mass of warriors. History records that they were simply overrun. As recently as 1995, several cairns were visible at this point, and belt buckles and buttons could be seen, lying exposed by heavy rain. (17)

In camp the 'Fall In' call was sounded for the third time. The remaining three companies of the 24th were extended 800 yards to the left and front of the camp facing both the plateau and the plain. The soldiers were positioned some three yards apart in a double line. Men of the NNC also formed a section of the line with the two 7-pound guns of the Royal Artillery between them. Curling wrote:

When we turned out again about 12, the Zulus were only showing on the left of our camp. All the time we were idle in the camp, the Zulus were surrounding us with a huge circle several miles in circumference and hidden by hills from our sight. We none of us felt the least anxious as to the result for, although they came on in immense numbers, we felt it was impossible they could force a way through us. (18)

The camp's earlier apprehension gave way to excitement; the attack was coming, and they, not Chelmsford's force, would have all the glory. In every previous battle fought by the 24th Regiment in Africa, the natives had fled when volley firing commenced; the British, however, had never fought the Zulus.

Pulleine and his camp officers could now see a massive force of Zulus pouring off the Nqutu Plateau and heading for the small conical hill one mile in front of the camp. They would shortly drive a wedge between Chelmsford and the camp. The full Zulu attack on Isandlwana had begun. Without giving any further orders, Pulleine went into his tent to write a letter. Various Zulu reports claim he was killed at the height of the battle while still writing at his desk.

The massed ranks of Zulu warriors streamed off the Nqutu Plateau then fanned out towards the over-extended British firing line protecting the camp. Meanwhile, some three miles further out on the plain, Durnford and his men began engaging the rapidly advancing Zulu left horn with controlled volley fire as, heavily outnumbered, they commenced a tactical withdrawal back towards the camp. Durnford's Rocket Battery, commanded by Major Francis Russell RA, had lagged behind Durnford due to the rough terrain. As the Zulus suddenly appeared over the hill immediately to their left, the battery managed to fire one ineffectual rocket before being overrun. Russell was mortally wounded and three gunners killed; their retainers fled, as did their pack mules. Durnford fell back, gathered up the battery's three survivors and withdrew through a gap in the Zulu attack back towards the camp, now less than one mile distant. The three survivors were able to mount spare horses and made their way back to the camp, only to find it being overwhelmed by the Zulus; they kept going and managed to escape. Captain Reginald Younghusband's 'E' Company was sent out from the camp towards the spur to cover the retreat of Cavaye and Mostyn's men as they withdrew under fire. Only one company would reach the temporary safety of the camp.

Meanwhile, the central body of the main Zulu force, consisting of some 15,000 warriors, rapidly advanced off the plateau to attack the thin line of British infantry. The two guns of the Royal Artillery deployed on the British left flank commenced firing. Several rounds of their case shot (shrapnel) hit home amidst the advancing Zulus causing much destruction, as confirmed by Lieutenant Higginson who later wrote that the fire 'swept them away'. Sadly, Lieutenant Roberts NNC had managed to get a group of his men to the safety of a stone cattle kraal when a direct hit from the artillery struck their position. The Zulus quickly observed the artillery's firing procedure, directed by Major Stuart Smith and Lieutenant Curling, and as each gun was prepared for firing the Zulus threw themselves to the ground; thereafter the shells passed over the Zulus and exploded with minimum effect. Having neutralised the effect of the artillery, the Zulus prepared to charge the British infantry line either side of the guns from the relative safety of dead ground to the immediate front of the British position. To the right of the guns, the three *amabutho* making up the main body, the iNgobamakhosi, uKhandempemvu and uMbonambi, all began to suffer heavily from British rifle fire. The officers and NCOs in the British front line calmly controlled their men's volley fire, and the Zulu main attack halted. The soldiers reportedly laughed and joked about the drubbing they were giving the Zulus, even though they could see the advancing warriors were over half a mile deep. Captain Edward Essex, one of the five Imperial officers to survive later wrote:

> I was surprised how relaxed the men in the ranks were despite the climactic tension of the battle. Loading as fast as they could and firing into the dense black masses that pressed in on them, the men were laughing and chatting, and obviously thought they were giving the Zulus an awful hammering. (19)

On the British front line, everything appeared under control and the men's spirits were high. Meanwhile, Durnford's men had been forced to withdraw by the massive Zulu left horn to a dried-up watercourse less than a mile from the camp, where they came under increasing pressure from the encircling Zulus. Durnford held the position for some fifteen minutes before observing that his men were seriously outnumbered. The Zulus began spreading around his position; he was in peril of being cut off from the camp and, worse still, his men were running out of ammunition. Durnford sent several men back to the camp with urgent requests for more ammunition and it was from the desperate actions of these men that the enduring 'ammunition boxes' myth was born. Durnford's men could not find their own ammunition carts and, understandably in the confusion of battle, the quartermasters supervising their own company supplies were reluctant to issue ammunition to Durnford's men. Durnford sent two of his officers, Lieutenants Henderson and Davies, to expedite the supply, but it was not forthcoming because the carbineers sent to carry the ammunition, Trooper Johnson and Bugler Jackson, had already been killed near the Nek (a shoulder joining two hills); so Durnford gave the order to begin the withdrawal back to the main camp.

Trooper Barker's eye-witness account illustrates the confusion and horror now present in the camp:

> I saw the soldiers who were left in camp literally surrounded by Zulus who had evidently come in from the rear, and as soldiers and natives repassed us in confusion we retired back to our Carbineer lines [Durnford's donga – a dry river bed]. The artillery now retreated in the direction of the Nek to the right of the camp.
>
> I mounted my horse, the Zulus now being busy all over the camp stabbing the soldiers, and made my way in the direction of the Nek in the rear of the camp. I was joined by W. Tarboton here, but being met by the Zulus we were obliged to retire back towards the camp [Durnford's donga], which was now a mass of Zulus. We then went in the direction we had seen an artillery carriage go, to the direct right of our lines, and saw the gun upset, it being immediately surrounded by Zulus. This point, from what I heard afterwards, was the only point the Zulus had not surrounded, and we two got through here. After riding for about half a mile or less, Tarboton asked me to return with him to look for his brother whom he had missed, and as I had lost my comrade Hawkins at the same time I willingly returned, but just as we got in sight of the camp, from a hill we both for the first time realised what had happened; the camp was completely surrounded and the people were being massacred by the Zulus. We were obliged to fly as Zulus were following fugitives up. (20)

This account suggests the route taken was the southern Fugitives' Trail; on their retreat towards the Nek they saw the Nek was already in Zulu possession so they retreated instead towards Durnford's *donga* before making off 'to the direct right of our lines', which strongly indicates the route south of Black's Koppie, not across the Nek from which they had just retreated. (See Wyld's 1879 map for details of the southern fugitives' route).

'G' Company 2/24th had been on camp guard duty that night and had not accompanied Chelmsford and their battalion to locate the Zulus. They had remained in camp to rest and were now occupying the extreme right end of the British line where they were easily checking the Zulus to their front. Their monocled officer, Lieutenant Charles Pope, saw that Durnford's men to the right were in danger of being engulfed by the Zulus' flanking advance and gave his men the order to move towards Durnford's position. It was a serious tactical mistake; Pope's advance left the British line seriously exposed to the advancing Zulus, and just as they might have reached a point where they could help stem the enemy, Durnford gave the order to retreat. Being mounted, Durnford's men quickly vacated their position and inadvertently left 'G' Company fatally exposed to the rapidly approaching Zulu left horn. Pope tried to hold the Zulu advance but his company was swiftly overwhelmed by the mass of several thousand charging warriors.

With the main Zulu advance stalled to the front of the main camp, the Zulu commanders on the overlooking heights of the iNyoni cliffs dispatched Chief Mkhosana kaMvundlana, a sub-commander of the Biyela, to exhort the warriors back into the attack. The Zulu chief, untouched by British bullets, strode among the prostrate warriors urging them to fight. Chief Muziwento recounted that his men were exhorted to fight with the words, 'Never did the king give you the command "Lie down upon the ground". His words were "Go and toss them to Maritzburg"'. (21) The uKhandempemvu rose to the attack. Chief Mkhosana was then shot dead, but he deserves to be remembered as the Zulu hero of the battle; but for Mkhosana, the Zulus attack might have faltered. In the final analysis, their attack was perfectly and courageously executed across several miles of rugged and difficult terrain; the British were powerless to meet the challenge.

As the Zulu masses closed with the British firing line, it was evident that even sustained volley fire was no longer effective. Yet, at the height of the main Zulu attack, all the 24th officers complied with their orders to hold their precarious and exposed positions even as the enemy closed with them. They would have quickly been fully aware of their vulnerability, but evidently all obeyed their orders to remain in extended line right up to the final bugle call to retreat. Just as the desperately awaited call sounded, the Zulus broke through their line. The Zulu left and right horns also completed their encirclement of the camp and, having joined up behind the British, advanced through the British camp to attack the retreating soldiers from their undefended rear. The centre companies of the 24th fought their way back towards the main camp area but began to lose men at a steady rate. They eventually reached the waggon park, where they tried to form a defensive square, assisted by the stretcher bearers who had been withdrawn from the front line by Surgeon Major Shepherd, the founder of the St John Ambulance. The two companies of 24th, positioned on the ridge to the left of the camp, had begun retreating back to the camp under pressure from the right horn. One company, commanded either by Lieutenant William Mostyn or Lieutenant Charles Cavaye, was soon overwhelmed and failed to make it back to the camp. Captain Reginald Younghusband's 'E' Company was forced back along the base of the cliff wall of Isandlwana until they reached a small plateau overlooking the waggon park. Having been furthest from the main Zulu attack, Younghusband had managed to keep his men together until the Zulus were about to overwhelm them. One Zulu later reported:

> The soldiers gave a shout and charged down upon us. There was an *induna* in front of the soldiers with a long flashing sword, which he whirled round his head as he ran, they killed themselves by running down. (22)

The most likely explanation is that Younghusband's men were trying to join up with the surviving 24th, now fighting back-to-back in the waggon park.

Major Smith and Lieutenant Curling were the officers in charge of the two 7-pound guns that day, and both rode sturdy artillery horses. Smith was shot through the arm but remained with the guns; he would shortly be killed in the flight from Isandlwana, while Curling became the only officer to have continuously engaged the Zulus until the camp fell. He survived to tell a remarkable tale and described his escape in a letter home:

> Of course, no wounded man was attended to, there was no time or men to spare. When we got the order to retire, we limbered up at once but were hardly in time as the Zulus were on us at once and one man was killed (stabbed) as he was mounting in a seat on the gun carriage. Most of the gunners were on foot as there was not time to mount them on the guns.

We trotted off to the camp thinking to take up another position but found it was in possession of the enemy who were killing the men as they ran out of their tents. We went right through them and out the other side, losing nearly all our gunners in doing so and one of the two sergeants. The road to Rorke's Drift that we hoped to retreat by was full of the enemy so, no way being open, we followed a crowd of natives and camp followers who were running down a ravine. The Zulus were all among them, stabbing men as they ran.

The ravine got steeper and steeper and finally the guns stuck and could get no further. In a moment the Zulus closed in and the drivers, who now alone remained, were pulled off their horses and killed. I did not see Maj. Smith at this moment but was with him a minute before.

The guns could not be spiked, there was no time to think of anything and we hoped to save the guns up to the last moment.

As soon as the guns were taken, I galloped off and made off with the crowd. How any of us escaped, I don't know; the Zulus were all around us and I saw men falling all round. We rode for about 5 miles, hotly pursued by the Zulus, when we came to a cliff overhanging the river. We had to climb down the face of the cliff and not more than half those who started from the top got to the bottom. Many fell right down, among others, Maj. Smith and the Zulus caught us here and shot us as we climbed down. I got down safely and came to the river which was very deep and swift. Numbers were swept away as they tried to cross and others shot from above.

My horse, fortunately, swam straight across, though I had three or four men hanging on his tail, stirrup leathers, etc. After crossing the river, we were in comparative safety, though many were killed afterwards who were on foot and unable to keep up. (23)

The Native Contingent on the line then broke ranks. They were ill-equipped, with only one rifle per ten men; they knew they faced certain death if they stayed, so they ran. The Zulus broke through the gap just after the call to retire on the main camp finally rang out across the battlefield. The ponderous British retreat back to camp began, but those fleeing from the firing line, hopeful of the camp's protection, found it already overrun from the rear by the Zulu right horn. While the Zulus had successfully manoeuvred and advanced their main body and left horn to attack the British, their right horn slipped unnoticed behind Isandlwana. The British only became aware of the right horn when, according to Commandant George Hamilton-Browne who watched the battle two miles from Isandlwana, they emerged in force from behind the mountain, driving the column's bellowing and terrified cattle through the waggon park and into the undefended rear of the British position. The scene in camp became a nightmare of gunfire, noise, terror, confusion and slaughter everywhere in sight; the pandemonium was further exaggerated by the lack of visibility.

British volley fire invariably reduced the visibility of the attacking Zulus to the defenders by creating a thick smokescreen, a vital factor usually overlooked by most authors. Lieutenant Wilkinson, a veteran of several Zulu War battles, subsequently made two relevant and revealing observations: firstly, 'we followed suit, firing volleys by sections in order to prevent the smoke obscuring the enemy'; and secondly, 'independent firing means in firing in twenty seconds, firing at nothing; and only helped our daring opponents to get close up under cover of our smoke'. (24)

An examination of some contemporary pictures of the battle, often painted from descriptions given by actual combatants, clearly reveals palls of smoke on various Zulu War battlefields. This effect can be seen in, amongst others, C.E. Fripp's *Isandlwana*, De Neuville's *Rorke's Drift*, Lieutenant Evelyn's two sketches of *Nyezane*, Crealock's *Final Repulse* [of Gingindlovu], Orlando Norie's watercolour of *Kambula* and the equally famous *Square at Ulund* in the *Illustrated London News* .

The original *Treatise on the British Martini-Henry* reveals no reference to any awareness of smoke by the British, although there are numerous references to the many major and minor mechanical difficulties which beset the development of both the weapon and its black powder cartridges. However, the 'smokescreen scenario' must not be overlooked, especially as the battlefield of Isandlwana sits in a wide bowl ringed by hills which, on a hot day, can be airless and still. It is easy to imagine the scene on the day of the British disaster; volley fire would soon have created a thick hanging smokescreen between the British line and the advancing Zulus. It could also account for the relatively small number of Zulu casualties, not only at Isandlwana but also at Rorke's Drift and subsequently through to the final battle at Ulundi. Two further references are relevant: firstly, Private George Mossop wrote perceptively of volley fire:

We were armed with Martini-Henry rifles charged with black powder, and each shot belched out a cloud of smoke; it became so dense that we were almost choked by it – and simply fired blindly into it. There was one continuous roar from cannon, rifles and the voices of men on both sides shouting. The smoke blotted out all view. It made every man feel that all he could do was to shoot immediately in front of him – and not concern himself with what was taking place elsewhere. (25)

Secondly, the problem of smoke is supported by an item in a contemporary army instruction manual: the *Appendix to Field Exercises: Rifle and Carbine Exercises and Musketry Instructions* issued by Horse Guards, July 1879. 'In firing volleys by sections it is well to commence from the section on the leeward flank, in order that the smoke may not inconvenience the remainder.' The British line at Isandlwana may well have fought and then withdrawn back to the camp in a fog of their own gunsmoke – only to encounter the Zulu right horn as its four thousand warriors charged from behind Isandlwana and into the unprotected rear of the British camp. The scene in the camp can only be described as total panic. A warrior from the iNgobamakhosi later recalled:

When I got in sight of [the camp] the whole place was a twisting mass of soldiers and natives fighting, the Mkandempemvu and Umbonambi were all killing, and then we attacked. One can remember little, and saw less, except for the twisting mass of men. (26)

As Lieutenant Raw rode through the chaos, he saw Lieutenant Stafford still on foot and shouted to him to get his horse as 'it was all up with us'. In the *Natal Mercury* 12 March 1924, Raw recalled that no one appeared to be in command. Lieutenant Nourse, who had lost his horse as the rocket battery was overrun, found a spare horse and headed for the Nek through which the camp's reserve cattle and horses were plunging, a scene he described as 'biblical'. Plunging his horse into the maelstrom, he escaped to tell the tale.

The ammunition myth
After Chelmsford's well equipped force was massacred by the spear-carrying Zulus, an acceptable explanation had to be found; being out-

generalled or out-fought by natives was not acceptable to the British. Chelmsford, together with his military and political advisers, urgently searched for a rational explanation, and the explanation they produced was both simple and logical – they reasoned that the soldiers on the line had run out of ammunition.

Survivors reported that Durnford's men had experienced ammunition supply problems, but Durnford retreated to the camp because his men were in danger of being surrounded. When the scene of the disaster was later visited, it was apparent that the Zulus had taken all the Martini-Henry rifles of the dead. They had also removed the boxes of ammunition that had remained on the ammunition carts; some of the boxes had been smashed open by the Zulus immediately following the battle. Other Zulus had removed ammunition from the pouches of dead soldiers, which encouraged the belief that the soldiers had exhausted their available supply before being overwhelmed. This belief was strengthened by the fact that smashed empty ammunition boxes lay around, and it was conveniently presumed that this was evidence of frantic British attempts to obtain further supplies. Collectively, this was a convincing argument that writers have perpetuated; the blame was laid at the door of incompetent officers or over-protective quartermasters.

The oft-discussed difficulty of opening ammunition boxes at Isandlwana is one of the most enduring myths of the Zulu war, probably because the tale remained unchallenged until the 1960s. There is adequate evidence both to refute these assertions and dispose of the myth. There are numerous survivors' reports that confirm extra ammunition was steadily moved out to the line before and during the Zulu attack. Private Wilson wrote that before the battle 'ammunition was beginning to be brought down to the companies'. Captain Essex confirmed that the quartermaster reputed to have denied ammunition to the line was actually shot dead even before boxes had been loaded on to a cart. Essex then saw the same cart deliver ammunition to the line. Much more ammunition was ferried out to the front line in 'Scotch carts' drawn by mules which, when fully loaded, could carry thirty boxes each containing six hundred rounds. Following the official archaeological excavation of the battlefield in 2000, a number of ammunition box lining handles were found along the firing line, indicating that boxes sent out by Captain Essex reached the front line where they were successfully opened. Zulu accounts confirmed that those survivors of the 24th Regiment who had retreated to the waggon park were all still firing 'furiously until their ammunition became exhausted, then all perished'. (25) Perhaps the inadvertent progenitor of the myth was General Sir Horace Smith-Dorrien, who wrote of an ammunition box difficulty nearly fifty years after the event. He obviously forgot that a few days after the disaster he had written, 'I was out with the front companies of the 24th handing them spare ammunition'. The myth grew to make an inexplicable defeat explicable; it also denied the enormous bravery and skill of the Zulus.

Once the Zulus were through the British line, the fighting and slaughter raged for little more than half an hour before sheer force of numbers overwhelmed the surviving soldiers. Whilst no soldier lived to tell the tale, several accounts survive from Zulu warriors interviewed after the battle:

Ah, those red soldiers at Isandlwana, how few they were, and how they fought! They fell like stones – each man in his place. (27)

They threw down their guns, when the ammunition was done, and then commenced with their pistols, which they fired as long as their ammunition lasted; and then they formed a line, shoulder to shoulder, and back to back, and fought with their knives. (28)

Some covered their faces with their hands, not wishing to see death. Some ran around. Some entered into their tents. Others were indignant; although badly wounded they died where they stood, at their post. (29)

One specific report clearly related to Durnford's last stand. There were no survivors from this group and no eye-witnesses other than Lieutenant Curling. However, Mehlokazulu, one of Chief Sihayo's sons, was present and gave a detailed statement of events when he was interviewed at Pietermaritzberg after the battle:

When we closed in we came onto a mixed party of men who had evidently been stopped by the end of our horn. They made a desperate resistance, some firing with pistols and others with swords. I repeatedly heard the word 'fire' but we proved too many for them, and killed them where they stood. When all was over I had a look at these men, and saw an officer with his arm in a sling and with a big moustache, surrounded by Carbineers, soldiers and other men I did not know. (30)

The Zulus killed the soldiers, their horses, cattle and those camp dogs they could catch; such was their fury. By about 1 pm only one British soldier remained alive. He was probably a survivor of Captain Younghusband's company. When they had fought their way towards the area of the waggon park, this soldier had climbed up the side of Isandlwana and taken refuge in a small cave. For another two hours, according to Zulu reports, he husbanded his ammunition and killed any Zulu who approached the cave. Eventually, the Zulus lost patience with this lone sniper and gathered a force armed with captured Martini-Henry rifles. They poured volley after volley into the cave until the soldier was hit. His body was discovered some ten months later by Captain Mainwaring's burial party, with a rope around his neck. Zulu folklore records their sorrow at having had to kill such a brave man, and his name and regiment remain unknown.

About sixty Europeans survived Isandlwana by escaping (the exact number is debatable), including five British officers who lived to tell the tale; these were Lieutenant Curling and four mounted transport officers – Captains Edward Essex and Alan Gardner, together with Lieutenants William Cochrane and Horace Smith-Dorrien. Apart from Curling, these officers had all been engaged on duties within the camp before they made good their escape.

In the early 1900s it was realised that a partial eclipse had occurred across southern Africa as the battle of Isandlwana drew to its bloody close. No Isandlwana survivors mentioned it, but that is understandable due to the smoke from the artillery and volley firing that preceded the defeat. No mention of the event was made at the time by any of the British military elsewhere in Zululand; it must be presumed that the eclipse was not perceptible to the naked eye at the time.

Chapter 6

Flight from Isandlwana

Zulus seemed to be behind, before, and on each side of us,
and as we hurried on we had to leave poor fugitives crying
and begging us not to leave them.
Trooper W. Barker, Natal Carbineers

The scene across the British position, as stabbing Zulus fought hand-to-hand with desperate soldiers, was unimaginably terrifying. British discipline had been replaced by a rout; it was every man for himself amidst the carnage. Nevertheless, some acts of selflessness were recorded: the Hon. Standish Vereker gave his horse to an injured man, which resulted in his own death moments later. Surgeon Major Peter Shepherd would have escaped on his horse had he not stopped to assist a severely wounded soldier; Shepherd was stabbed through the neck by a passing Zulu. With the British force so heavily outnumbered, it was remarkable that anyone should have escaped back to the safety of Natal, although of the sixty or so Europeans who did escape the majority were camp followers who departed before the battle was underway, or colonials who were mounted and could outpace the Zulus. Lieutenant Horace Smith-Dorrien, who was one of only five Imperial officers to escape, was in camp as the Zulus attacked and wrote of his escape to his father:

> I was out with the front companies of the 24th handing them spare ammunition. Bullets were flying all over the place, but I never seemed to notice them. The Zulus nearly all had firearms of some kind and lots of ammunition. Before we knew where we were, they came right into the camp, assegaing everybody right and left. Everybody then who had a horse turned to fly. The enemy were going at a kind of very fast half walk and half run. On looking round we saw that we were completely surrounded and the road to Rorke's Drift was cut off. The place where they seemed thinnest was

where we all made for. Everybody went pell-mell over the ground covered with huge boulders and rocks until we got to a deep *spruit* or gully. How the horses got over, I have no idea. I was riding a broken kneed old crock which did not belong to me, and which I expected to go on its head every minute. We had to go bang through them at the *spruit*. Lots of our men were killed there. I had lots of marvellous escapes, and was firing away at them with my revolver as I galloped along. The ground there down to the river was so broken that the Zulus went as fast as the horses and kept killing all the way. There were very few white men; they were nearly all mounted niggers of ours flying. This lasted until we came to a kind of precipice down to the river Buffalo. I jumped off and led my horse down, there was a poor fellow of the Mounted Infantry, a Private, struck through the arm, who said as I passed that if I could bind up his arm and stop the bleeding he would be alright. I accordingly took out my handkerchief and tied up his arm. Just as I had done it, Maj. Smith of the Artillery came down by me wounded, saying, "For God's sake get on, man, the Zulus are on the top of us". I had done all I could for the wounded man as I turned to jump on my horse. Just as I was doing so, the horse went with a bound to the bottom of the precipice, being struck with an assagai [sic]. I gave up all hope, as the Zulus were all round me, finishing off the wounded, the man I had helped and Maj. Smith among the number. However, with the strong hope that everybody clings to that some accident would turn up, I rushed off on foot and plunged into the river, which was little better than a roaring torrent.

Lieutenant William Cochrane was also in the camp when it was overrun by the Zulus. He echoed the desperate attempts to escape in a letter to his family:

I made in the direction which I had seen taken by the mounted men, guns and Royal Artillery, and natives on foot. I was cut off by the enemy, who had now reached the line of retreat; but with a good horse, hard riding, and good luck, I managed to reach the Buffalo River. The Zulus seemed perfectly fearless; they followed alongside, having desperate fighting with those retreating, mostly our natives on foot. On several occasions they were quite close to me, but I was fortunate enough to escape, while others dropped at my side. They fired at us the whole way from the camp to the river, but having mounted the bank on the opposite side we were safe.

One officer, sadly unidentified, subsequently sent a descriptive account of the battle to *The Times,* who published it on 10 April 1879. He also added that he had been escorting a shipment of gold (probably to pay or bribe wavering Zulu chiefs). What happened to the gold is not recorded, although immediately after the war an escort of British cavalry arrived at the hardware store at Greytown to collect a heavy box marked 'Horseshoes' deposited for safe keeping in the confusion after the battle of Isandlwana. When the storekeeper signed the officer's receipt he saw, to his astonishment, that he had been caring for a wooden case of gold sovereigns.

With the exception of Lieutenant Curling who vainly tried to save the artillery guns, no British front-line soldier or officer survived. Much controversy was thus caused when, a few days after the battle, it was discovered that two mounted officers of the 24th Regiment, Lieutenants Coghill and Melvill, had not only managed to escape from the camp but had actually reached Natal on horseback before then being killed. Their departure from the battlefield while their regiment's soldiers were still fighting for their lives, and the circumstances in which the two officers died, were to become the subject of much speculation and debate, as well as a harsh statement from Chelmsford's successor, Sir Garnet Wolseley. Only three Isandlwana Victoria Crosses were awarded, and curiously, every recipient had fled the battlefield. A Victoria Cross was awarded immediately to Private Wassall, but the awards to Lieutenants Coghill and Melvill would be delayed for nearly thirty years.

Because there were some survivors, it has often been argued that the Zulus never completely surrounded Isandlwana. This argument is based on the fact that a number of survivors were able to flee through a gap in the Zulu encirclement and escape towards Natal, albeit over the very rough terrain known today as the Fugitives' Trail. In fact, the Zulus did complete their encirclement and blocked the British line of retreat back to Rorke's Drift, but a section of the iNgobamakhosi then detached themselves from the closing right horn to chase fleeing NNC natives trying to escape across the boulder-strewn terrain. This caused a temporary gap through which the escaping Europeans were able to follow, only for most to run into Zulus who killed them. It was through this gap that Lieutenant Curling and Major Smith rode alongside the two artillery guns, only to observe them careering out of control down a steep slope, where the guns overturned amidst the Zulus. Curling and Smith, independently mounted, were able to escape the incident and rode on; Smith was killed further along the Fugitives' Trail, while Curling escaped. The only Europeans to reach Natal did so on horseback, and it can be positively argued that most of these survivors, with the exception of Curling, left Isandlwana before the main battle was under way – but which route did they take to escape the slaughter raging across the camp?

Contemporaries and modern researchers have collectively related how the battlefield fugitives tried to flee back to the safety of Natal by first crossing the Nek between Isandlwana and Black's Koppie. This choice of route is strange, even for fugitives consumed with panic, as they would have been fleeing into the full force of the densely packed advancing Zulus now attacking the camp across the Nek from the undefended rear of Isandlwana. Obviously this was the route taken by some of the fugitives when the iNgobamakhosi detached themselves from the completed encirclement and created a temporary gap; but what route did the fugitives take before the gap opened? Standing on the battlefield, it is clear that the obvious escape route is to the left (south) of Black's Koppie and not across the Zulu-occupied Nek.

From most points on the battlefield the area left of the Nek offered the fugitives a view of Natal some six miles distant, and the route lay downhill. The uphill track across the Nek was the known route that had recently brought everyone to Isandlwana, but would that have been a sufficient incentive in the face of advancing Zulus? When the author examined the map of the battle drawn by the Queen's cartographer, James Wyld, submitted to the War Office on 31 March 1879, it was clear that, to those interviewed in the making of the map and with matters recently in their minds, there were two fugitives' trails: one each side of Black's Koppie, and both leading to the safety of Natal. This alternative route has hitherto been ignored by historians, but more recent research in South Africa into the accounts of Captain William Barton NNH and Private Wassall suggest they also took this route. (1) In April 2010 the author and Dr David Payne attempted to follow the southern route. It was boulder-strewn and difficult to follow, and no cairns could be found. Indeed, it is logical that none was built, as no one taking this route died;

but the extreme African elements and the long grass made such searching impossible. There is still further research to be conducted into this second fugitives' trail.

During the 2000 archaeological investigation of Isandlwana, the author brought to the attention of the archaeologists a freshly eroded cairn near the beginning of the Fugitives' Trail, a mere 400 yards from the Nek. A recent storm had exposed the cairn's stones and a small flood had eroded the side of the cairn. After careful work, the site revealed numerous horse bones and fragments of rotted leather straps and metal buckles. Just below these items were found human remains – the bones of Curling's Royal Artillery drivers who died when the Zulus overwhelmed their gun carriage. The artefacts and bones were replaced with due care and reverence.

Coghill and Melvill

Lieutenants Teignmouth Melvill and Nevill Cóghill were two 24th officers who escaped from Isandlwana but were killed while attempting to save the Regimental Colour of the 1/24th. Both officers were subsequently awarded the Victoria Cross for their efforts, but not until 1907, nearly thirty years later. Much has been written about their gallantry but nothing is known about their escape from Isandlwana camp.

The eminent British historian of the time, Sir Reginald Coupland, wrote of Coghill and Melvill (always as Melville), that these two officers:

> Had charged themselves with saving the Colours of the 24th and then, after their six-mile flight on horseback across impossibly rocky terrain, they reached the river together and plunged straight into it. (2)

It is highly probable that Coupland had studied and then relied on the original report written by Lieutenant Colonel Richard Glyn, then isolated at Rorke's Drift, in his capacity as the Officer Commanding the 3rd Column (Coupland even copied Glyn's incorrect spelling of Melvill's name). This highly emotive but fascinating report, the earliest record of the fate of these two officers, was written by Glyn after the enquiry into the disaster of Isandlwana and, no doubt, after much anguish and personal reflection on his part. At the time of the Zulu attack on the camp, Glyn was with Chelmsford at Mangeni. This report, based on hearsay only, is his emotional justification of his officers' actions at Isandlwana. The full report by Glyn, dated 21 February 1879, is produced in full as Appendix C. The official history of the 24th Regiment, similarly based on hearsay, records the event as follows:

On the fateful 22nd January 1879, when it was evident that all was lost in Isandhlwana camp, Lieutenant and Adjutant Melvill, 1st battalion 24th, received special orders from Lieutenant Colonel Pulleine, to endeavour to save the Colour. "You, as senior subaltern", that officer is reported to have said, "will take the Colour, and make your way from here". Accompanied by Lt. A.J.A. Coghill, 1st Battalion 24th, who was orderly officer to Colonel Glyn, but had remained in camp on account of a severe injury to his knee, Melvill rode off with the Colour, taking the same direction as the other fugitives. Both officers reached the Buffalo (river) although, owing to the badness of the track, the Zulus kept up with them and continued throwing their spears at them. The river was in flood, and at any other time would have been considered impassable.

They plunged their horses in, but whilst Coghill got across and reached the opposite bank, Melvill, encumbered by the Colour, got separated from his horse and was washed against a large rock in mid-stream, to which Lieutenant Higginson, Native Contingent, who afterwards escaped, was clinging. Melvill called to him to lay hold of the Colour, which Higginson did, but so strong was the current that both men were washed away. Coghill, still on his horse and in comparative safety, at once rode back into the stream to their aid. The Zulus by this time had gathered thick on the bank of the river and opened fire, making a special target of Melvill, who wore his red patrol jacket. Coghill's horse was killed and his rider cast adrift in the stream. Notwithstanding the exertions made to save it, the Colour had to be abandoned, and the two officers themselves only succeeded in reaching the opposite bank with great difficulty, and in a most exhausted state. Those only who know the precipitous character of the Natal side at the spot, can fully realise how great must have been the sufferings of both in climbing it, especially of Coghill with his wounded knee. They appear to have kept together, and to have got to within twenty yards of the summit when they were overtaken by their foes and fell. On 3rd February, a search party found the bodies of Melvill and Coghill covered with assegai wounds and with several dead Zulus around them. Next day the flood, having subsided, the Colour, on its pole, was recovered further downstream. For their gallantry in the saving of the Colour, Lieutenants Melvill and Coghill were later each awarded a posthumous Victoria Cross. (3)

This official history tallies almost exactly with the contemporary report, also based on hearsay, of Captain Penn Symons, 2/24th, who wrote:

They [Coghill and Melvill] were greatly exhausted, partly from the quantity of water they had swallowed, and partly from their struggle in the river. For a moment they laid down on the water's edge, and then getting over the first 200 yards of the bank which is flat, they began to climb the side of the ravine which was exceedingly steep. Lieut. Coghill was lame from an old injury to his knee, and on this account had been left in camp on this day. They had gone but a little way up when they saw that the Zulus were crossing after them. They scrambled on until Lt. Coghill said "I am done, I can go no further". Lt. Melvill said, "Neither can I". Lt. Higginson begged of them to shoot as they still had their revolvers, he, having lost his rifle in the river, went on, and at the top of the bank found some Basutos who were keeping up a fire on the advancing Zulus. (4)

It would appear that Captain Penn Symons' subjective report was based largely on comments made by Higginson, adjutant of the 3rd Battalion Natal Native Contingent, on his arrival at Helpmekaar after fleeing from Isandlwana. Higginson stated that he had left Coghill and Melvill after the three of them had safely reached the Natal bank. It is probable that all three believed they were then safe, as Higginson initially related how he, being the fittest, left the two exhausted British officers in order to find some horses. He claimed to have found two spare horses and, on reaching a vantage point, saw the bodies of Coghill and Melvill surrounded by Zulus. Unable to help them, he then rode off to Helpmekaar.

Curiously, local rumours have long persisted that four bodies were found at the spot where Coghill and Melvill died. Lieutenant Hillier of the NNC throws more light on the subject as he was present when the bodies were discovered several days later. His unabridged account of what he saw, published in the press on 28 February, makes interesting reading:

You will see my name in General Orders as one of those that recovered the colors [sic] of the 1-24th Regiment. Major Black, of the 2-24th Regiment, came and asked for volunteers to go and search for the colors of the 1-24th Regiment, as they were known to be lost in a dangerous part of the Drift. It was thought that there might be a fight, so 20 men volunteered. Well armed, we rode out and, crossing over the hill overlooking the Drift, we came across the bodies of poor Lieuts. Melvill and Coghill; they lay behind the bodies of two soldiers, where they had made a stand. Coghill was quite naked except for his boots and a gold ring on his finger, which Captain Parr took off. Poor Melvill had everything on, but was much disfigured. We buried them and read the Service over them. (5)

After the battle, and in line with the military custom of the time, the death of two ordinary soldiers alongside the officers would not have been deemed relevant or significant. The author, aware of this account, searched the area around the graves of Coghill and Melvill; there are, indeed, two cairns nearby. The story has an interesting twist because Sergeant Cooper of the 1/24th is officially recorded as being an Isandlwana casualty, but his family papers and memorial service documents indicate he was killed at Rorke's Drift. Fugitives' Drift is much closer to Rorke's Drift than Isandlwana. Cooper is not recorded in any of the accounts as having died during the fighting at Rorke's Drift, but the logical hypothesis is that he died nearby – possibly at Sotondose's Drift (re-named Fugitives' Drift after the battle) alongside Coghill and Melvill. This hypothesis is supported by a letter sent from the Officer in Command at nearby Helpmekaar, Major Upcher, to Cooper's married sister, a Mrs Clements, informing her of his death. Had Cooper been killed at Isandlwana this would not have happened. But could Cooper have made good his escape along the Fugitives' Trail and across the Buffalo River before being killed? If he had been able to catch or cling to a fleeing horse the answer has to be 'yes'. Curling wrote that his horse pulled four soldiers across the flooded river. If Cooper's body had been discovered and buried where it fell near those of Coghill and Melvill, notification of Cooper's death, especially since he was a sergeant, would have been passed to Major Upcher and thus generated his letter to Mrs Clements.

As with many details about the battle of Isandlwana, the death of Cooper remains shrouded in uncertainty, and so the questions remain: how near to Rorke's Drift was Sergeant Cooper when he was killed, or was his body that of one of the two soldiers actually discovered along with those of Coghill and Melvill and buried under one of the adjacent cairns? What caused Major Upcher to write specially to Cooper's sister on 11 April 1879, bearing in mind the first serious attempt to tidy the Isandlwana battlefield did not take place until 21 May of that year? Why did Cooper's family always believe he had been killed at Rorke's Drift? And if one of the two soldiers' bodies was indeed that of Cooper, who was the fourth soldier seen there by Lieutenant Hillier? The author has frequently walked the route between Fugitives' Drift and Rorke's Drift, alone or with David Rattray (the final time just a month before David Rattray's death), and most recently in April 2010 accompanied by Dr David Payne. No evidence of any cairns has ever been found beyond those where Coghill and Melvill were killed at Fugitives' Drift. It is possible that Cooper could have been one of the two soldiers who made a stand with Melvill and Coghill. Only a DNA analysis will provide the definitive answer. (6)

Meanwhile, protected by the covering fire of Lieutenant Raw's Mounted Basutos who had safely gained the Natal bank, two Troopers, Barker and Tarboton, had managed to swim their horses across the flooded Buffalo River to join them. The group then rode up the steep Natal side of the bank until they were out of range of the Zulu marksmen on the far bank. Looking back, they saw a distant figure scrambling on foot towards them. While his companions rode on, Barker rode back down the hill and met the figure, who turned out to be Higginson. As his horse was in no state to carry them both back up the steep slope, Barker surrendered his mount to the exhausted officer but implored him to wait for him at the top of the hill. Higginson gave his promise then spurred the horse up the hill, leaving Barker to follow on foot. With natives closing in around him (no doubt the same men who in due course killed Melvill and Coghill), Barker struggled to the summit only to find that Higginson had galloped off, leaving him to his fate. The exhausted Barker was forced to run for his life; he was pursued for another three miles before Lieutenant Raw arrived and drove the pursuers off.

In the meantime, Higginson had come across Tarboton, Lieutenants Raw and Henderson and some Basutos who had waited on the Helpmekaar track for Barker to rejoin them. Perhaps certain that Barker must by this time have been overtaken by the 'Zulus', Higginson at first insisted that he had found the horse down at the Buffalo River. Tarboton, though, immediately recognised Barker's horse, which Higginson relinquished in exchange for a spare Basuto pony. Higginson having set off for Helpmekaar to make his report, the group rode back towards the river until they came upon the exhausted Barker still running for his life. Within a few days, the truth of Higginson's escape from the scene became well known; Higginson, now with a black eye, quietly disappeared into obscurity.

Over the years, writers have invariably accepted that the original stories relating to Coghill and Melvill riding together to save the Colour were correct, and little additional comment was added to the contemporary reports of the day. Several modern authors have gone somewhat further and described how, at the height of the battle, Melvill had ridden with Colonel Pulleine to his HQ tent housing the Queen's Colour of the 1/24th (the Regimental Colour was at Helpmekaar; the two Colours of the 2/24th were in Colonel Glyn's tent, which was quickly engulfed by Zulus). According to one military author, Pulleine apparently emerged from his tent, handed the cased Colour to Melvill and 'ordered him to take it to a place of safety'. Melvill then apparently 'placed the staff across the saddlebow, saluted, wheeled his horse and plunged into the stream of refugees who were fleeing the camp'. (7) This description portrays a melodramatic scene, but sadly without any empirical evidence.

The popular press perpetuated many of these stories, although on 1 March 1879 the highly respected *Illustrated London News* drew its own rational conclusion as to why Coghill left the battlefield. It wrote that Mr Young, a surviving officer of the NNC who fled early in the battle alongside his natives, also saw Coghill leave Isandlwana. Young wrote, 'It appears that Lt. Coghill was dispatched for assistance as he was acting that day as staff officer to Colonel Pulleine'. (8)

The Curling letters also throw some light on the matter. Curling mentions seeing both Melvill and Coghill at separate times during his escape, and his initial encounter with Melvill indicates that the Zulu right horn had already entered the camp before the order to retire was given to the firing line. Curling wrote that the guns were positioned 'about four hundred yards beyond the left front of the Natal Native Contingent Camp' and that, 'on the order being given to retire, the guns were limbered up and were trotted away finally galloping through the camp being invaded by the Zulus'. The distance from the guns' position to the waggon park is approximately 1,500 yards, which in panic and among fleeing soldiers would have taken three to four minutes to cover on horseback. Melvill had already left with the Colour as Curling caught up with him some distance from the camp. Curling was riding his own charger which, by his own account, was a splendid animal which did not put a foot wrong and carried him all the way down to and across the Buffalo River without faltering.

Lieutenant Coghill's departure from the battlefield
Although an officer of the 24th on the day of the battle, Coghill was staff officer to Colonel Glyn, commander of No. 3 Column. He did not, however, accompany Glyn due to an 'old injury to his knee', and accordingly stayed at Isandlwana camp. As the Zulu attack was pressed home, several staff officers rendered valuable assistance to the failing British line. Captain Essex, who survived, subsequently reported that he had spent some time supervising the flow of additional ammunition to the front line before the Zulus broke into the camp. Coghill was probably unable to assist anyone due to his injured knee. As yet, there is no evidence, oral or written, official or unofficial, to indicate that Coghill was with Melvill when Melvill departed from the battlefield at Isandlwana with the Colour.

Survivors' reports indicate that Coghill left Isandlwana well before Melvill took charge of the colour from Pulleine, yet, curiously, some five miles from the camp Coghill specifically informed Curling that Pulleine had already been killed. Lieutenant Smith-Dorrien was near Melvill as the two officers were jointly negotiating a marshy patch, and Smith-Dorrien looked up and recognised Coghill at least half a mile ahead. There are other eyewitness reports of Coghill and Melvill being seen at different points along the Fugitives' Trail, but never together. It is known that Coghill, considerably incapacitated by his injury, left the camp on a stray horse. Had he left later with Melvill, it is unlikely that he could have maintained the same pace as Melvill, who was riding his own 'splendid' mount. On the approach to the river, Curling had a brief discussion with Coghill and later wrote, 'I was with Maj. Smith at this time, he told me he had been wounded in the arm. We saw Lt. Coghill, the ADC and asked him if we could not rally some men and make a stand, he said he did not think it could be done'. (8)

It is also probable that Coghill's departure from Isandlwana was rather less well organised than Melvill's. Coghill certainly did not manage to collect his own horse, which would indicate a degree of chaos in the headquarters area. Instead, he seized another horse and thus made his escape, but only just, as several survivors saw some Zulus attempt to assegai Coghill but settle instead for spearing and injuring his horse. (9)

Lieutenant Higginson reached the river ahead of Coghill and Melvill but, having lost his horse in mid-stream, was clinging for dear life to a large rock protruding from the swirling water. He recalled that Coghill and Melvill reached the river independently and at different locations, with Coghill successfully crossing the river upstream of Melvill's approach. The combination of Coghill's incapacity, the rough terrain and his riding an unfamiliar and wounded horse, conspired to slow his progress to the place of the fateful incident about to unfurl. Coghill reached the safety of the Natal bank and was recovering from his ordeal as Melvill was swept into view clutching the Colour. Melvill had put his horse into the surging river and was immediately swept from the saddle. Still clutching the colour, Melvill was carried towards the rock supporting Higginson. Melvill called to Higginson to grasp the Colour but the force of the water caused Melvill to drop it; his subsequent impact with Higginson left both officers struggling in the water but protected by the lee of the rock. The struggle was observed by Coghill who put his horse into the river in an attempt to reach his fellow officers; he had nearly reached them, under a hail of Zulu rifle fire, when his horse was shot dead. The three officers then struck out for the Natal bank and safety.

Higginson first mentions Coghill after he and Melvill were swept from the now famous 'coffin rock', and not before. Donald Morris, a meticulous researcher, also makes no mention of Coghill and Melvill being together until Melvill was actually in the river with Higginson and after they had been clinging to the rock for some time. Morris continues, 'Lieutenant Coghill, in a blue patrol jacket had reached the Natal shore in safety a few minutes before'. (10) Obviously no one knows why Coghill departed the battlefield; he was an ambitious officer who was highly regarded by senior officers of the 24th, including Colonel Glyn and Lord Chelmsford. As a staff officer, Coghill would have been fully aware that considerable reserves, consisting of two companies of the 1/24th, were already en route from Helpmekaar to Rorke's Drift. He could not have known that those reserves, on learning the unbelievable news of the British defeat, would turn back to Helpmekaar when only three miles from Rorke's Drift. It is possible that Coghill left Isandlwana early in the battle, intending to summon help from these reserves, which he would have believed were either at Rorke's Drift or even closer to Isandlwana.

Lieutenant Melvill and the Colour

There is no actual evidence, either primary or secondary, that Lieutenant Colonel Pulleine ever dispatched Melvill with the Colour; likewise, there is nothing to substantiate the classic words attributed to Pulleine in a variety of films and books, imploring Melvill, 'You, as senior subaltern, will take the Colour, and make your way from here'. This story is one of the legends of Isandlwana and originated in the hearsay account by Colonel Glyn, subsequently copied in a report in an obscure Natal newspaper signed by 'A gentleman whose testimony may be relied upon'. As to its author's identity and truthfulness, we will probably never be sure, but it certainly joined the growing collection of heroic scenes adored by the Victorians. It might just be possible that Melvill, an officer with a fine reputation, seized the initiative from the inexperienced Pulleine, who before that fateful day had never heard a shot fired in anger. There is plentiful evidence that, once the Zulus entered the camp, terror and panic took an immediate hold and resistance lasted for minutes only. It is probable that Melvill took the one symbol that could restore order, the Colour, in a brave attempt to rally the 24th as the Zulus were progressively overwhelming them. Traditionally, the primary role of the Colour was as a rallying point for one's own troops in the noisy confusion and smoke of battle, and Melvill would have been only too aware of this purpose. He may then have realised his task was impossible and sought to save the Colour. In any event, Melvill managed to leave Isandlwana in relatively good order. He had the Colour, he rode his own horse and he still possessed his revolver and sword. We know that he lost his sword during the flight to the river, as Chelmsford's interpreter, Brickhill, remembered being asked by Melvill if he had seen his lost sword. Melvill probably departed the scene just as the camp was being overrun and just ahead of Curling, making him one of the last to leave the stricken position; this also accounts for Melvill's arrival at the river so long after the other fugitives.

The question posed has to remain unanswered. What is clear is that Melvill reached the river with the Colour, lost it in mid-stream and then, having been saved by Coghill, lost his life trying to save Coghill. There is little doubt that Melvill could have escaped on foot with Higginson, but chose instead to assist Coghill.

What role was played by the two soldiers who died alongside the officers is not known; they may well have arrived at the spot after Higginson departed. Higginson's initial report soon reached Glyn at Rorke's Drift. Using the report, a search party found the bodies of Coghill, Melvill and the two soldiers the following day and buried them where they had fallen. There are three cairns close to the graves of the officers and the supposition is that the soldiers were buried close to, but apart from, the officers – a normal practice at the time. It later occurred to Glyn that the Colour could still be in the vicinity of the bodies, and on 3 February he dispatched a party to search the river banks. Lieutenant Harford and Captain Harber soon discovered the Colour's case and further down the river found the Colour's pole protruding out of the water. Harber waded into the river and pulled the pole, still attached to the Colour, out of the water. As he recovered the Colour, the gold-embroidered centre scroll fell back into the water. In a moving ceremony at Rorke's Drift the Colour was restored to Colonel Glyn, the officer to whom it had originally been presented in June 1866.

Of the Regimental Colour left in camp, the crown, which was detachable, was found in March on the Natal side of the Buffalo River among the debris of a farm burnt by the Zulus. Its case was recovered from the dried-up bed of the Manzimnyama stream.

Higginson received no recognition for his endeavours to save either the two officers or the Colour from the Buffalo River. He was a colonial officer, his story was not corroborated, and then there was the unworthy incident of the horse stolen from Trooper Barker and Higginson's broken promise to him.

Who killed Coghill and Melvill?
Following the initial British attack on Sihayo's homestead, a number of surviving Zulus were detained for questioning, invariably a rough and brutal process. These captives were released during the following day or so, and a number of them took refuge with relatives living in the vicinity of Fugitives' Drift on the Natal bank of the Buffalo River, then known as

Sothondose's Drift. These men, resentful of the British action and grieving for their chief's son and friends killed in the attack, were not well disposed towards the British. As the few British survivors from Isandlwana crossed the river, these very same Zulus observed them; the time for revenge had arrived. Local Zulu folklore holds that Coghill and Melvill were both killed by these previously friendly local natives and not by Cetshwayo's Zulus. It was well known that the Zulus were reluctant to cross the fast flowing and turbulent Buffalo River. Apart from being reluctant to disobey Cetshwayo's order not to invade Natal, most warriors could not swim.

Author Ron Lock wrote that many of the fugitives, including Melvill and Coghill, were killed by the prisoners released by Chelmsford the previous day, a fact which was kept secret at the time but was well known to Chelmsford's staff. One member of Chelmsford's staff actually wrote that:

> Some of them got right down to the river six miles off and were killed by a lot of scoundrels whom the General had taken prisoner a few days before. (11)

What is not disputed is that three officers, Coghill, Melvill and Higginson, all ended up in the Buffalo River. All of them could have survived, but a combination of circumstances proved fatal for two of them so that only Higginson escaped. It is apparent that Melvill refused to leave Coghill to his fate, and both were killed just below the crest of the ridge overlooking the river. Amazingly, Coghill still had his sword and revolver; Melvill had drawn his revolver but it was useless – the cylinder had fallen out at Isandlwana and was allegedly found by a member of a later burial party. It is evident that Coghill, being mounted and having safely reached the Natal bank, could easily have escaped had he left Melvill to his fate in the river. Likewise, once Melvill was on the Natal bank, he could have easily reached safety had he accompanied Higginson to search for horses instead of remaining with the lame Coghill.

Chelmsford's and Wolseley's view of events

In the following months, Chelmsford remained unhappy about the circumstances surrounding the deaths of Coghill and Melvill. He was well aware of the implications of certain officers' conduct – those who had escaped Isandlwana and others who had subsequently deserted their men – so he was understandably cautious before making any official comment.

Most notable of the recent desertions was that of Lieutenant Henry Harwood, who abandoned his heavily outnumbered men in the midst of the Ntombe Drift battle on 12 March. This followed the desertion of two officers, Lieutenants Avery and Holcroft, who were part of Major Dartnell's force sent to scout ahead of Isandlwana; both disappeared and were never seen again. The circumstances of Lieutenant Adendorff's departure from Isandlwana, where he was on picket duty, and his arrival at Rorke's Drift are also uncertain. There is even the possibility that he deserted Rorke's Drift moments before the Zulu attack. Zulu war author, Michael Glover, wrote, 'Chard did not notice Adendorff's defection and reported that he stayed to assist in the defence. Nevertheless, the evidence is overwhelming that he decamped. He was later arrested in Pietermaritzburg'. (12) More seriously, on the afternoon of the battle at Isandlwana, Captain Stevenson deserted from Rorke's Drift, leaving Lieutenants Chard and Bromhead to face the attacking Zulus. Likewise, Major Spalding never explained why he left Rorke's Drift for reinforcements only hours before the Zulus attacked the position. On 14 May 1879 Lord Chelmsford wrote to the War Office:

> It is most probable that Melvill lost his life endeavouring to save Coghill rather than vice versa. He (Coghill) could hardly walk and any exertion such as walking or riding would have been likely to render him almost helpless. He could not have assisted, therefore, in saving the Colours of the 1/24th, and as I have already said I fear he was a drag on poor Melvill. As regards the latter (Melvill) I am again puzzled how to reply to your question. I feel sure that Melvill left camp with the Colours under orders received. He was too good a soldier to have left without. In being ordered to leave, however, he no doubt was given the best chance of saving his life which must have been lost had he remained in camp. His ride was not more daring than that of those who escaped. The question, therefore, remains had he succeeded in saving the Colours and his own life, would he have been considered to deserve the Victoria Cross? (13)

The new British Military Commander, Sir Garnet Wolseley, was to write even more strongly on the issue:

> I am sorry that both of these officers were not killed with their men at Isandlwana instead of where they were. I don't like the

idea of officers escaping on horseback when their men on foot are killed. Heroes have been made of men like Melvill and Coghill, who, taking advantage of their having horses, bolted from the scene of the action to save their lives. It is monstrous making heroes of those who saved or attempted to save their lives by bolting or of those who, shut up in buildings at Rorke's Drift, could not bolt, and fought like rats for their lives which they could not otherwise save. (14)

Why were Coghill and Melvill awarded the Victoria Cross?
The criteria for the award of a posthumous Victoria Cross prior to 1879 are confusing. Much of this confusion arose over men who died during the Indian Mutiny before the Victoria Cross could be conferred. Due to the long delays in the transmission of news between India and London, one GOC, Lord Clyde, had even requested that a supply of Victoria Crosses should be dispatched to him. His request was considered but refused by the War Office. Even after 1879, General Harman, Military Secretary at the War Office, wrote to the Foreign Secretary in 1888 concerning a request for a Victoria Cross for a deceased ensign:.

> Ensign Phillipps would have been recommended for the VC had he survived, but he was not recommended prior to his decease and there are only precedents for the issue of the Cross to the relatives of persons upon whom it had been provisionally conferred, who had been recommended for it whilst alive. (15)

This doctrine prevailed until the end of the nineteenth century, though Sir Evelyn Wood recommended that Captain Ronald Campbell would have received the Victoria Cross had he survived the battle of Hlobane. Wood's relevant War Office file contains a pencilled note: 'Gen W [presumably Wolseley] does not wish this question raised'.

With regard to Coghill and Melvill, it is interesting that no recommendation was submitted from the commander in the field. Colonel Glyn's emotive dispatch praised their conduct but made no specific recommendation. The Duke of Cambridge suggested to the Secretary of State for War that the terms of the dispatch merited the issue of memoranda to the effect that they would have been recommended to the Queen for the award of the Victoria Cross had they survived. Exactly the same situation applied to the recommendation made by the Indian Government on 15 May 1879 for the Victoria Cross to be awarded to Lieutenant Walter Hamilton for his action at Futtehabad. This attempt to bend the rules, as in the case of Coghill and Melvill, also failed.

There can be no doubt that Melvill richly deserved his award on at least two counts: firstly, for denying the Colour to the enemy and, secondly, for remaining to assist the injured Coghill. The case of Coghill is only marginally less clear although, sadly, the awkward question concerning the authority for his flight from the battlefield remains unanswered. He probably left Isandlwana, under orders, early in the battle to summon help from the reserves he fully expected to be at nearby Rorke's Drift or even closer to Isandlwana. He also surrendered his only chance of escape by plunging back into the river, under heavy enemy fire, to assist Melvill and Higginson who were floundering in mid-stream.

On 19 May 1879 Disraeli, the Prime Minister, notified Melvill's widow Sara that Queen Victoria had awarded her a pension of £100 a year 'in recognition of the heroic conduct of your late husband in saving the Colours of the 24th Regt. on the field of Isandlana [sic]'. Melvill's father received the following letter from Major General Dillon, War Office, and dated 21 April 1879:

Sir,

I am directed by the Field Marshal Commanding in Chief to inform you that his Royal Highness [the Duke of Cambridge] perused with melancholy interest the report forwarded to him by Lord Chelmsford from Colonel Glyn, shewing how the Queen's Color [sic] of the 1st Battalion 24th Foot would have fallen into the hands of the enemy on the 22nd January but for the gallant behaviour of your son Lieutenant & Adjutant Melvill and Lieutenant Coghill of that Regiment. His Royal Highness in communicating this dispatch to you desires me to assure you, of his sincere sympathy with you in the loss of your son, whose gallant death in the successful endeavour to save the Colour of this regiment, has gained the admiration of the army.

It is gratifying to His Royal Highness to inform you that, if your son had survived his noble effort, it was Her Majesty's intention to confer upon him the Victoria Cross, and a notification to that effect will be made in the London Gazette. (16)

In 1907 the rules for the award of a posthumous Victoria Cross were changed; perhaps the continuous pressure on King Edward VII from Coghill's father, Sir Jocelyn Coghill, and Sara Melvill, influenced the change. On 15 January 1907 the *London Gazette* published the names of a number of families who were to receive a posthumous Victoria Cross; the list included the names of Melvill and Coghill, Melvill for attempting to save the Colour, Coghill for attempting to save Melvill and the Colour. Sadly, Sir Jocelyn Coghill died just before the awards were announced.

The Isandlwana Victoria Cross

Private 427 Samuel Wassall of the 80th Regiment of Foot (Staffordshire Volunteers) earned the only Isandlwana Victoria Cross. On 13 June 1877 Wassall joined the 80th Regiment in South Africa. The Imperial forces were short of mounted troops at the time, and a call went out for volunteers from the various regiments and detachments. Along with a number of soldiers from the 80th Regiment, Wassall volunteered and was accepted. It was not long before he was assigned to Carrington's Horse and saw action in the South African Border wars.

At the outbreak of the Zulu War, Wassall was still with the mounted infantry, and his squadron was allotted to No. 3 (Central) Column. On 11 January 1879 Chelmsford's column, containing Carrington's Horse, crossed into Zululand. On the 22nd Chelmsford divided his forces; the mounted infantry and the 1/24th remained behind with Pulleine to protect the Isandlwana camp. When the Zulus attacked the encampment, only those on horseback had any chance of escape. With the way to Rorke's Drift cut off, the only means of escape was across the rough countryside to the river border some six to seven miles distant. It will be recalled that the river was in flood, and crossing was going to be a formidable task even without the attacking Zulus. The point of the river known from that day as 'Fugitives' Drift' was where Wassall saved the life of a drowning comrade, Private Westwood, whilst under enemy fire.

After his escape from Isandlwana, Wassall was unofficially attached to the Northern Column under Colonel Wood VC. Westwood was still recovering in hospital at Helpmekaar from his near-drowning when he overheard two officers discussing an unrecorded event of 'unparalleled bravery' in the river by an unknown soldier. Although weak, Westwood managed to provide his saviour's name, but it took the army several weeks to trace Wassall. In the meantime, Wassall had also fought with Colonel Buller at Hlobane, the second major British disaster of the war. Wassall survived both. In the *London Gazette* dated 17 June 1879 the War Office gave notice:

> That the Queen has been graciously pleased to signify Her intention to confer the decoration of the Victoria Cross on the undermentioned Officers and soldier of Her Majesty's Army, whose claims have been submitted for Her Majesty's approval, for their gallant conduct during the recent operations in South Africa, as recorded against their names.

One of these was Samuel Wassall of the 80th Regiment of Foot. On 11 September 1879, Wassall, along with Robert Jones of the 24th Regiment (for his part in the defence of Rorke's Drift), were presented with their Victoria Cross medals by Sir Garnet Wolseley GCMG, KCB. Wassall was twenty-two years and nine months old and was the youngest serving soldier then to hold the award. His VC was the first awarded during the Zulu War. He was also granted a pension of £10 per annum for life. His citation for the award was published in the London Gazette on 17 June 1879:

> For his gallant conduct in having, at the imminent risk of his own life, saved that of Private Westwood, of the same Regiment. On the 22nd January 1879, when the camp at Isandhlwana was taken by the enemy, Private Wassall retreated towards the Buffalo River, in which he saw a comrade struggling, and apparently drowning. He rode to the bank, dismounted, leaving his horse on the Zulu side, rescued the man from the stream and again mounted his horse, dragging Private Westwood across the river under a heavy shower of bullets. (17)

When he left the army, Wassall moved to Barrow-in-Furness and lived with his brother William at 18 Exeter Street. He was for a time employed in the electrical department of the Barrow shipyard. He married Rebecca Round on 10 April 1882 at the parish church of St. Matthew's. They were blessed with seven children, all of whom later married. Wassall died at the age of seventy and is buried at St. James's Church, Barrow-in-Furness, in the same grave as his wife. Their graves were unmarked until 1985, when

A British soldier on guard in Zululand (*W.W. Lloyd*, On Active Service)

The position of the Zulu left horn as they attacked Isandlwana (*Author's collection*)

Isandlwana before the battle (*AZWHS*)

Isandlwana after the battle (*AZWHS*)

'Well seasoned material', from Lloyd's 1879 paintings (*Author's collection*)

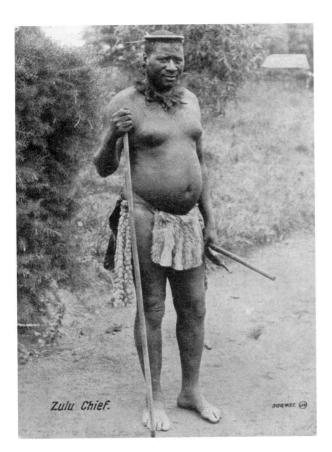

A Zulu chief in 1879
(*Author's collection*)

Zulu warriors in 1879 (*Author's collection*)

A visit to Isandlwana in May 1879 (*Ian Knight*)

The position of Cavaye and Mostyn on the spur above Isandlwana as the Zulus attacked (*Author's collection*)

The north side of Isandlwana – Capt. Shepstone's grave and his men's cairns (*Author's collection*)

Ngwebeni Valley where Zulus assembled, five miles from Isandlwana (*Author's collection*)

Durnford's donga – where Durnford held the Zulu left horn until overwhelmed (*Author's collection*)

The South Africa campaign
medal of Lt. Henry Curling
RA. A rare Isandlwana
survivor's medal (*Author's
collection*)

The 24th Regimental Memorial at Isandlwana (*Author's collection*)

Lt. Charlie Raw (right) and Lt. Vause after the war. Raw died at Pietermaritzburg aged thirty-two (*Author's collection*)

The memorial at Fugitives' Drift to Lts. Coghill and Melvill (*Author's collection*)

A message from Col. Pulleine during the Zulu attack (*Author's collection*)

'Report just come in that the Zulus are advancing in force from left front of camp.'

A second message from Pulleine during the attack (*Author's collection*)

'Zulus are advancing on your right in force. Retire on camp in order. E Coy will support your right. NNC on your left.'

Artefacts collected after the battle (*Author's collection*)

The Zulu memorial at Isandlwana (*Author's collection*)

Mangeni Falls, where Chelmsford learned fate of Isandlwana. Members of the AZWHS in the background (*Author's collection*)

The author presenting David Rattray with the campaign medal to Trooper Pollard – top of the memorial list (*Author's collection*)

Isandlwana and the memorial to the Natal Carbineers (*Author's collection*)

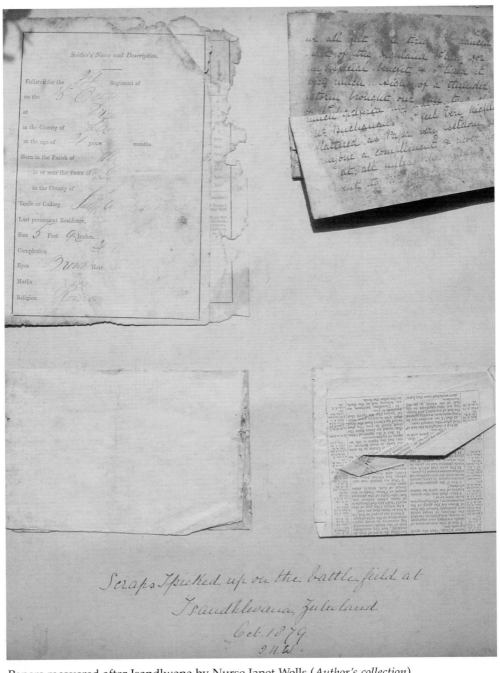

Papers recovered after Isandlwana by Nurse Janet Wells (*Author's collection*)

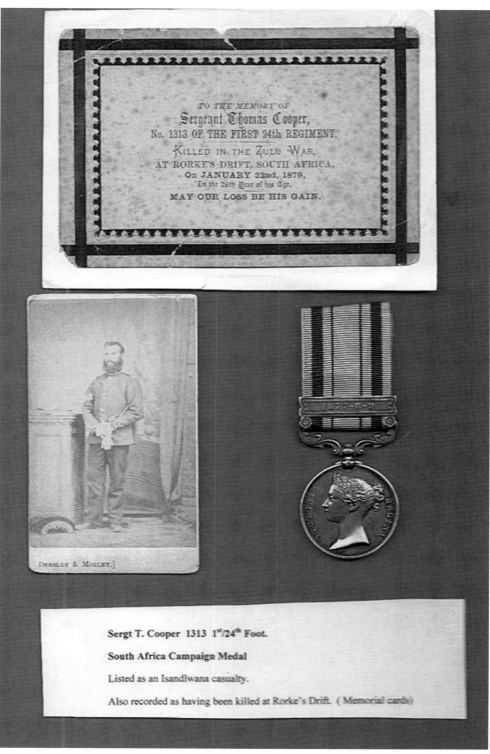

TO THE MEMORY OF
Sergeant Thomas Cooper,
No. 1313 OF THE FIRST 24th REGIMENT,
KILLED IN THE ZULU WAR,
AT RORKE'S DRIFT, SOUTH AFRICA,
On JANUARY 22nd, 1879,
In the 29th Year of his Age.
MAY OUR LOSS BE HIS GAIN.

DERSLEY & MOSLET.]

Sergt T. Cooper 1313 1st/24th Foot.

South Africa Campaign Medal

Listed as an Isandlwana casualty.

Also recorded as having been killed at Rorke's Drift. (Memorial cards)

Sgt. Cooper's medal and memorial card (*Author's collection*)

A prize cheque for seizing Zulu cattle, issued to Corporal Pato on 6 June 1879 (*Author's collection*)

The Buffalo River at Fugitives' Drift – the border between Zululand and British Natal (*Author's collection*)

a fine marble headstone was erected by his regiment. Wassall's account of his escape and citation is reproduced in full at Appendix D.

Nearly an Isandlwana VC

Chased for six miles over extremely rugged terrain, the mounted survivors (those on foot were soon overtaken and killed) reached the Buffalo River. This fast-moving river was in full spate, and many who had survived the dangers of the trail perished beneath the swirling waters.

Trooper William Barker was one who managed to cross safely and began to climb the steep slopes on the Natal bank. Here he joined Lieutenant Charlie Raw's Mounted Basutos, who were giving covering fire. The group then moved out of range of the Zulus on the far bank. The danger, however, was not past, for the discontented relatives of the Zulus, who lived in the vicinity, now attacked the survivors as they reached the Natal bank.

Looking back, Barker saw a distant figure scrambling on foot towards them. Thinking it was a colleague, Barker left his companions and rode back down the hill. The struggling figure was Lieutenant Higginson, the Adjutant of 2/3rd Natal Native Contingent, and it will be recalled that Barker insisted the officer took his exhausted horse, as it was incapable of carrying them both up the steep slope, but obtained Higginson's promise that he would wait for him at the top of the hill. It will also be recalled that Higginson reneged on his promise, in the belief that Barker had been killed, and then rode off to 'look for horses' for Melvill and Coghill. But Trooper Barker had not been killed; when Raw and his companions rode back towards the river to check for any survivors they came upon Barker still running for his life. He had been pursued for about three miles, managing to fire the occasional round to keep the natives at a distance.

Within a few days the truth of Higginson's escape became well known. And there it would have ended but for a visit paid on 17 December 1881 to the Natal Carbineers by the outgoing Military Commander, Sir Evelyn Wood. During his speech to the officers he said:

> I have only now heard of a gallant act performed by a straggler, whose late arrival is well explained by his having, during the retreat, given up his horse to an officer, who was exhausted. Into this matter, it will be my pleasure to enquire more.

Thus Trooper, now Sergeant, William Barker, was recommended by Wood for the Victoria Cross. But there had already been a reaction in Whitehall over the seemingly lavish dispensing of the Cross, and it cannot have been a surprise for Wood to receive the following reply:

Major General Sir Evelyn Wood VC
Sir
I am directed by the Field Marshal Commanding in Chief to acknowledge your letter of the 6th instant, and to acquaint you in reply, that statements re: Trooper Barker, Natal Carbineers, at the battle of Isandlwana, on 22 January 1879, having carefully been considered, His Royal Highness desires me to state that, while Trooper Barker's conduct on the occasion referred to is deserving of every commendation, there does not appear to be sufficient ground, according to the terms of the statute, for recommending him for the distinction of the Victoria Cross.

The disembowelling myth

As part of the Zulus' battle ritual, warriors invariably disembowelled and occasionally mutilated the bodies of their slain enemies. These were acts that horrified British soldiers, who initially believed that disembowelling was a process of torture. In fact, it was a post-combat ritual which reflected the extent to which death in battle was linked to the spiritual world of the Zulus.

After battle, freshly slain bodies were repeatedly stabbed, a practice known as *ukuhlomula*. Inflicting this on a fallen enemy was a ritual to mark a participating warrior's role in the kill. Warriors who had been involved in the fighting but had not actually killed an enemy were still entitled to share the glory that was attached to the victory – stabbing the corpse after it was dead and 'washing the spear' in blood acknowledged this.

The associated custom of disembowelling a fallen enemy – *qaqa* – was directly related to the Zulu view of the afterlife and its relationship with the world of the living. Part of this ritual involved slitting open the stomach of the slain enemy. Under the African sun any corpse will quickly putrefy, and the gases given off by the early stages of decay cause the stomach to swell. In Zulu belief, this was the soul of the dead warrior vainly trying to escape to the afterlife. The victor was obliged to open the stomach of his victim to allow the spirit to escape, failing which the victor would be

112

haunted by the ghost of his victim, who would inflict unmentionable horrors upon him, including causing his own stomach to swell until eventually, the victor went mad.

Mehlokazulu kaSihayo, an attendant of King Cetshwayo, was present at Isandlwana with the iNgobamakhosi regiment. In his account of the war, which was recorded in September 1879, he made various references to the subject of stripping and disembowelling the dead:

> As a rule we took off the upper garments, but left the trousers, but if we saw blood upon the garments we did not bother. All the dead bodies were cut open, because if that had not been done the Zulus would have become swollen like the dead bodies. I heard that some bodies were otherwise mutilated. (18)

At Isandlwana some bodies were disembowelled immediately. Trooper Richard Stevens of the Natal Mounted Police survived the battle, and recorded his shock at the practice:

> I stopped in the camp as long as possible, and saw one of the most horrid sights I ever wish to see. The Zulus were in the camp, ripping our men up, and also the tents and everything they came across, with their assegais. They were not content with killing, but were ripping the men up afterwards. (19)

One aspect of Zulu ritual that did result in mutilation of the dead was the removal of body parts from a fallen enemy to add to the ritual medicines used to fortify the Zulu army before battle. These medicines were known as *intelezi*, and were sprinkled on the warriors by *izinyanga*, war-doctors, before the army set off on campaign. Incorporating into *intelezi* parts from a dead enemy, especially one who had fought bravely, would be an enormous boost to Zulu morale, thus ensuring supremacy in battle. Since a number of *izinyanga* accompanied the army that triumphed at Isandlwana, they would certainly have taken the opportunity to collect the raw materials for such medicine from dead soldiers. Archibald Forbes' graphic account of the state of the bodies at the time of the first burial expedition to Isandlwana in May 1879 is highly suggestive:

> Every man had been disembowelled, some were scalped, and others subject to yet ghastlier mutilations. (20)

At Isandlwana these mutilations included the disarticulation by the

Zulus of the dead soldiers' jaws, complete with beards, for trophies. Facial hair was relatively unknown to the warriors, and the luxuriant beards worn by many soldiers fascinated them. Despite the deep-seated fears of the British that these mutilations were carried out before death, and therefore amounted to torture, there is no evidence that this was in fact the case. Interestingly, after Isandlwana, the practice of shaving became widespread throughout the army. Soldiers accepted the necessity of dying for their country, but were reluctant to become trophies after death on the battlefield.

The gulf of cultural misunderstanding on this point was so wide that after Isandlwana any Zulu who fell into British hands was doomed.

Chapter 7

After Isandlwana

I have terrible news to tell you . . .
Private Houseman, 2/24th Regiment

Chelmsford's return to Isandlwana

January 22 began frustratingly for Chelmsford's force, including four companies of the 2/24th who found themselves chasing elusive groups of Zulus. As the morning wore on, disquieting messages began to reach Chelmsford's staff officers that there might be a problem at Isandlwana. As early as 9.30 am a message was received from Pulleine that the Zulus were advancing towards the camp. A junior staff officer, Lieutenant Berkley Milne RN, was dispatched to a nearby hilltop with his telescope; he saw nothing amiss. Chelmsford then set off to scout the area between Magogo Hill and the Mangani waterfall. Accompanied only by a small escort, he did not think it prudent to inform his staff officers of his whereabouts, and when subsequent messages arrived from Isandlwana, Chelmsford could not be found until 12.30 pm. Distant firing could now be heard from the direction of Isandlwana, so Chelmsford and his staff rode to the top of a nearby hill and observed the camp through field glasses. Nothing untoward could be seen, partly because of the thick heat haze and because the battle at the camp was taking place inside a long valley. Chelmsford assumed that any Zulus there had long been rebuffed, but he nevertheless decided to ride back towards the camp, leaving Glyn to concentrate the force and organise the new campsite near Mangeni, a location considered by Chelmsford to be ideal as a bivouac site for the night

Colonel Arthur Harness RA was with the guns that accompanied Chelmsford's force, and during the morning he heard gunfire from the camp and realized that Isandlwana was probably under serious attack. He spontaneously ordered those under his command to march back to the camp. His force had only travelled a mile and a half when a message from

115

Chelmsford ordered him to about-turn to the new campsite. Meanwhile, Russell arrived on the scene and informed Chelmsford that a message had arrived to the effect that Durnford was also engaging the Zulus. An uneasy Chelmsford and his staff set off towards the camp to ascertain the situation. After a few miles they came across Commandant George Hamilton-Browne's battalion observing the camp; Chelmsford again ordered Hamilton-Browne to advance just as Commandant Rupert Lonsdale arrived to report that the camp had been lost. Lonsdale had ridden back to the camp having suffered from a fall and sunstroke; as he approached the camp in a dazed state he suddenly realised it was in Zulu hands. Only two hundred yards from the camp he turned and, riding for his life, escaped across the plain towards Chelmsford's force. Based on hearsay, much has been erroneously written about Lonsdale's injury. Harford's recently discovered letters mention the incident and he puts the record straight:

> It was now nearing the 11th January, the date fixed for the troops to move across the border. Lord Chelmsford had arrived at Rorke's Drift and Lonsdale rode over to have an interview with him but received no definite orders with regard to the movements of the Contingent. However, one morning I had occasion to go to Rorke's Drift myself, to see the Adjutant-General, Major Clery. Luckily, arriving at a very early hour, and having completed my work with him, I was on the point of mounting my pony to ride back to camp, when Major Clery said, "You will have everything ready, Harford, won't you, for the General today?" "Good Heavens, Major", I said, "This is the first I've heard about his coming!" "You don't mean to say that Lonsdale never told you about it?" he replied, "He is going to inspect you at twelve o'clock. The General gave Lonsdale his orders days ago."
>
> Well, I rode off as hard as I could go, to camp. I found Lonsdale sitting in his tent, looking over his Masonic orders and paraphernalia, and, on my breaking the news to him as quickly as I could, he said, "Good God! I forgot all about it. Shout for my pony, like a good chap." I also got a change of ponies. Kaffirs were sent out in all directions to call in the men who were drilling, many of them miles away. As soon as the ponies were ready, we jumped on, Lonsdale saying, "You take that way; I'll take this", and we went off

at a gallop. We had scarcely parted company when Lonsdale's pony shied at something and threw him off. I saw the fall. He appeared to have struck his head and then, rolling over on his back, lay quite still with one of his arms projecting in the air at right angles to his body. I got off at once and ran to his assistance, only to find that he was unconscious, and rigidly stiff. I shouted for the doctor, and as soon as he had come up with some natives and a stretcher, I galloped off again to collect the men. Eventually, after a real race for it, everybody was got in; but Hamilton-Browne and Cooper were still getting their Battalions formed up on parade when the General and staff made their appearance.

I had, of course, to ride out and tell the General what had happened. So we first went to Lonsdale's tent, and finding that he was still unconscious, orders were given for his removal to Helpmekaar hospital. It was found afterwards that he had received concussion of the brain. Through his interpreter, he expressed his pleasure at what he had seen, and gave some sound advice on matters of discipline, especially behaviour towards women and children and prisoners.

On the following day we moved to Rorke's Drift, where Major Black, of the 2nd Battalion, 24th Regiment was given temporary command until Lonsdale returned. (1)

Due to his troops being so widely spread, it was not until 6.30 pm that Chelmsford could muster his force about three miles from Isandlwana. In darkness they advanced towards the silent camp and fired several rounds of shrapnel to dislodge any remaining Zulus; at about 9 pm they reoccupied the corpse-strewn position. The Zulus had gone; there were no survivors from the 1,350 men left there that morning. Worse was to come: Chelmsford's attention was drawn to the distant glow of fire at the British camp seven miles distant at Rorke's Drift. Zulu camp fires could be seen in the nearby hills, and Chelmsford's weary force settled down in a position of all-round defence, expecting an attack at any time.

Private Houseman of the 2/24th Regiment wrote home and his letter clearly identifies the feelings of the surviving soldiers:

I have terrible news to tell you, on 22 all our 1st Bn of Regt were cut up [words missing].
We have lost 200 men and officers.

They surrounded the camp and took everything that we had, we are quite naked. We took and fought our [words missing] at night and killed thousands of their [words missing].
They cut open terrible, we kept tumbling over our poor fellows all cut open from their throat down. We are keeping our own [words missing]. We are making sacks to put on our backs.
They burnt all [words missing] destroyed – it is horrible to think of it.
Everything we had, money and all, we are quite helpless, they took all our rations and ammunition.
Write back at once and direct. T Houseman 2/24th Regt. Zululand, South Africa.
God Bless you all, Amen.
You have heard no doubt of the news in the papers. Out of one company we lost 91 men, 3 got away only. (2)

Just before dawn, Chelmsford's exhausted force moved out of Isandlwana towards Rorke's Drift, which had been left with 'B' Company 2/24th. Shortly afterwards they learned that the outpost, with its 8 officers and 131 soldiers under the command of Lieutenant John Chard RE, had survived a night of Zulu attacks. The Zulus at Rorke's Drift had probably intended to make one last attack on the outpost at dawn, but to their sheer disbelief saw Chelmsford's column advancing out of the mist. This caused them much confusion, as they believed the whole of Chelmsford's force had been destroyed. The Zulus abandoned their attack on Rorke's Drift and wearily made their way back into Zululand. Eleven Victoria Crosses and five Distinguished Conduct Medals were later awarded for the defence of the outpost.

Chelmsford paused at Rorke's Drift before setting off to Pietermaritzburg to explain to a startled world how the Zulus had defeated him. By this time, even Chelmsford must have realised the extent of his own luck. But for his splitting of the force on the 22nd, thus precipitating the Zulu attack, the whole column would most likely have been annihilated. Had the Zulus been able to attack the whole force on the following dawn, as they had originally intended, the unprotected camp with the full sleeping force of 5,000 British troops under canvas would have stood little chance against 25,000 charging Zulus.

The Isandlwana Court of Inquiry – blaming Durnford

Of course I know that a dead set was made against your brother. Lord Chelmsford and staff, especially Colonel Crealock tried in every way to shift the responsibility of the disaster from their own shoulders onto those of your brother. (3)

The dust had hardly settled on the carnage of Isandlwana when Colonel Durnford was cast as the prime scapegoat, as the above letter to his brother shows. Within days of the defeat, several damning memoranda had been written:

a. Lord Chelmsford's Order Book dated Wednesday, 22 January 1879:'Camp entered. No wagon laager appears to have been made. Poor Durnford's misfortune is incomprehensible'.

b. Major Francis Grenfell, one of Lord Chelmsford's staff officers who was still in Natal on the day of the battle wrote to his father: 'The loss of the camp was due to [the] officer commanding not Colonel Pulleine, but Colonel Durnford of the Engineers who took command after the action had begun and who disregarded the orders left by the General'.

c. On 27 January, five days after the battle, Sir Bartle Frere was advising the Colonial Secretary in London: 'In disregard of Lord Chelmsford's instructions, the troops left to guard the camp were taken away from the defensive position they were in at the camp, with the shelter which the wagons, parked [laagered] would have afforded'. And a few days later, 'It is only justice to the General to note that his orders were clearly not obeyed on that terrible day at Isandlwana Camp'. (4)

Following the British defeat at Isandlwana, Lord Chelmsford convened a Court of Inquiry that met on 27 January 1879 at Helpmekaar, just ten miles from Rorke's Drift. The Court President was Colonel F.C. Hassard, with Lieutenant Colonel Law RA and Lieutenant Colonel Harness RA as Court members. Harness was a crucial witness to events but he was prevented from giving evidence to the Inquiry by Chelmsford, who insisted on his inclusion amongst the jurors. Colonel Glyn, another vital witness, was not permitted to attend or give evidence. The nature of the

Inquiry was most unusual when compared with standard military procedure; the court's brief was merely to 'enquire into the loss of the camp'. Although a number of officers and men had been required to make statements after their escape from Isandlwana, the Court only recorded the evidence of Majors Clery and Crealock, Captains Essex, Gardner, Cochrane, Curling and Smith-Dorrien, and NNC Captain Nourse. It was subsequently argued, within the army and by the press, both in the UK and South Africa, that insufficient evidence was heard, in order to divert blame away from Chelmsford. Harness was later to defend himself by stating, 'I am sorry to find that it is thought more evidence should have been taken. Of course, I know Lord Chelmsford thought so, for he sent an order that it should be done; but he does not know, nor does the general public know, that a great deal more evidence was heard, but was either corroboratory of evidence already recorded or so unreliable that it was worthless'. He also wrote that, 'It seemed to me useless to record statements hardly bearing on the loss of the camp but giving doubtful particulars of small incidents more or less ghastly in their nature'. The final line of his report indicated his defensive attitude: 'The duty of the Court was to sift the evidence and record what was of value: if it was simply to take down a mass of statements the court might as well have been composed of three subalterns or three clerks'. (5)

As author Ian Knight wrote, 'Of course, the modern historian is left to ponder by what criteria Harness decided which statements were unreliable and worthless'. (6) A moot point indeed.

Harness saw the Court, at best, as a means of obtaining information about the defeat for Lord Chelmsford. However, it served no real purpose apart from giving Chelmsford time to prepare his explanatory speech before he returned to England to present his case to Parliament. The initial observations of the Court certainly enabled the blame for the British defeat to be laid squarely upon the NNC and Durnford. At the Inquiry Colonel Crealock gave false evidence, stating that he had ordered Durnford, on behalf of Chelmsford, to take command of the camp; this persuasive evidence totally exonerated Chelmsford. With regard to the NNC, the Court had heard confusing evidence as to their location and actions on the battlefield, yet they based their findings on the evidence of Captain Essex, who had clearly stated that he did not know their location. The Court declined to listen to several surviving NNC officers who did know.

Durnford was the perfect scapegoat – he was dead. The fact that Durnford was not from an infantry regiment of the line also went against him. He was deemed by the Inquiry to be the senior officer present and therefore responsible, despite the fact that he had explicitly followed orders given to him by Chelmsford. The finding of the Court conveniently accepted, on Crealock's false evidence, that Durnford had been in charge, and accordingly highlighted Durnford's various deficiencies to the point that the Deputy Adjutant General, Colonel Bellairs, forwarded the Court's findings to Chelmsford with the following observation:

> From the statements made to the Court, it may be gathered that the cause of the reverse suffered at Isandhlwana was that Col. Durnford, as senior officer, overruled the orders which Lt. Col. Pulleine had received to defend the camp, and directed that the troops should be moved into the open, in support of the Native Contingent which he had brought up and which was engaging the enemy. (7)

Not content with blaming Durnford, Chelmsford's staff then began focusing their attention on Colonel Glyn, Chelmsford's second-in-command, now conveniently isolated from any news at Rorke's Drift. Glyn was sent a number of official memoranda requiring him to account for his interpretation of orders relating to the camp at Isandlwana. Glyn recognised the trap and returned the memoranda unanswered but with the comment, 'Odd the general asking me to tell him what he knows more than I do'. Glyn finally accepted all responsibility for details, but declined to admit any responsibility for the movement of any portion of troops in or out of camp. The acrimony continued, with Chelmsford even suggesting that it was Glyn's duty to protest at any orders with which he did not agree. Glyn maintained his dignity and his position by stating that it was his duty to obey his commander's orders. Little was said beyond this point; Glyn remained silent and loyal to his General but Mrs Glyn robustly defended her husband in the coming months.

There was no defence for the NNC and no defence for Durnford. Chelmsford finally damned Durnford's reputation in his speech to the House of Lords on 19 August 1880, by stating that:

> In the final analysis, it was Durnford's disregard of orders that had brought about its [the camp's] destruction. (8)

It was thereafter widely believed that Durnford had failed to assume command of the camp from his subordinate Pulleine and then irresponsibly taken his men off to chase some Zulus. Most historians' accounts of Durnford's actions at Isandlwana are, at best, uncertain about his orders and the exact sequence of events; or they suppose that Durnford was seeking either to warn Chelmsford of the presence of the Zulus or prevent Chelmsford's force being cut off from their base at Isandlwana. In one of the most famous works on the Zulu war, Major the Hon. Gerald French DSO wrote [his italics]:

> As to Lord Chelmsford's orders to Colonels Pulleine and Durnford before leaving the camp on the morning of January 22nd, the evidence adduced before the Court of Inquiry conclusively proved that the former was directed to *defend the camp*, whilst the latter was to move up from Rorke's Drift and *take command of it* on his arrival. Colonel Durnford would consequently, on assuming command, take over and *'be subject to the orders given to Colonel Pulleine by Lord Chelmsford'*. (9)

Durnford was now damned beyond redemption. It is probable that we will never know exactly what happened immediately prior to the battle. It is possible that the five surviving British officers' reports were influenced by the nature of the Inquiry. After all, it would have been abundantly clear to these five officers that Chelmsford and his influential staff were doing everything in their power to deflect blame away from Chelmsford and on to others, some conveniently dead. These junior officers were in an obvious predicament, and may well have felt inclined to 'toe the line' in support of their General. They were undoubtedly fully aware that their own departure from the Isandlwana battlefield could still be the subject of uncomfortable enquiries. They would certainly have known that Colonel Glyn had been ignominiously relieved of his column duties and transferred to the command of the outpost at Rorke's Drift, thus effectively isolating him from the Inquiry and its aftermath. Despite the possibility of behind-the-scenes pressure on the surviving officers to support their General, Lieutenant Curling nevertheless gave damning evidence of the chaos and confusion at Isandlwana, both before and during the battle. On 28 April he wrote to his mother from the Victoria Club at Pietermaritzburg:

I see they have published the proceedings of the Court of Inquiry: when we were examined we had no idea this would be done and took no trouble to make a readable statement, at least only one or two did so. (10)

Who had command?

Notwithstanding the decision of the Court to exonerate Chelmsford, it seems right to raise the question – who actually had command at Isandlwana? At first sight, this difficult question appears to have been a matter of some confusion between Durnford and Pulleine. Durnford had requested clarification of the orders he had received the day before, but Chelmsford had not replied. Neither had Chelmsford specifically ordered Durnford to remain, or take charge, at the Isandlwana camp. Having requested clarification, it is probable that Durnford expected to receive fresh orders on his arrival at the camp, yet nothing awaited him. Durnford then set about following his current order to initiate action against Matyana, the chief of the area beyond Isandlwana. It is clear from Lieutenant Cochrane's evidence that Pulleine accepted Durnford's decision to leave the camp, the situation being outside the framework of the orders left to him by Chelmsford. Only Pulleine had orders to 'defend the camp'. Had Chelmsford intended that the two columns should merge, it is inconceivable that he would not have referred to such an important policy change in his orders.

It was later 'leaked' by Chelmsford's staff that Durnford and Pulleine had had words over the issue of taking Imperial troops from the camp, but Cochrane, who claimed he was present, denied that this was so. Durnford's suggestion had been persuasive rather than officious.

Cochrane wrote that Pulleine was apparently distressed when Durnford wanted to relocate two Imperial companies beyond the inlying pickets, yet it is inconceivable that Durnford would have wanted the two infantry companies with him. Slow-moving foot soldiers would obviously have been more of a hindrance than a help to his fast-moving mounted force. It seems more likely that Durnford wished both to strengthen the weak position to the north of the camp and to protect the rear of his mounted men who would be operating on the Nqutu Plateau. Pulleine's concern was apparently shared by some of the camp's officers who felt that the removal of such a large part of the camp's force did not accord with Chelmsford's orders. Cochrane recalled that Lieutenant Melvill, the adjutant of the 1/24th, approached Durnford and said, 'Colonel, I really do not think Colonel Pulleine would be doing right to send any men out of camp when his orders are to defend the camp'. Durnford replied: 'Very well, it does not much matter. We will not take them'. (11)

No one knows the objective behind Durnford's request. It must, nevertheless, have been clear to all the officers present, especially Durnford and those of the 24th, that the northern aspect was a blind spot in the camp's defences. After Durnford's departure to intercept the advancing Zulus, two companies of the 1/24th were subsequently dispatched from the camp to the spur to the north, and although the idea for the order could be said to have come from Durnford, Pulleine quite clearly thought it was necessary. In any event, one of the two companies so dispatched was soon overrun by the speed of the Zulu attack; the other just made it back to the camp before it too was annihilated.

Looked at critically, the questions of who was in charge and why Pulleine and Durnford acted as they did are difficult to answer, especially in the light of the Inquiry's deliberations. The truth may never be known, but additional evidence is now available which goes some way towards clarifying the situation. The whole question of Durnford's orders has previously hinged upon the supposition that Durnford received specific orders from Chelmsford. After Isandlwana Chelmsford reproduced, from memory, his recollection of this particular order for his official report and backdated it to 19 January; it is included below, using Chelmsford's remembered words.

Head Quarter Camp
Near Rorke's Drift, Zululand
19 January 1879

No 3 column moves tomorrow to Insalwana Hill and from there, as soon as possible to a spot about 10 miles nearer to the Indeni Forest. From that point I intend to operate against the two Matyanas if they refuse to surrender. One is in the stronghold on or near the Mhlazakazi Mountain; the other is in the Indeni Forest. Bengough ought to be ready to cross the Buffalo R. at the Gates of Natal in three days time, and ought to show himself there as soon as possible.

I have sent you an order to cross the river at Rorke's Drift tomorrow with the force you have at Vermaaks. I shall want you to operate against the Matyanas, but will send you fresh instructions on this subject. We shall be about 8 miles from Rorke's Drift tomorrow.

Chelmsford knew that the actual order had never been found, and no one challenged his account. In 1885, in an extraordinary twist of fate, the Commanding Officer of the Royal Engineers in Natal, Colonel Luard, heard rumours of a cover-up involving the surreptitious removal of Chelmsford's written orders to Durnford from his (Durnford's) body by Shepstone. Luard cautiously advertised his fears in the *Natal Witness* newspaper and on 25 June 1885 he received the following remarkable reply:

P.M.B. 25 June 85
F. Pearse & Co
14 Cole St.

E.D. Natal Witness Office

Dear Sir
    Referring to yr. Advertisement wh. Appeared a few weeks ago in the Natal Witness respecting relics of the late Colonel Durnford. I write to inform you that I have in my possession a document which was picked up by my brother A. Pearse late trooper in the Natal Carbineers. It appears to be the instructions issued by Lord Chelmsford to the late Colonel on taking the field.
    I have written to my brother to ascertain whether he is willing to part with it in the event of your wishing to have it in your possession.

        Yours truly

    (signed)   F. Pearse

The weather-stained orders were promptly delivered to Luard. They were in two parts: the first was Chelmsford's original order dated 19 January 1879, and it is on this order that Durnford must have based so much of his decision making when he arrived at Isandlwana. The original text is reproduced below (where a word is unreadable, a possible interpretation is shown in **bold**), and the order leaves little doubt what was in Chelmsford's mind when he wrote it. It differs considerably from Chelmsford's recollection, printed above.

> Lieut. **Colonel Durnford** R.E
> **Camp** Helpmakaar
> 1. You are requested to move the troops under your immediate command viz.: mounted men, rocket battery and Sikeli's men to Rourke's Drift tomorrow **the** 20th inst.; and to encamp on the left bank of the Buffalo (in Zululan**d**).
> 2. No. 3 Column moves tomorrow to the Isandhlana Hill.
> 3. Major Bengough with his battalion Native Contingent at Sand Spruit is to hold himself in readiness to cross the Buffalo at the shortest possible notice to operate against the chief Matyana &c. His wagons will cross at Rourke's Drift.
> 4. Information is requested as to the ford where the above battalion can best cross, so as to co-operate with No. 3 Column in clearing the country occupied by the chief Matyana.
>
> By Order, H. Spalding. Major DAAG
> Camp, Rourke's Drift 19.1.79

This penultimate order to Durnford precedes the final order received on the morning of the 22nd. The order clearly states that Durnford's column is to cooperate with the central column and that Bengough's battalion, part of Durnford's force, must be ready to move from the border to the Mangeni area of Chief Matyana; his waggons are to accompany Durnford which indicates an imminent rendezvous.

Chelmsford's final orders to Durnford, signed and sent by Crealock, were received by Durnford at Rorke's Drift on 22 January. Because they are so ambiguous, they are reproduced exactly:

You are to march to this camp at once with all the force you have with you of No. 2 Column.

Major Bengough's battalion is to move to Rorke's Drift as ordered yesterday. 2/24th, Artillery and mounted men with the General and Colonel Glyn move off at once to attack a Zulu force about 10 miles distant.

Armed with this instruction, which clarified his orders from the General dated 19 January, Durnford's mind was clear. He was not instructed to take command of the camp at Isandlwana; indeed, he was free to use his independent No. 2 Column as he thought fit. On his arrival at Isandlwana and seeing the Zulus approach in force, he had no alternative but to attempt to block Zulu progress towards the camp.

Durnford was clearly ordered to 'cooperate with No.3 Column by clearing the country occupied by the Chief Matyana'. In essence, Durnford did exactly as he was ordered. At 11.15 am Durnford dispatched Captain Barton, who had been attached to Durnford's column for General Duties, with the remaining two troops of Zikhali's Horse led by Lieutenants Raw and Roberts, to the hills to the north to sweep away those thousand or so Zulus who could be seen there. Barton accompanied Roberts; Captain Shepstone, Durnford's staff officer, went with Raw. At about 11.30 am the rocket battery arrived and Durnford gave them orders to be prepared to move out of camp in fifteen minutes. At 11.45 am Durnford left the camp. He took with him Lieutenant Harry Davis's Edendale troop and Lieutenant Alfred Henderson's BaSotho mounted men, the rocket battery under Major Russell supported by 'D' Company and the 1/1st NNC under Captain Nourse. Durnford's waggons bringing his ammunition and supplies had not yet arrived, but he must have been confident that the Zulus would not stand and fight. The worst he would have expected was a brief skirmish. This makes sense, as Durnford's highly mobile No.2 Column was ideally placed to drive the Zulus away from the camp.

Trooper A. Pearse discovered these papers on or near Durnford's body while seeking the body of a brother, also a trooper, who had been seen to escape from Isandlwana but then inexplicably to return to collect his bridle, and was never seen alive again. (12) The papers were in poor condition, having been subjected to several months of exposure; at the time of their discovery some parts were so fragile that they could not easily be unfolded or read. The details on the envelope and the location where it was found were clearly sufficient for Pearse to realize that the envelope contained Chelmsford's instructions to Durnford, and in due course Pearse forwarded the papers to the editor of the *Natal Witness*.

At some point in time, as yet unknown, the envelope and its contents were then forwarded to the Royal Engineers Museum at Chatham. It is possible that Frances Ellen Colenso, the daughter of Bishop Colenso (Anglican Bishop of Natal), sent them to Chatham, as the envelope still bears the initials F.E.C.

The second order found on Durnford's body, copies of which had, presumably, been sent to all the Column commanders, relates to the specific tactics to be used when engaging Zulus and is dated 23 December 1878. Whilst it is not relevant to the present argument, the fact that Durnford kept it on his person indicates his intention to obey his orders fully. He would still have been smarting from Chelmsford's earlier rebuke and his threatening reminder to obey future orders, following his (Durnford's) unauthorised excursion across the border with Zululand. The full order is reproduced in Appendix F.

The discovery of the evidence he was seeking galvanised Luard into action, and he wrote a remarkable letter to Sir Andrew Clarke, Head of the Corps of Royal Engineers in which he indicated his view that he could vindicate Durnford. The whole letter is reproduced unabridged and uncorrected in Appendix G.

The result was that Shepstone finally agreed to attend a new Court of Inquiry. The Acting High Commissioner in South Africa was quick to see the implications for Chelmsford and wrote to Luard before the Court was convened at the end of April 1886, 'I have taken measures to limit proceedings and to prevent, I trust, the possibility of other names, distinguished or otherwise, being dragged into it'. (13)

When the Inquiry commenced, it was, curiously, limited to the investigation of whether or not papers had been removed from Durnford's body. Various important witnesses were refused leave to attend by the army or the civil authorities, and Luard's case crumbled. Shepstone was cleared and Luard was obliged to apologise to him. And there the matter rested.

In June 1998, a report made by Captain Stafford of the NNC came to light. This report was written in 1938, when Stafford was in his late seventies, and records his memory of the battle at Isandlwana, where he was one of Durnford's staff officers. Two interesting points are made by Stafford. Firstly, his account of the initial meeting between Durnford and Pulleine reveals that Durnford was concerned at Pulleine's disposition of the troops so far from the camp. Stafford wrote:

> Col. Durnford and Capt. Shepstone entered Pulleine's tent whilst I remained outside. From what I could hear, an argument was taking place between Pulleine and Durnford as to who the senior was. Col. Pulleine appeared to give way and I heard Durnford say, "You had orders to draw in the camp". Alas there was no time for this as the fighting had already commenced. I can never understand to this day why this was not done. (14)

Secondly, Stafford relates how Durnford deployed his force to stem the advance of the main Zulu force. It would appear that Durnford was anticipating the camp being attacked and acted accordingly. Stafford records how the Zulus advanced at speed and forced Durnford's men back towards the camp. This was with the exception of Lieutenant Roberts of Pinetown who had managed to get his men into a cattle kraal on the edge of a ridge. Stafford subsequently heard that Roberts and his men had been shelled by British artillery and that Roberts met his death as the result of this 'friendly fire'.

Pulleine now faced the rapidly approaching Zulu army; it was too late to react, the troops were deployed too thinly and too far from the camp. His total misunderstanding of Zulu tactics ensured their victory, as did Pulleine's deployment of his manpower so far away. The reason, as seen from the missing orders, was because he was obeying to the letter the orders he had received from Chelmsford, orders given to all five Column commanders which detailed the tactics to be used in the event of a Zulu attack. If further evidence is required, then it should be pointed out that identical tactics had coincidentally been used that very same morning on two separate occasions: only fifty miles from Isandlwana at Nyzane, where Colonel Pearson's Coastal Column came under a sustained Zulu attack, and by Colonel Wood during a skirmish at Hlobane. Pulleine had no battle experience and faithfully deployed his force according to Chelmsford's orders. Such tactics were doomed to fail in a defensive position. They were never used again against the Zulus.

Was there a conspiracy to blame Durnford? Perhaps not intentionally, but after Durnford's death circumstances appear to have conspired against him. Chelmsford initiated the Court of Inquiry, and its terms and purpose were, at best, curious. Certainly Crealock deliberately lied when he told the Court that he had issued orders to Durnford to 'take command of it' (the camp), when in fact this was not the case. The Court's findings enabled Chelmsford to escape the blame, and his account to the House of Lords relied on those findings to pin the blame on Durnford. Sadly, Chelmsford always stood by his report to Parliament and joined his staff in their attempt to blame Glyn – but this tactic backfired when Glyn defused the accusation by accepting partial blame.

At last there is sufficient evidence to prove that Durnford behaved correctly and bravely in following his General's faulty orders. His reputation should now be seen in the same light as his military record, which was exemplary. Incidentally, it is known that Durnford's daughter moved to South Africa and subsequently married a local farmer, whose name is not recorded.

On 28 March 1880 Sir Charles Dilke, MP for Chelsea, spoke   in Parliament of:

> The gallant fellows who fell in that miserable affair at Isandlwana –
> 53 officers and nearly 1,400 men – through the gross incompetence
> of a General upon whose head rests the blood of these men until he
> has been tried by Court Martial and acquitted.

Lord Chelmsford's orders to Column commanders

A modern examination of these long-lost documents confirms that both Pulleine and Durnford obeyed Chelmsford's orders fully. It is also evident that, after Isandlwana, Chelmsford's written orders that Durnford received on the day of battle were ambiguously 're-worded' by Crealock to vindicate Chelmsford and his staff and to incriminate Durnford. One must presume that Chelmsford's staff believed that the actual orders had been destroyed; indeed, there has been no trace of these latest orders until recently.

Among the papers found on Durnford's body was his personal copy, as commander of No. 2 Column, of Chelmsford's General Orders; these relate to the specific tactics to be used when engaging the Zulus and are dated 23 December 1878. These orders may well have been re-issued, because the previous '1878' orders were generally disregarded and were mockingly known as 'Bellairs Mixture', a combination of the Deputy

Adjutant General's name with that of a popular patent medicine. Presumably these same new orders were sent to all of the five Column commanders, because they referred to the tactics to be used in anticipation of a Zulu attack. It is these orders that may now answer the question that has baffled historians since Isandlwana: why did Pulleine deploy his manpower so far from the camp?

These orders, found on or near Durnford's body, were hand-written and signed by Chelmsford. They are dated Monday, 23 December 1878 and must, therefore, have replaced Chelmsford's original *Regulations for Field Forces in South Africa 1878*. They are reproduced in Appendix F in their exact form, using the original, unabridged and grammatically uncorrected text.

A review of the General Orders

A comparison of item 18 in Chelmsford's Orders with the known Isandlwana line of defence reveals a strong similarity, also seen in Pearson's tactics at Nyezane only a few hours earlier. Presumably to avoid ambiguity, Chelmsford even drew a diagram of his required deployment in the face of a Zulu attack. This is particularly relevant in the light of the similar formations adopted on 22 January at Nyezane and Isandlwana. Furthermore, many writers have discussed the lack of camp defences at Isandlwana; these orders totally omit any reference to prepared defences in camp.

Colonel Pulleine's deployment of his experienced troops in an extended line so far out from the Isandlwana camp was referred to contemptuously by many contemporary writers and has mystified most military historians. Pulleine had no battle experience and had little warning of the impending disaster – yet the deployment was clearly not his own idea. No historian has ever produced evidence that the experienced 1/24th officers ever challenged the extended deployment so far from the camp, although Captain Stafford NNC recalled in his memoirs that when Durnford arrived at Pulleine's tent, Durnford expressed considerable alarm at the distant disposition of British troops. As the senior officer at Isandlwana, it was logical that Pulleine would follow Chelmsford's orders and so he deployed his men according to the plan drawn in these orders. No wonder that the officers of the 24th thus deployed did not openly demur.

A comparison of these orders with the Isandlwana dispositions prior to the Zulu attack reveals a pattern in exact accordance with Chelmsford's orders. Perhaps this is another reason why these orders were never referred to by Chelmsford's staff officers at the subsequent Inquiry, or thereafter. Their publication would have completely vindicated Pulleine. There is a distinct possibility that the five junior officers who survived Isandlwana were unaware of the existence of these orders, which may also account for their previous non-publication. In effect, the distribution of these orders was very restricted and they would have been easy to conceal subsequently.

At exactly the same time as the attack on Isandlwana, Colonel Pearson and his No. 1 Column were advancing into Zululand from near the mouth of the Tugela River. Early on the morning of 22 January 1879, Pearson's Column was attacked near the Nyezane River. Pearson would presumably have made his troop dispositions according to Chelmsford's instructions, i.e. the same instructions issued to Durnford and Glyn (and inherited by Pulleine). There should therefore be some correlation between Pearson's and Pulleine's troop dispositions, at Nyezane and Isandlwana respectively, and Chelmsford's diagram.

Pearson's initial troop deployment at Nyezane

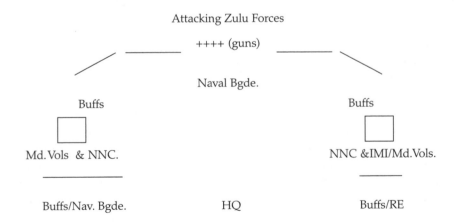

Attacking Zulu Forces

++++ (guns)

Naval Bgde.

| Buffs | | Buffs |

Md. Vols & NNC.   NNC &IMI/Md.Vols.

Buffs/Nav. Bgde.   HQ   Buffs/RE

AFTER ISANDLWANA

Pulleine's initial troop deployment at Isandlwana

Attacking Zulu Forces

++++ (guns)

| Mostyn | Porteous | Wardell | Pope |

NNC & Zikhali Horse   Lonsdale's NNC

Younghusband   HQ

Both Pulleine's and Pearson's troop deployments in the face of attacking Zulus (on the very same day but fifty miles apart), as represented above, are too like Chelmsford's orders for the similarity to be coincidental. Bearing in mind the terrain over which Pearson's men were deployed and the fact that the diagram is a simplified version of their disposition, the similarities between his and Chelmsford's deployment order eighteen are plainly visible. Likewise, only two days later on 24 January, Colonel Wood's northern column, forty miles to the north of Isandlwana, dispersed a strong force of Zulus near Hlobane Mountain using identical tactics.

Pulleine had no battle experience and he appears to have faithfully deployed his force according to these orders – orders that the other Column commanders had also received and on which Pearson had similarly acted on the very same day as Isandlwana. The whereabouts of Pulleine's original orders are unknown for certain, although a second set of orders, also taken from the battlefield as a souvenir by a member of the burial party, was discovered in early 2000. These orders are identical to those taken from Durnford's body but have no addressee. Likewise, the whereabouts of the identical orders to the other three Column commanders (Pearson, Woods and Rowlands) are not known. Indeed, there is no known mention, official or otherwise, of these original orders.

Clearly, any acknowledgement of them would have been highly embarrassing to Chelmsford and his staff, and there is no known evidence that Chelmsford ever mentioned the existence of these orders in any private or official correspondence. Pulleine's reputation, like that of Durnford, should now be seen in the same light as both their military records, exemplary and beyond reproach.

Perhaps the final word on Chelmsford comes from the War Office. In a memorandum to the Commander in Chief of the Army, the Duke of Cambridge, his Adjutant General Sir Charles Ellice wrote a lengthy but considered overview of the defeat at Isandlwana, after examining all available evidence and reports. His overview ended by making a number of crucial observations, abbreviated below. He wrote:

> To this belief in the crushing effect of our weapons and the small probability of the enemy venturing upon a flank attack in the open, is evidently due to the immediate causes of the defeat at Isandlwana, viz.
> a. Rorke's Drift had not been put in a proper state of defence before operations commenced.
> b. The non-preparation of a defence at Isandlwana either by wagons or building a small redoubt.
> c. Departing the camp in the early hours of the 22nd with a significant force leaving the camp defences, notwithstanding that Durnford had been called up.
> d. Not searching the north-east knowing there was a large force of Zulus approaching from the east.
> e. Not considering the possibility/likelihood of a serious attack on the camp, and
> f. Dividing the camp defenders and not creating a laager, or massing the troops in a square with sufficient ammunition. (15)

Several points spring to mind: in item c., Durnford was ordered to reinforce the camp, not to take command. This therefore discredits Crealock's statement that Durnford was ordered to 'take command'. The final item seems directed at Pulleine, but in his defence Pulleine tried to follow Chelmsford's written orders which were, as it turned out, defective – especially as Chelmsford had ignored all intelligence warnings of the Zulu army's approach.

Recently discovered letters from Lieutenant Curling

In 1998 three bundles of faded letters were about to be discarded when it was realised they related to the Zulu War. They were the letters of Lieutenant Henry Curling RA, the only British officer to have fought on the front line at Isandlwana and survived. These letters provide a fascinating insight into what really happened, as well as casting some doubt on the previously accepted theories of the RA guns' final position after the British defeat. His letters reveal the chilling terror and chaos of Isandlwana as well as the appalling conditions endured by the few survivors:

23rd January 1879

My dear Mama,

Just a line to say I am alive after a most wonderful escape.
In the absence of the General, our camp in Zululand was attacked by overwhelming numbers of Zulus. The camp was taken and out of a force of 700 white men only about 30 escaped. All my men except one were killed and the guns taken. Major Smith who was with me was killed. The whole column has retreated into Natal again and we are expecting hourly to be attacked.

Of course everything has been lost, not a tent or blanket left.

Your aff son

H T Curling

This letter was written the day after the battle, and was entrusted to the officer carrying the official dispatch to Pietermaritzburg, but it probably did not arrive at Curling's home in Ramsgate until early March. The dispatch was telegraphed to Cape Town and carried by special steamer to St Vincent, whence it was telegraphed to London; it arrived in the early hours of 11 February 1879. A Reuters dispatch arrived slightly earlier, their man in St Vincent having persuaded the telegraphist to give his message priority, and reached Mr. Dickinson, the night editor, at 1 am. He rushed it to the newspapers via a fleet of hansom cabs and *The Times* printed the report in their second edition on the 11th, so Ramsgate probably got the news on the 12th, three weeks after the battle. The report included a list of the officers killed, including Major Stuart Smith, who was known to be a comrade of Curling, so his parents would have been anxious for many days on his behalf.

Curling's next letter home was dated 2 February 1879 and was printed in the *Standard* on 27 March. This letter is reproduced in Appendix H and confirms his evidence to the Court of Inquiry.

Curling's evidence to the Court of Inquiry

From Lt. Curling to Officer Commanding no 8 [sic – N5?]

Sir,

I have the honour to forward the following report of the circumstances attending the loss of 2 guns of N. Brigade, 5th Battery, Royal Artillery, at the action of Isandala [sic] on January 22nd.

'About 7.30 a.m. on that date, a large body of Zulus being seen on the hills to the left front of the camp, we were ordered to turn out at once, and were formed up in front of the 2nd Battalion 24th Regiment camp, where we remained until 11 o'clock when we returned to camp with orders to remain harnessed and ready to turn out at a minutes notice. The Zulus did not come up within range and we did not come into action. The infantry also remained in column of coys [companies]. Col. Durnford arrived about 10 a.m. with Basutos and the rocket battery; he left about 11 o'clock with these troops, in the direction of the hills where we had seen the enemy. About 12 o'clock, we turned out, as heavy firing was heard in the direction of Col. Durnford's force. Major Smith arrived as we were turning out, and took command of the guns. We trotted up to a position about 400 yards beyond the left front of the Natal Contingent camp, and came into action at once on a large body of the enemy about 3/4000 yds. off. The 1st. Battn. 24th Regt. soon came up and extended in skirmishing order on the flanks and in line with us.

In about a quarter of an hour, Major Smith took away one of the guns to the right, as the enemy were appearing in large numbers in the direction of the drift, in the stream in front of the camp.

The enemy advanced slowly, without halting; when they were 400 yards off, the 1st/24th advanced about 30 yards. We remained in the same position. Major Smith returned at the time with his gun, and came into action beside me. The enemy advancing still, we began firing case, but almost immediately the infantry were ordered to retire. Before we could get away, the enemy were by the guns, and I saw one gunner stabbed as he was mounting on to an axle-tree box. The limber gunners did not mount but ran after the guns. We went straight through the camp but found the enemy in possession. The gunners were all stabbed going through the camp, with the exception of one or two. One of the two Sergeants was also killed at this time. When we got on to the road to Rorke's Drift, it was completely blocked by Zulus. I was with Major Smith at this time, he told me he had been wounded in the arm. We crossed the road with the crowd, principally consisting of natives, men left in camp and civilians and went down a steep ravine leading towards the river.

The Zulus were in the middle of the crowd, stabbing the men as they ran. When we had gone about 400 yds. we came to a deep cut in which the guns stuck. There was, as far as I could see, only one gunner with them at this time, but they were covered with men of different corps clinging to them. The Zulus were in them at once and the drivers pulled off their horses. I then left the guns. Shortly after this I saw Lt. Coghill, who told me Col. Pulleine had been killed.

Near the river I saw Lt. Melvill, 1/24th, with a colour, the staff being broken.

I also saw Lt. Smith-Dorrien assisting a wounded man. During the action, cease firing was sounded twice.'

I am, etc.,

H.T. Curling, Lt. RA

The crux of the difference between Curling's version and that accepted by modern historians is that the latter believe that the horses and limbers plunged into a transverse *donga* beside Black's Koppie, whereas Curling consistently maintained that the guns ran along the rocky ground for some 400 yards and then stuck. Lieutenant Milne RN, Chelmsford's naval liaison officer, recorded in his *Report on Proceedings, 21st-24th January, 1879,* 'There is a report that one gun was seen to tumble into a nullah but whether it was spiked or not is not known'. Lieutenant Cochrane's report, published in the *London Gazette* on 21 March, can be interpreted either way:

> The guns moved from left to right across the camp and endeavoured to take the road to Rorke's Drift: but finding this in the hands of the enemy, turned off to the left, came to grief in a 'Donga', and had to be abandoned.

The Court of Inquiry's evidence is suspect because Lieutenant Colonel Harness, one of the Court's three members, insisted that it should not express an opinion. He also stated that a lot more evidence was heard, but was ignored in the record as being repetitive or worthless (Harness had arrived at Helpmekaar on 24 January and doubtless interviewed Curling at length before his evidence was recorded on the 26th. The Court opened on the 27th). All concerned from Chelmsford downwards had a vested interest in putting the best possible interpretation on the sorry story. Curling's evidence may have been considered too damaging to record in full, knowing it would subsequently be open to thorough examination.

Lieutenant Smith-Dorrien later wrote:

> I came on the two guns which must have been sent out of camp before the Zulus charged home. They appeared to me to be upset in a donga and to be surrounded by Zulus. I caught up Curling and spoke to him, pointing out that the Zulus were all around, and urging him to push on, which he did. (16)

The strongest support for Curling's version of events is to be found in Captain Essex's evidence to the Court of Inquiry, written at Rorke's Drift on 24 January and handed in on or after the 27th:

> The retreat became in a few minutes general, and in a direction towards the road to Rorke's Drift. Before, however, we gained the neck near the Isandula Hill, the enemy had arrived on that portion of the field also, and the large circle he had now formed closed in on us. The only space which appeared opened was down a deep gully running to the South of the road, into which we plunged in great confusion. The enemy followed us closely and kept up with

us, at first on both flanks, then on our right flank only, firing
occasionally, but chiefly making use of the assegais. It was now
about 1.30 p.m.: about this period, 2 guns with which Major Smith
and Lt. Curling R.A. were returning with great difficulty, owing to
the nature of the ground, and I understood were just a few seconds
late. Further on, the ground passed over on our retreat would, at
any other time, be looked upon as impractical for horsemen to
descend, and many losses occurred, owing to horses falling, and
the enemy coming up with the riders: about half a mile from the
neck, the retreat had to be carried on in single file, and in this
manner, the Buffalo river was gained at a point about 5 miles below
Rorke's Drift. (17)

It is perhaps significant that Curling wrote after his return to the
battlefield in May that the gun limber was 'just where I left it'. Curling was
not in command, and wrote on 2 February 1879 that Smith's return 'of
course relieved me of all responsibility as to the movement of the guns'.
Hence, apart from any loyalty to a dead brother officer, he was almost in
the position of an impartial observer. And though Smith was wounded
before the retirement, he was still able to do his duty up to the time he was
killed near Fugitives' Drift. Lieutenant Smith-Dorrien recalled that whilst
he was tending a wounded man there, there was a shout, 'Get on, man, the
Zulus are on top of you'! Smith-Dorrien continued:

I turned round and saw Major Smith RA who was commanding the
section of guns, as white as a sheet, and bleeding profusely; and in
a second we were surrounded, and assegais accounted for poor
Smith, my wounded MI [mounted infantry] friend and my horse.
With the help of my revolver, and a wild jump down the rocks, I
found myself in the Buffalo River. (18)

Apart from the question of the exact point where the guns were
abandoned, Curling's report and letters are certainly consistent. It is not
surprising that the Inquiry disregarded his evidence, as his account
confirmed Pulleine's inability, probably as a result of his lack of fighting
experience, both to prepare for the Zulu attack and then to take
appropriate measures to counter it. On 28 April Curling wrote to his
mother from the Victoria Club, Pietermaritzburg:

I am sorry to say our column is still to be commanded by the

General [Lord Chelmsford]. I feel these disasters have quite upset his judgement or rather that of his staff and one does not feel half so comfortable under his command as with a man like Col. Wood. Our column is likely to be the one that will have all the fighting.

Indeed, Chelmsford formally sought to be returned to the UK on the grounds of ill health. On 9 February 1879 he wrote:

In June last I mentioned privately to His Royal Highness The Duke of Cambridge, Commander in Chief, that the strain of prolonged anxiety and exertion, physical and mental was even then telling on me – What I felt then, I feel still more now. (19)

The *Standard* was moved to write:

No such appeal to the Authorities of England for dismissal from a position to which Lord Chelmsford felt himself unequal had ever before been addressed to them by a General in the field commanding Her Majesty's troops. (20)

He was not replaced until after the Battle of Ulundi on the 4th July 1879.

Curling moved to Wesselstrom in the Transvaal early in October 1879 where he remained until the end of November. He was promoted Captain and posted to a battery in 'Caubul [Kabul] – in time to earn another medal'. He had hoped that he would be able to secure home leave before sailing to India, but it was not to be, and in a letter dated 25 January 1880 from Pinetown he wrote that he expected to sail for India and the Afghan war on 4 February.

After the Afghan war, Curling served in India and at Aldershot, and in 1896 was Lieutenant Colonel OC RA in Egypt. He retired to Kent, where he became a respected Justice of the Peace; he never spoke of Isandlwana.

Re-formation of the 1st Battalion 24th Regiment and the sinking of the *Clyde*

As soon as tidings of the disaster at Isandlwana reached England, volunteers were called for to re-form the First Battalion, and a draft of 520 non-commissioned officers and men was furnished by the following units: 1st battalion 8th, 1st battalion 11th, 1st battalion 18th, 2nd battalion 18th, 1st battalion 23rd, 2nd battalion 25th, 32nd, 37th, 38th, 45th, 50th, 55th,

60th, 86th, 87th, 103rd, 108th, and 109th. When they collected at Aldershot, under the command of Lieutenant Colonel H.F. Davies of the Grenadier Guards, most of the men were raw recruits and many had never fired a Martini-Henry rifle. The draft embarked at Woolwich, in the *Clyde*, on 1 March 1879; Captains Brander and Faraquhar Glennie and Lieutenant T. J. Halliday, 24th Regiment, and a number of special service officers proceeded with the draft.

The *Clyde* had an uneventful voyage until 4 April 1879, when she ran upon a reef seventy miles east of Simon's Bay, between Dyer's Island and the mainland. The sea was perfectly smooth at the time, and the troops were all got safely on shore by 11.30 am, except for two companies which were left on board two hours longer to look after the baggage. These companies had not long landed when, with the rising of the tide, the ship slid off the reef and suddenly went down, all clothing, books and other personal property in her being lost. The chief officer of the *Clyde* had previously been dispatched to Simon's Bay, where he arrived at 10 pm the same night, and early on the morrow the *Tamar* arrived, took the draft on board, returned to Simon's Bay and on 7 April started for Durban, arriving there on the 11th. The troops were at once landed and marched up country, reaching Pietermaritzburg on 18 April, Ladysmith on 29 April, and Dundee on 4 May.

At Dundee the 1st Battalion was re-formed with 'D' and 'G' companies 1/24th, which had remained at Helpmekaar, under command of Brevet Major Russell Upcher.

The acting officers of the re-formed battalion were:

Brevet Lieutenant Colonel W. M. Dunbar, commanding.
Major J. M. G. Tongue. Acting-Major Wm. Brander.
Captains Brevet-Major Russell Upcher (A company), Rainforth, (G company), A. A. Morshead (B company), L. H. Bennett (D company), Hon. G. A. V. Bertie, Coldstream Guards (E company).
Lieutenants W. Heaton, (F company), C. R. W. Colville, Grenadier Guards (C company), R. A. P. Clements, (Acting Quartermaster), Weallens, W. W. Lloyd.
Sub-Lieutenants W. A. Birch, J. D. W. Williams, W. C. Godfrey, M. E. Carthew Yorstoun, Robt. Scott-Kerr, R. Campbell, Hon. R. C. E. Carrington. Captain C. P. H. Tynte, Glamorgan Militia, Lieutenant St. Le Malet, Dorset Militia, Lieutenant E. P. H. Tynte, Glamorgan Militia, E. R.

Rushbrook, Royal East Middlesex Militia, Second Lieutenant Lumsden, 2nd Royal Lanarkshire Militia.

On 13 May 1879, the reconstituted 1/24th, again under the command of Colonel Glyn, marched to join Major General Newdigate's division, and on 7 June was formed into a brigade with the 58th and 94th regiments, under Colonel Glyn. The brigade marched towards Ulundi, and on 27 June arrived within ten miles of the Zulu capital. Leaving two companies in laager at Entonganini, the remainder of the battalion advanced with its division, carrying ten days' rations and no tents, towards Umsenbarri; they joined General Wood's column, and formed laager and built a stone fort, Fort Nolela, on the banks of the Mfolozi. All the mounted men, including the mounted infantry under Lieutenant and Local Captain E. S. Browne, 24th Regiment, crossed the river and reconnoitred as far as Ulundi. In the battle which followed there, Glyn's brigade was present, with the exception of the 1/24th, which Chelmsford considered to lack any battle experience and left in the entrenched camp on the Umvolozi, under Colonel Bellairs. On 4 July, the Zulu power now being regarded as broken, the brigade retraced its steps to Entonganini, where it lay during the great storm of wind and cold of 6 July 1879. It subsequently returned to Landman's Drift.

On 26 July the battalion received orders to march back to Durban and embark for England. Moving by Dundee, Greytown, and Pietermaritzburg to Pine Town, it encamped, and there, at a brigade parade on 22 August 1879, the Victoria Cross was presented to Lieutenant E. S. Browne, 'H' (late 'B') company, having rejoined from St. John's River. The battalion, under command of Colonel Glyn, numbering 24 officers, 46 sergeants, 36 corporals, 11 drummers and 767 privates, then embarked in the transport *Egypt* on 27 August, landed at Portsmouth on 2 October, and marched into quarters in the New Barracks, Gosport.

Many of the surviving 'D' Company (Upcher) and 'B' Company (Rainforth) 1/24th soldiers found it difficult to mix with the new recruits and, once back in England, most of the recruits chose to return to their original regiments rather than remain as 24th soldiers.

Mental health of British soldiers in Zululand
Following Isandlwana, a number of soldiers fell victim to stress and anxiety – today known as post-battle fatigue syndrome and post-

traumatic stress. Such soldiers were gathered into groups and, often in handcuffs, repatriated to Britain for distribution to mental homes or to the care of their families. One group of about thirty such souls was collected at Durban to await embarkation on a UK-bound troopship. The men were transferred by lighter to the ship, but before the accompanying orderlies could board, a storm blew up and the ship was forced to sail without them. Some panic ensued in port, and the orderlies were sent overland to meet the ship at Capetown.

On board, the returning soldiers took pity on the 'inmates', and following much exchanging of uniforms, the inmates mingled among the hundreds of healthy soldiers. The captain, aware of events, formed a board of NCOs to trace the inmates. They failed. When the ship docked at Durban, it was impossible to differentiate between the two groups and no further action was taken. The ship sailed on to England without the orderlies.

Chapter 8

The Re-invasion and Destruction of Zululand

Further disasters – but a glimmer of hope
The British public had certainly had more than its fair share of disasters to absorb. The original invasion of Zululand was considered of such little significance that only one of the London newspapers bothered to send a correspondent to cover it. Instead, all eyes were focused upon the campaign in Afghanistan where, in the event, the British had a comparatively easy advance.

After reports from Charles Norris-Newman of the *Standard* about a stunning British defeat at a place called Isandlwana, interest swung away from events on the North-West Frontier. Correspondents were ordered to make haste to Natal and attach themselves to Lord Chelmsford's command; for the next few months, reports from Zululand dominated the news and heightened the public's awareness of the war. With the gentlemen of the press attaching themselves to the new invasion force on the border of Zululand, the news-hungry British public looked forward to reading about a resounding victory over Cetshwayo's impis. Instead, they were treated to yet further catastrophes that had descended on the luckless head of Lord Chelmsford.

On 7 March a convoy of eighteen waggons loaded with ammunition and supplies for the second invasion reached Myer's Drift on the Intombe River in northern Zululand. The officer in command was Captain David Moriarty, and after two days of driving rain he had only managed to get two waggons across the river. He tried to form a waggon laager encompassing both sides of the river, but in the early hours of 12 March several thousand Zulus attacked the camp. Within minutes, Moriarty and most of his men, seventy in all, were killed; only the dozen or so soldiers on the far bank had time to form themselves into a small tight defensive group. Their officer, Lieutenant Henry Harward, mounted the only available horse and abandoned his surviving men, ostensibly to obtain help. The survivors, under the command of Sergeant Anthony Booth, slowly fought their way towards the main British position some four miles away. Mounted troopers from the nearby garrison rode to their rescue, but Harward was court-martialled for deserting his men. Sergeant Booth was awarded the Victoria Cross for his part in saving the survivors.

On 28 March further Zulu success occurred at Hlobane mountain in northern Zululand. The same *amabutho* that had triumphed at Isandlwana just two months before utterly defeated a large British mounted force under Colonel Redvers Buller. However, flushed with victory, the Zulu army moved on to attack Colonel Wood's entrenched position at neighbouring Kambula Hill the following day, only to suffer a serious defeat. Moreover, just a few days later, and at the other end of the country, the Zulu forces investing Pearson's column at Eshowe were scattered at Gingindlovu. At both ends of the country, therefore, the Zulus had been broken, and their total casualties over these three battles numbered nearly 3,000 dead and many more wounded. In the blink of an eye all the strategic advantages that King Cetshwayo had earned at Isandlwana had been lost, and the war had turned decisively against him.

Kambula and Gingindlovu shook the king's faith in his army's ability to bring the war to a successful conclusion by purely military means. Holding back the British, he said, was like 'warding off a falling tree'. While his warriors dispersed to undergo the necessary post-combat purification rituals and to heal their wounds, the king tried to reopen diplomatic contacts with the British in a final attempt to discover what terms they would accept for peace.

Burying the Isandlwana dead, and the second invasion

On 14 March 1879, seven weeks after the battle, the first formal visit was undertaken to the Isandlwana battlefield. The party was led by Major Black of the 24th, Commandant Cooper and Major Dartnell, accompanied by several 24th officers together with the Natal Native Contingent, and a party of the Natal Mounted Police. On crossing into Zululand they were immediately observed by Zulus who shadowed them to Isandlwana. The Zulus then opened fire, causing the party to retire to Rorke's Drift. Nothing was achieved other than to view the dreadful scene of the wrecked camp and the decomposing bodies scattered around.

ISANDLWANA

On 15 May Black returned to Isandlwana, this time as a freshly promoted Lieutenant Colonel. His party again stayed but twenty minutes to count and assess the condition of the waggons, before following the Fugitives'Trail to the Buffalo River. It was on this survey of the trail that the body of Major Stuart Smith was found near the river and buried under a pile of stones. In 2007 members of the Anglo Zulu War Historical Society visited the area, armed with contemporary sketches, in an attempt to find Smith's grave. As the area is remote, heavily overgrown and very rocky, in spite of their very best efforts no trace of Smith's grave could be found.

By April it was obvious to Lord Chelmsford that the war was turning in his favour, but he and Sir Bartle Frere needed a decisive victory in the field to erase the stain of Isandlwana. Throughout March and April a steady stream of reinforcements had arrived in Durban and Chelmsford now had far more troops at his disposal than he had hoped for at the beginning of the campaign. With the Zulu capacity to mount an offensive broken, he was now in the best position to lead a fresh invasion of Zululand. King Cetshwayo's principle homestead at Ulundi, in the heart of Zululand, remained Chelmsford's target.

Chelmsford had learned much from the disastrous first invasion of January. Whereas his original columns had been weak and failed to take proper precautions on the march, he intended the new columns to be veritable juggernauts. They would be much stronger, and would not only protect their halts with improvised laagers each night but would also establish a chain of fortified posts in their wake to guard their lines of communication.

For this second invasion of Zululand, Chelmsford planned to make two main thrusts. The first would follow the coastline northwards into Zululand, using troops from Pearson's old column. This force was designated the First Division and was under the command of Major General Henry Crealock, one of several Major Generals who had been sent to South Africa as reinforcements. Crealock was an experienced officer whose younger brother, John North Crealock, was Chelmsford's Assistant Military Secretary. Chelmsford planned that his second main thrust would come from the north-west, following roughly the line of the former Centre Column. However, as Chelmsford wished to spare his men the sight of the battlefield of Isandlwana, where the dead still lay unburied, he planned a new line of communication through the village of Dundee, crossing the Mzinyathi and Ncome Rivers upstream of Rorke's Drift. This column would thus bypass Isandlwana to rejoin the old planned line of advance near Babanango Mountain. It would be called the Second Division and was composed of troops fresh out from England. Although Chelmsford planned to accompany this column, it was to be commanded by another new arrival, Major General Edward Newdigate, who, like Glyn before him, would find himself with little real opportunity to exercise his authority. A new cavalry division, consisting of the 1st (King's) Dragoon Guards and 17th Lancers commanded by Major General Frederick Marshall, was to be attached to the Second Division. Evelyn Wood's column was re-designated the Flying Column. Its orders were to effect a junction with the Second Division and advance in tandem with it to Ulundi.

Meanwhile, Chelmsford was greatly concerned by the lack of transport waggons, while the accumulation of reinforcements created further logistical demands. The Natal authorities were becoming more and more reluctant to cooperate with Chelmsford's requests; they were increasingly worried that the ordinary commercial economy of the colony would grind to a halt as transport drivers abandoned their regular work for the easy pickings offered by the army. Many of the waggons accumulated by the old Centre Column were still lying abandoned on the field of Isandlwana, so Chelmsford decided to recover any serviceable transport from the battlefield. On 21 May he dispatched General Marshall to bury the dead and recover any undamaged waggons. A force of 2,490 men was dispatched, including the 17th Lancers, the King's Dragoon Guards and four companies of the 24th. They were accompanied by a sizeable force of natives with 150 army horses to bring the waggons back. The complete force assembled at Rorke's Drift and set off at daybreak. A detachment of Lancers made a detour to Sihayo's kraal to clear the area and, unopposed, met up with the main force at Isandlwana. Major Bengough's natives were deployed in skirmishing formation to search the slopes of the Nqutu Plateau, while the main force, led by the marching 24th, approached the devastated camp site. Once General Marshall was satisfied the area was free of Zulus, the solemn but ghastly task of burying the dead commenced. The whole area was strewn with human bones, some covered with parchment-like skin; the scene was made grimmer still by the ravages of vultures and predatory animals, including the formidable pack of soldiers' dogs, which had reverted to the wild (see Appendix I). Most of the bodies were unrecognisable; others had been desiccated by the hot African sun, which left their features still shockingly recognizable. Captain Shepstone pointed out the face of Colonel Durnford, who was buried where he fell.

The party recovered forty-five waggons along with a large supply of stores that had been ignored by the victorious Zulus. Apart from the bodies of men of the 24th Regiment, the dead were now buried. Colonel Glyn of the 24th had requested that the bodies of his regiment should be buried by his own men at some later time. It was not until 20 June that a party of the 2/24th under Lieutenant Colonel Black returned to undertake the task; it took the burial party until 26 June to complete their work, digging shallow graves and marking their positions across the battlefield with piles of large stones. On the 25th a burial party from the Natal Carbineers was permitted to search for their lost comrades. They found the bodies of Lieutenant Scott and Troopers Davis, Borain, Lumley, Hawkins, Dickinson, Tarboton and Blaikie on the Nek. Nearby were Moodie, Swift and Jackson. Trooper Macleroy was found a mile along the Fugitives' Trail, where he was buried. The following day Quartermaster London and Troopers Bullock, Ross and Deane were found in the main camp area. The bodies of only two members of the Carbineers remained missing. Sadly, the heavy rains which are a feature of the area soon eroded the grave sites and re-exposed the bodies to the elements.

During the second invasion of Zululand, a young British nurse, Janet Wells, had been sent from England as part of a group of six nurses to assist army doctors. Due to her experience in the Russo-Turkish war of 1878 she was sent to Utrecht in northern Zululand, where she worked under the supervision of Dr Fitzmaurice. On the cessation of hostilities, she was directed to return to Durban by pony trap, via Rorke's Drift, where the remaining garrison were known to be suffering from various gastric complaints. On arriving at Rorke's Drift she ordered all water used by the soldiers to be boiled; the men recovered within days. With some spare time on her hands, she walked and rode around the mission station, visited the graves of Coghill and Melvill and undertook a full tour of Isandlwana. At Isandlwana she collected various souvenirs still littering the battlefield, including a soldier's identification papers, part of a Bible and abandoned official documents (see Appendix J). At the two drifts, she collected herbs and wild flowers which she carefully pressed into her scrapbooks. (3)

Complaints continued to be received from visitors to the battlefield that bones could still be seen, usually following heavy rain; so on 19 September, on instructions from the new British commander, General G.P. Colley, Brevet Major C. Bromhead (brother of Bromhead VC) set up camp at Isandlwana to collect and burn the debris and rebury bodies and bones which had become exposed. Where Bromhead's party found the greatest concentration of bodies, three large stone cairns were built. Isolated human bones were collected on to canvas sheets dragged around the battlefield by parties of soldiers; when sufficient bones had been gathered, they were buried and the site marked with a cairn. The burial party also used waggons to recover military equipment left strewn across the battlefield; this was taken back to a site near Fort Melvill and buried. Despite these efforts, reports of exposed bodies continued to reach army headquarters. On 20 February 1880 General Sir Garnet Wolseley instructed Lieutenant O'Connell of the 60th Rifles to return to the battlefield, where his party worked from 13 to 26 March collecting up any bones that they found and burying them in communal pits. Cairns were built to identify these locations.

After the Zulu War, a steady stream of visitors began to make their way to the battlefields; that stream continues to this day. Most of the early visitors continued to be disturbed by discovering Isandlwana battlefield was still littered with debris from the battle – smashed boxes, parts of waggons, rotting clothing and, most distressingly, scattered bleached human bones. Over the next two years further protests about the condition of the battlefield, mainly from civilian visitors, continued to reach the Governor General of Natal. This resulted in the employment of Alfred Boast, a civil servant, to organise the proper clearing of the site. The task took one month and was completed on 9 March 1883. Boast even removed the skeletons of the artillery horses killed in the ravine during the flight along the Fugitives' Trail, although some eroded cairns have since been found to contain the bodies of both men and horses. The bodies of Captain Anstey and Durnford were recovered and re-buried by their families, Anstey at Woking and Durnford at Pietermaritzburg. Boast submitted a report from Greytown on 13 March in which he described how 298 graves were dug, containing between two and four skeletons each. Cairns were built on the graves, and where possible, the identity of the fallen was marked. (4)

The largest cairn on the site of the Nek, no doubt where many of the 24th Regiment died, was chosen as the site of the 24th's regimental memorial, the concrete work being built over the cairn. Today, the concrete around its base is showing signs of erosion and the original cairn stones are clearly visible.

The second invasion

From the first, Crealock's coastal column suffered from a serious lack of transport; they were dubbed 'Crealock's Crawlers' by the rest of the army. The health of Crealock's troops also deteriorated rapidly which seriously slowed his progress. Outbreaks of enteric fever, typhoid and dysentery soon hospitalised a worryingly high proportion of his men. Nevertheless, Crealock achieved some of his objectives when he destroyed two large Zulu homesteads containing over 900 huts. The Zulus made no attempt to distract the British from burning these two important complexes, which suggests their capacity to resist was weakening. The King now realised the grim truth that, while many Zulus remained loyal to him, with so many of their young men now dead they stood little chance of resisting the huge British column which was steadily occupying their country.

Chelmsford's advance commenced on 31 May and was very different in character to that of Crealock's coastal division. Almost immediately further tragedy struck. It was not another great defeat at the hands of the Zulus but the death of the young exiled heir to the throne of France, Prince Louis Napoleon. The Zulus had deployed a large number of scouting parties to observe British progress; the main British advance was therefore accomplished in the face of almost constant skirmishing. On 1 June a small patrol including Lieutenant Jaheel Brenton Carey of the 98th Regiment and the exiled Prince Imperial of France set out from the Second Division to select a suitable camping ground for Chelmsford's force. Despite the fact that the area had already been swept for Zulus and the Flying Column was only a few miles away, the patrol was ambushed at a deserted homestead and the Prince was killed. Although the Prince's death created a scandal, it was an incident of minor importance in the course of the war. At home, it created a greater stir than the defeat at Isandlwana and resulted in a story that was set to run and run. The ingredients for headlines were potent: 'Brave young descendant of the century's outstanding leader forced into exile while serving with his adopted country in a far-off place', 'A violent death and cowardice by the British officer who abandoned him', 'A grieving widowed mother', 'Queen Victoria's involvement and the end of a dynasty'. In fact, the public's mood was largely one of *schadenfreude,* all the more so because a Frenchman was involved!

By this time, Chelmsford had become increasingly ruthless in his determination to bring the war to a conclusion by any means possible. The soldiers regularly burned any Zulu homestead they came across, whether it had a military connection or not, and drove off whatever cattle they could find.

At the end of June Chelmsford established camp on the banks of the White Mfolozi River overlooking King Cetshwayo's capital. A flurry of last-minute diplomatic activity by the Zulu king took place. Chelmsford was not concerned with Cetshwayo's diplomatic overtures so much as his own urgent need to bring the war to a close. His replacement, Sir Garnet Wolseley, was already in South Africa, and both wanted the glory of the final battle. Wolseley sent Chelmsford several desperate telegrams attempting to halt the British advance; Chelmsford ignored them.

At first light on 4 July 1879 Chelmsford led the fighting men of the Second Division and Flying Column across the river to bring the second invasion of Zululand to its dreadful and inevitable conclusion. They engaged with and defeated the Zulu army at Ulundi in a brief, one-sided battle dominated by the Gatling machine-gun. By this stage, the marching troops were unrecognizable as such; their faces were weatherbeaten, their uniforms were in tatters, many of their red jackets had disintegrated and long hair and beards were common.

King Cetshwayo escaped but was finally captured by a patrol on 28 August. The British forces then marched out of Zululand and left its people to their fate. Starved of good news and needing a lift, the British nation cheered; the public welcomed home the worn-out regiments that had suffered so greatly during this mismanaged campaign. There were plenty of heroes to fête and their names became known in every household. Queen Victoria, after years of mourning widowhood during which she refused to involve herself in the nation's affairs, was pleased to pin decorations and orders on the fresh tunics of her brave soldiers. For several weeks the nation enjoyed being proud of its army, until memories faded and fresh news succeeded old. Sir Bartle Frere was recalled, his credibility ruined. He defended his position to the end; on his death-bed his last words were: 'Oh, if only they would read "The Further Correspondence", they must understand'. (1) Lord Chelmsford survived the wrath of the press, and, being a favourite of Queen Victoria, still more honours came his way, although Disraeli refused to receive him. He died of a heart attack in 1906 while playing billiards at his club.

King Cetshwayo was exiled to Capetown, from where he frequently petitioned Queen Victoria to grant him an audience. He was described in Parliament as:

> A gallant Monarch defending his country and his people against one of the most wanton and wicked invasions that ever could be made upon an independent people. (5)

He finally arrived in England in July 1882 and was presented to Queen Victoria at Osborne House on the Isle of Wight. As a result of the meeting, Cetshwayo was escorted back to Zululand and re-instated as King of the Zulus. During Cetshwayo's three-year absence, Wolseley had independently restructured Zululand into thirteen chiefdoms – a classic case of 'divide and rule'. It was never in the newly-appointed chiefs' interest to accept King Cetshwayo in his former role, and in 1883 his homestead was attacked by rival Zulus, causing him to flee. He took refuge under the protection of the British resident at Eshowe but died on 8 February 1884; it is believed his own people poisoned him.

Meanwhile, the debacle of the Zulu War convinced the Boers that the British army was not invincible. Encouraged by widespread discontent throughout the Transvaal, the Boer community made preparations to resist further British influence. Within a few months they commenced limited military action against the British. It was a conflict that quickly developed into the First Boer War. Zululand itself remained in turmoil until 1906, when the country erupted in a ferocious civil war from which it never recovered.

Identification of bodies at Isandlwana: an archaeological perspective
The mortal remains of soldiers who fell at the Battle of Isandlwana on 22 January 1879 have, since the first attempts at burial, been repeatedly re-exposed by the combined effects of heavy rain and associated erosion. In the four years after the battle, the battlefield was visited by a number of, at best, clumsy burial parties. Many of the cairns visible at Isandlwana today

are most likely the results of Boast's work, superimposed upon and modifying the efforts of the earlier burial parties, especially that of Major Bromhead. Some cairns mark the place where an officer is known to have fallen, but none of the cairns, except Shepstone's, mark the resting place of any individual soldier.

The dearth of artefacts and the casual re-interment procedures that have occurred, collectively suggest that Boast's cairns have limited archaeological value. However, they provide a powerful visual and emotional reminder to visitors of the scale of the British defeat.

Zulu accounts of the battle

Rightly, the reader may question why so few Zulu accounts exist. Firstly, the Zulu language in 1879 was oral and not written. Secondly, any Zulu account would have been recorded by Chelmsford's staff, who would not record anything that discredited Chelmsford. Furthermore, such Zulus would have been apprehensive for their safety and compliant under questioning; methods of interrogation used were such that those under questioning eventually gave the answers being sought.

Notes

Introduction
(1)   General Sir Richard Hart at the unveiling of the Regimental Memorial at Isandlwana, March 1914
(2)   Hansard, 25 March 1878
(3)   *The South Wales Borderers*, Atkinson, C.T., Cambridge University Press, 1937
(4)   *Zulu: Isandlwana & Rorke's Drift, 22-23 January 1879*, Knight, Ian, Windrow & Greene, 1992
(5)   *There Will Be an Awful Row at Home About This*, Knight, Ian, West Valley Books, 1987
(6)   *Daily News*, 12 February 1879, *Graphic*, 15 February 1879, *Annual Register for the Year 1879* and *Pall Mall Gazette*, 12 February 1879, all make the link with the Indian Mutiny.

Chapter 1
(1)   Evidence of a less severe form of syphilis among medieval monks in Britain and elsewhere indicates that a type of non-sexually transmitted syphilis was already common in Europe. The Spanish introduced the virulent form.
(2)   There were several other notable elevations from the ranks including Luke O'Connor, who won the VC at the Battle of the Alma as a sergeant and rose to become a major general. Major General Sir Hector MacDonald rose from the ranks in the Gordon Highlanders. Colonel Philip Eyre commanded the South Staffordshires that he had joined as a private. He was killed leading his Regiment at the Battle of Kirbekan in the Sudan in 1885.
(3)   Report by Captain Essex, courtesy of the AZWHS

Chapter 2
(1)   *Shaka Zulu*, Ritter, E.A., Penguin, 1955
(2)   'Political Power within the Zulu Kingdom', Cope, R.L., *Journal of Natal and Zulu History*, 1985
(3)   *South Africa*, Trollope, A., Tauchnitz, 1878, quoted in AZWHS Journal 1, 1997

Chapter 3
(1)   *Zulu Battle Piece*, Copeland, R., Collins, 1948
(2)   Letter from Cetshwayo on learning of the annexation of the Transvaal, courtesy of the AZWHS
(3)   *Landdrost* – a Boer regional official, usually elected
(4)   Blue Books C.2222
(5)   Ibid.
(6)   *From Midshipman to Field* Marshal, Wood , E., Methuen & Co,1906
(7)   *Lord Chelmsford's Zululand Campaign*, Army Records Society Vol. 10,1994

(8)   The cartridge was named after Colonel E.M. Boxer (Royal Artillery) who developed this projectile at the Royal Laboratories. Fired at a target at 500 yards, the bullet rose 8 feet from a Martini-Henry compared with 15 feet from the old Enfield muzzle-loader.

(9)   Not all mounted troops were armed with carbines. The Mounted Infantry under the command of Lieutenant Edward Browne VC carried Martini-Henry rifles.

(10)   *A Treatise on the British Martini-Henry*, Temple, B.A., Greenhill Books, 1983

(11)   Ibid.

(12)   Colonel R. Buller VC, Memorandum to the Royal Laboratory, 11/6/1880

(13)   *Précis of the Zulu War Intelligence Division*, War Office, Appendix 1.

(14)   *The Red Soldier*, Emery, F., Hodder & Stoughton, 1977

(15)   *The Story of the Zulu Campaign*, Ashe & Edgell, Sampson Low, 1880

(16)   *The South Wales Borderers 24th Foot 1689-1937*, Atkinson, C.T., Cambridge University Press, 1937. See also Appendix J for a review of the nationality of the two battalions of the 24th Regiment serving in South Africa during the Anglo-Zulu war. *Field Regulations South Africa 1878 Connected with the Zulu War of 1879*, prepared by the Intelligence Branch of the War Office and published in 1881

(17)   *Anatomy of the Zulu Army*, Knight, Ian, Greenhill, 1995. These rifles were prized as status symbols.

(18)   Ibid.

(19)   As reported in *The Zulu War*, Clammer, David, Pan Books, 1975

(20)   *Fight us in the Open*, Laband, John, Shuter and Shooter, KwaZulu Monuments Council edition, 1985

(21)   Ibid.

Chapter 4

(1)   *Natal Colonist*, 17 April 1879

(2)   Letter from Chelmsford to Sir Theophilus Shepstone, 21 July 1879, in *Lord Chelmsford's Zululand Campaign 1878-1879*, Laband, John, Alan Sutton Publishing Ltd for the Army Records Society, 1994

(3)   Letter from Chelmsford to Colonel H.E. Wood, 23 November 1878, Killie Campbell Library, Durban

(4)   It is interesting to note Harford's comment about RD being used as a fort and entrenched as early as 11 January. This supports August Hammar's account of Witt's house being prepared for defence at the same time. Also, during the intense aftermath of the Zulu War when Chelmsford came under pressure to explain certain aspects of the defences of camps, he wrote in his own defence:

> The labour of getting troops and supplies across the Buffalo river, and of making the roads passable for wheeled transport, absorbed nearly the entire strength of No. 3 Column from its arrival on the banks of the river, to its advance to Sandlwana. I know, however, that Colonel Glyn had given orders to

Lieutenant Chard, Royal Engineers, to construct an entrenched post on the Natal side, and that *it had been commenced by the detachments left behind before the column moved off* [author's italics]. So long as the force was in occupation of the position at Sandlwana it covered directly the ford on the Buffalo River.

(5)   PRO WO 33/34 56333. Letter from Chelmsford to Colonel H.E. Wood, 16 January 1879, Killie Campbell Library
(6)   From an unpublished narrative by Captain (later Lieutenant General) W. Penn Symons in the 24th Regimental Museum at Brecon. Penn Symons, a 2/24th officer, was killed at Talana in the Second Boer War in 1899. He was requested by Queen Victoria not to publish this account in Chelmsford's lifetime.
(7)   *The Harford Diaries,* Payne and Payne, Ultimatum Tree, 2010
(8)   *In Zululand with the British in 1879,* Norris-Newman, C., W.H. Allen, 1880
(9)   *There will be an Awful Row at Home About This,* Knight, Ian, West Valley Books, 1987
(10)   From an unpublished narrative by Captain (later Lieutenant General) W. Penn Symons in the 24th Regimental Museum at Brecon
(11)   Information from the King's own intelligence reports, p 63 of *A Zulu King Speaks,* Webb, C. de B. and Wright, J.B. (eds), University of Kwazulu Natal Press, 1987
(12)   PRO WO 33/34 S 6333
(13)   See Higginson, WO 33/34 S6333
(14)   Harford's own handwritten account inserted into Norris-Newman's presentation copy to Harford of *With the British in Zululand in 1879*
(15)   *A Soldier's Life,* Durnford, A.W., Sampson Low, 1882

Chapter 5

(1) *The Later Annals of Natal,* Hattersley, A.F. (ed.), Longmans, 1938
(2) Hillier's letter to his father published 28 February 1879 in the *Telegraph and Eastern Standard* courtesy of private correspondence, Lock & Quantrill. This report may well be the same as that of Captain Edward Essex 75th (Stirlingshire) Regiment, Director of Transport for No 3 Column.

> 'about eight A.M . . . a report arrived from a picquet stationed at a point about 1,500 yards distant, on a hill, to the north of the camp, that a body of enemy's troops could be seen approaching from northeast.' WO 33/34, No 69, Chelmsford to Secretary of War, Court of Enquiry.

(3)   *The Natal Carbineers 1855-1911,* Stalker, Rev. J. (ed), Davis, 1912
(4)   Ibid.
(5)   *The Curling Letters of the Zulu War,* Greaves, A. & Best., B., Pen & Sword Books, 2004
(6)   PRO ADM 16486 S6333
(7)   Archives of 24th Regimental Museum, Brecon

(8)   *A Lost Legionary in South Africa*, Hamilton-Browne, G., Naval & Military Press, 2009
(9)   Ibid.
(10)   *The Red Book*, referring to the *Natal Witness* report
(11)   AZWHS Journal 3, 1998
(12)   Pope's diary, later found on the battlefield
(13)   Lieutenant Charles Raw's personal account in *Running the Gauntlet*, Mossop, G., Nelson, 1937
(14)   *Isandhlwana: Zulu Battle Piece*, Coupland, R., Collins, 1948
(15)   *Zulu Victory*, Lock & Quantrill, Greenhill, 2002
(16)   Brickhill, Court of Enquiry
(17)   In 1990 the author was taken to the site by the Isandlwana battlefield curator, George Chadwick. The cairns were repaired and the exposed artefacts replaced.
(18)   *Curling Letters*, AZWHS
(19)   *The Red Soldier*, Emery, Frank, Hodder & Stoughton, 1970
(20)   *The Natal Carbineers 1855-1911*, Stalker, Rev. J. (ed), Davis, 1912
(21)   *Fight us in the Open* , Laband J., Shuter and Shooter, 1985. Many authors have written that the Zulus were ordered not to cross into Natal. This corrects the myth.
(22)   *The Red Soldier*, Emery, Frank, Hodder & Stoughton, 1970
(23)   *Curling Letters*, AZWHS
(24)   AZWHS Journal 3
(25)   *Running the Gauntlet*, Mossop, G., Nelson, 1937
(26)   *A Sketch of the Kaffir and Zulu War 1880*, Hallam-Parr, H., Naval & Military Press, 2004
(27)   *Reasons of Defeat at Isandlwana 1879*, Hallam-Parr, H., Knight, Ian (ed), MI, 1986
(28)   Ibid.
(29)   Ibid. – account by Muziwento, a Zulu warrior
(30)   Statement of Mehlokazulu when interviewed post-war by the British at Pietermaritzberg

Chapter 6
(1)   Lock & Quantrill – correspondence with author, October 2010
(2)   *Zulu Battle Piece*, Copeland R., Collins, 1948
(3)   *The South Wales Borderers*, Atkinson, C.T., Cambridge University Press, 1937
(4)   Ibid.
(5)   *Telegraph and Eastern Province Standard*, 28 February 1879
(6)   'Without hesitation I would say that, on the balance of probability, he (Cooper) was the soldier – or one of the two soldiers – who made a stand with Melvill and Coghill'. Personal letter to the author, October 2010, from South African author and expert on the Anglo Zulu war, Ron Lock.
(7)   *The Washing of the Spears*, Morris, D., Cardinal, 1964
(8)   *The Curling Letters of the Zulu War*, Greaves, A. and Best, B., Pen & Sword Books, 2004
(9)   Numerous references. Coghill wrote that he injured his knee chasing some

chickens during the reconnaissance of the Mangeni Falls on 20 January. Why a staff officer would chase a chicken, even for his Commander's supper, has long stretched many a military man's imagination. What is not generally known is that Coghill suffered from a previous assegai wound to his knee sustained during high jinks in the officers' mess. Lieutenant Daly, 1/24th, had been demonstrating his dubious skill at assegai throwing and speared Coghill in the knee. Perhaps this accounts for the several descriptions of Coghill's knee injury being 'old'.

(10)   There is no special significance in Coghill's jacket being blue, other than the fact that it may have saved his life on the ride along the Fugitives'Trail. The 24th's officers had a choice of regimental jackets to wear in the field, so just as many could have been wearing blue as were wearing red. Cetshwayo had ordered the Zulus to concentrate on red-jacketed personnel in the mistaken belief that only they were the Imperial troops. The red jackets were dyed from the extract of the root of the madder plant.
(11)   Major Grenville, letter to his father, 3 February 1879, AZWHS Journal 17
(12)   *Rorke's Drift,* Glover, M., Wordsworth Military Library, 1997. If Ardendorff fought at Rorke's Drift, he was the only person to see action at both Isandlwana on the 22nd and Rorke's Drift on the 22nd and 23rd. Likewise, the Rorke's Drift lists prepared by Dunbar and Bourne make no mention of him.
(13)   *The Zulu War – Then and Now,* Knight, Ian, Plaistow Press, 1993
(14)   Ibid.
(15)   AZWHS Journal 6, 1999
(16)   AZWHS Journal 2, 1997
(17)   *The Zulu War and the 80th Regiment of Foot,* Hope, R., Churnet Valley Books, 1997
(18)   Account by Mehlokazulu, *Natal Mercury,* 27 September
(19)   Richard Stevens, letter dated 27 January 1879, AZWHS Journal 17
(20)   Archibald Forbes, *Daily News,* 10 July 1879

Chapter 7
(1)   *The Harford Diaries,* Payne & Payne, Ultimatum Tree, 2010
(2)   Private letter in possession of the author
(3)   Letter to Edward Durnford from Inspector George Mansel, KCAL 89/9/32/10
(4)   Blue Books C.2242
(5)   Ibid.
(6)   *The Sun Turned Black,* Knight, Ian, Waterman, 1995
(7)   Blue Books C.2242
(8)   Ibid.
(9)   *Lord Chelmsford and the Zulu War,* French, G., Unwin Brothers, 1939
(10)   *Curling Letters,* AZWHS Journal 3, 1998
(11)   Cochrane report, AZWHS unpublished papers
(12)   Ibid.
(13)   AZWHS Journal 4, 1998
(14)   Stafford letters, AZWHS Journal 14

NOTES

(15)   For the full report see PRO WO 30/129 56316
(16)   *Memories of Forty-Eight Years Service*, Smith-Dorrien, H., Murray, 1925
(17)   Blue Books Essex report inquiry
(18)   *Memories of Forty-Eight Years Service*, Smith-Dorrien, H., Murray, 1925
(19)   *Lord Chelmsford's Zululand Campaign*, Army Records Society Vol. 10, 1994
(20)   AZWHS Journal 2, 1997

Chapter 8

(1)   *Sir Bartle Frere: a Footnote to the History of the British Empire*, Worsfold, W.B., Butterworth, 1923. The further correspondence relates to personal letters in the official Blue Books.
(2)   For a description of Cetshwayo in Parliament see Hansard Vol. CCXLIX , 14 August 1879
(3)   At the request of the Duke of Sutherland, Chairman of the Stafford House South African Aid Committee, and with the approval of the military authorities, Sister Janet and six nurses set off for Zululand, most with less than 24 hours notice. On the evening of 12 February 1879, the party, under the command of Dr Stoker, departed from Paddington Station and proceeded to Dartmouth, sailing in the *Dublin Castle* at noon the following day.

On arrival at Durban, the nurses were appointed to various military hospitals. Due to her experience, although aged just twenty, Sister Janet was appointed to take charge of the Base Field Hospital at Utrecht that supported Sir Evelyn Wood's column. Sisters Ruth and Elizabeth were assigned to the hospital at Durban, Mary and Annette went to Pietermaritzburg and Edith and Emma to Ladysmith. Sister Janet's journey involved arduous travel in mail carts, covering the 217 miles to Utrecht in five days over badly rutted roads; in one incident the cart overturned, leaving Sister Janet with a dislocated arm and associated bruising.

At Utrecht, Sister Janet quickly settled into her role and wrote home that, 'it was a delightful experience to nurse the English soldiers' after her horrendous experiences in the Russo-Turkish war. She described the hospital as 'a collection of good huts outside the laager, and a range of tents inside the walls'. She not only had the care of the base hospital but frequently had to ride out to the outlying camps to attend the wounded. On one occasion, she and her guide eluded a Zulu scouting party by hiding overnight in the bush. By 6 September the last of the wounded from Ulundi were fit enough to be transferred to Newcastle, and this ended Sister Janet's work in the field. Those moved to Newcastle included fifty wounded and sick soldiers along with four cases of typhoid.

Many of the wounded from Hlobane and some from Ulundi had passed through her care. Sister Janet also treated the few wounded Zulus who managed to reach the hospital; the most noted case was reported in the *Daily Telegraph* on 3 October 1879. The paper related that a wounded Zulu named 'Pashongo' was admitted to the care of Sister Janet having suffered serious bullet wounds to a knee. The Zulu was reported to have won the hearts of those who attended him by his cheerfulness, patience and natural manner. The *Daily Telegraph* quoted a memorandum from Sister Janet to Surgeon General Ross in which she observed that, 'the Zulu had so gained the goodwill of the hospital orderlies that they would come in twenty times a day to turn and ease him and to lift him up in their arms to give him ease. Every effort was made to save his life, but it was necessary to amputate the leg and the operation was followed by blood poisoning, of which he died, a better man than many a so-called Christian'.

On 11 September 1879 Sister Janet attended the parade for the presentation by Sir Garnet Wolseley of Victoria Crosses to Major Bromhead and Private Jones of the 24th Regiment. After the parade, Sister Janet was personally complimented by the Commander-in-Chief on the manner in which she had nursed the wounded. He then requested that she accompany the Army's Sekhukhune expedition. At Landman's Drift she briefly attended Captain Hardy before he died of his wounds. The press estimated that some 3,200 soldiers passed through her hands.

In a memorandum from Surgeon Major Fitzmaurice A.M.D., Senior Medical Officer at Utrecht, to Stafford House, Sister Janet came in for special praise. He wrote, 'Miss Wells proved herself to be a thoroughly accomplished nurse; her attention to her duties and kindness to the sick and wounded under her care has been most praiseworthy, and she carries with her on leaving this station the gratitude alike of patients and staff.'

On her arrival home, and in time for her 21st birthday, Queen Victoria insisted that she be decorated. In 1883 she received the Royal Red Cross, later known as the nurses' Victoria Cross, to complement her South Africa medal; the citation reads: 'for special devotion and competency displayed in nursing duties with Her Majesty's troops'. The Russian government had, in the meantime, awarded her the Imperial Order of the Red Cross of Russia.

For an account of her visit to Isandlwana, see Appendix J.
For a full account of Sister Janet Wells' experiences, see *Sister Janet*, Best, B., Pen & Sword Books, 2005.

(4)   Paper 1078/1883, Natal Archives. There are a number of reasons why the Isandlwana battlefield continues to hold its secrets. These include the dearth of artefacts, the degradation of skeletal remains due to the acidic soil and the insensitive re-interment procedures adopted by the early military burial parties. Even Boast's cairns have limited archaeological value as they cannot represent the position where men actually fell in battle. However, the 298 whitewashed cairns across the battlefield continue to have a strong visual and emotional effect on visitors. Over the years, a number of regimental and family memorials have been erected at Isandlwana; in March 1914 a memorial to the 24th was erected by the regiment. It was not until 2001 that a memorial to the Zulus was built at Isandlwana.

(5) Hansard Vol CCXLIX, 14 August 1879

Battlefield Participants

Notable figures involved in the
battle of Isandlwana

I British & auxiliaries

Chelmsford, General Lord

Frederic Augustus Thesiger, descended from a Saxon gentleman who emigrated to England and became secretary to an influential English statesman, was born on 31 May 1827. He succeeded to the title Lord Chelmsford on 5 October 1878. Thesiger's father, also Frederic, was a lawyer and Tory MP who became Lord High Chancellor of England and was ennobled as the first Baron Chelmsford. The first Baron married Anna Maria Tinling in 1822 and had four sons and three daughters, of whom Frederic was the eldest. His education at Eton was followed by the purchase of a commission, initially into the Rifle Brigade, and then into the Grenadier Guards. He was subsequently promoted to the rank of Captain and appointed ADC to the Commander of Forces in Ireland. In 1855 he joined his regiment in the Crimea but missed the battle of Inkerman. He ended his posting to the Crimea as Deputy Assistant Quartermaster General.

Further promotion brought him the Lieutenant Colonelcy of the 95th Regiment, and it was with his new regiment that he sailed for India in 1858. The Indian Mutiny had all but been suppressed, but the regiment was involved in mopping-up operations in Central India during 1859. As a competent staff officer, Chelmsford was appointed Deputy Adjutant General.

When General Sir Robert Napier was ordered to mount an expedition against King Theodore of Abyssinia in 1868, he chose Chelmsford to be his Deputy Adjutant General. It was a well organized and successful expedition, and the Anglo-Indian force suffered few casualties. Chelmsford emerged from the campaign with much credit, being mentioned in dispatches and made Companion of the Bath for his tireless staff work. He was also appointed ADC to the Queen and made Adjutant General of India. In 1861 he married Adria Heath, the daughter of an Indian Army General; she eventually bore him four sons. He became friendly with the Governor of Bombay, Sir Henry Bartle Frere, a man who would have considerable influence on Chelmsford's subsequent life. After sixteen years service in India, Chelmsford was recalled home. With little in the way of family wealth, the prospect of the expensive entertaining befitting an officer of his rank was a source of worry to him.

When offered the post of Deputy Adjutant General at Horse Guards, he felt obliged to decline and made known his wish to take a command again in India, where the cost of living was much lower. Instead, he was promoted to Brigadier General commanding the 1st Infantry Division at Aldershot pending a suitable overseas posting.

He accepted the first vacancy, to South Africa, and it was his first independent active service command in thirty-four years. He renewed his association with Sir Bartle Frere, now the High Commissioner for South Africa, and shared Frere's vision of a Confederation of southern African states under British control.

When Chelmsford arrived at the Cape in February 1878 the fighting against the Xhosa was entering its final stages. His subsequent experiences against a foe that relied on hit-and-run tactics rather than becoming involved in full-scale battles confirmed his low opinion of the fighting capabilities of black Africans. Chelmsford did, however, show himself to be a commander who did not shirk hard work, often riding great distances over rugged country to break remaining resistance. Although the Cape Frontier campaign left Chelmsford wary of the ability of colonial officers, he was generally held in high regard. As a tactician he had proved competent if uninspired.

With the successful conclusion of the Frontier war, Chelmsford followed Frere's political agenda in mounting the invasion of Zululand. Chelmsford had initially planned to invade with five columns, but a lack of resources forced him to reduce his force to three offensive and two defensive columns. He decided to accompany the Centre Column in person, a decision which effectively deprived its designated commander, Colonel Glyn, of a meaningful role. He also failed to address the friction which developed between his own staff and Glyn's.

Chelmsford's force invaded Zululand on 11 January 1879. On the 12th he attacked and destroyed the stronghold of Chief Sihayo kaXongo. Because of the poor state of the tracks, he delayed advancing to his next objective, Isandlwana, until the 20th. On arriving, he personally rode out to scout the Mangeni hills for signs of a Zulu presence. Although he was later criticised for not placing the camp at Isandlwana on a defensive footing, he argued that he had not intended it to be permanent and was, indeed, already planning to advance by the 22nd.

That plan was interrupted by the discovery of a Zulu decoy force near Mangeni on the evening of the 21st. Receiving the report in the early hours of the 22nd, Chelmsford split his command and moved to support his reconnaissance. Unfortunately, as a result, Chelmsford spent most of 22 January skirmishing in the hills twelve miles from Isandlwana, while the Zulus attacked and destroyed his base.

The disaster nearly crushed him. Worn down by the relentless personal attacks on him in the newspapers, he fluctuated between confidence and despair and contemplated resigning. His friends advised him to retire on health grounds but, with Wood's decisive victory at Khambula and the arrival of fresh regiments of Imperial troops, Chelmsford recovered his determination to defeat the Zulus. He personally chose to lead the column to relieve Colonel Pearson's besieged force at Eshowe. At the battle of Gingindlovu, he displayed the Victorian officer's disdain for enemy fire by remaining standing to encourage the troops, many of whom were newly arrived and raw recruits.

With Eshowe relieved, Chelmsford was able to plan a fresh invasion of Zululand which proved successful. Nevertheless, another misfortune befell this luckless commander. During a routine reconnaissance by a small patrol, which included the Prince Louis Napoleon, a group of Zulus opened fire on the party and in the scramble to safety, two troopers were killed and the Prince was caught and slain. When the news broke in the British newspapers, the shock was even greater than that of Isandlwana. Chelmsford could not be blamed for the Prince's death but, following all the previous disasters, his culpability was implied.

Sir Garnet Wolseley was sent to Zululand to supersede Chelmsford but arrived too late to prevent Chelmsford disobeying Wolseley's direct order not to attack Cetshwayo. Chelmsford inflicted a crushing defeat on the Zulus at Ulundi on 4 July, before handing over his command on a high note; he then resigned. He sailed home on the RMS *German* in the company of Wood and Buller, his most effective and reliable commanders.

Back in England, the military establishment rallied to his support and he enjoyed the continued confidence of the Commander-in-Chief, the Duke of Cambridge, and of Queen Victoria herself. Chelmsford was showered with honours. His rank of Lieutenant General was confirmed and the Queen used her influence to have him appointed Lieutenant of the Tower and later Gold Stick. He later became a full general and Colonel of the Sherwood Foresters, then of the 2nd Life Guards. Edward VII made the ageing general a GCVO.

On 9 April 1905, at the age of 78, Lord Chelmsford had a seizure and died while playing billiards at the United Services Club.

Clery, Cornelius Francis
Clery was born in Ireland in 1838 and educated in Dublin and at Sandhurst

before joining the 32nd Regiment as an ensign in 1858. He was promoted Lieutenant in 1859 and Captain in 1866. In 1868 he entered the Staff College. He passed out in 1870 and took up a post as instructor – later professor – of tactics at Sandhurst. He served on the staffs of Ireland and Aldershot before sailing to the Cape in 1878 as a special staff officer with the rank of major. He served briefly in the Griqualand West and 1878 Sekhukhune expeditions before being appointed to the Zululand invasion force, where he took up the job of principal staff officer to Colonel Glyn of the Centre Column.

On 20 January it fell to Clery to mark out the position of the camp at Isandlwana when the column arrived there. Clery was with Glyn during the skirmishing of 22 January at Mangeni, and following the Isandlwana disaster sought to shield Glyn from attempts by Chelmsford's staff to make him a scapegoat. Following Captain Campbell's death at the battle of Hlobane on 28 March, Clery was transferred to Wood's column as staff officer and Deputy Acting Adjutant. He served with Wood's column throughout the war and was present at the battle of Ulundi on 4 July. Clery returned home in August 1879. In 1882 he served in the Egyptian campaign as Assistant Adjutant and Quartermaster General, and in 1884 he served in the Sudan under General Sir Gerald Graham as a Brigade Major in the fighting against the Mahdists around the Red Sea port of Suakin.

Clery received the CB for his Sudanese service and was promoted Brigadier General. He remained in Egypt until 1887, when he returned to England as Commandant of the Staff College. He was promoted to Major General in 1894 and given command of a brigade in Aldershot. With the outbreak of the Second Anglo-Boer War in 1899 he was sent to South Africa in command of a division with the rank of Lieutenant General but, by now elderly, allowed his strategy to be dictated by Buller, with disastrous results at Colenso on 15 December 1899, from which Clery's reputation suffered. He left southern Africa in October 1900 with a KCMG but retired from the army in February 1901. He died in 1926.

Curling, Henry Thomas

Henry Thomas Curling was born at Ramsgate on 27 July 1847. He was educated at Marlborough before entering the Royal Military Academy, Woolwich at the age of seventeen. Despite being short-sighted, he was commissioned into the Royal Artillery in 1868. He was sent to South Africa in 1878 with N Battery, 5th Brigade. On 22 January 1879 Curling remained behind at Isandlwana camp with the guns while Lord Chelmsford and half of the No. 3 Column marched to Mangeni to meet the Zulu army, which

Chelmsford wrongly believed to be approaching Mangeni. Curling was on the front line when the main Zulu army attacked the camp and supervised the firing of the guns until the Zulus overran their position. He ordered the withdrawal of the guns back to the camp, but although the horse-drawn guns reached the camp it was now in possession of the Zulus. The two gun-teams ploughed through the Zulus, losing many men to the stabbing masses, and emerged on the far side of camp, only for the guns to crash and overturn among the rocks. The Zulus fell on the surviving artillerymen, but being mounted Curling managed to escape.

He wrote a dramatic report, which was ignored by the official enquiry on the grounds that it contained 'nothing of value'. In fact, his harrowing account is very detailed and describes exactly what happened. It is the sole account from a front-line survivor (see Appendix H).

After the Zulu War, Curling was promoted to Captain, sent to Afghanistan and stationed at Kabul with C/3 Battery. His new wife then died of fever, he returned to England after three years without leave, and was promoted Major at Aldershot. In 1895 he was promoted to Lieutenant Colonel and appointed CO of the RA in Egypt. He retired as a Colonel in 1902 and died a widower at Ramsgate on New Year's Day 1910. His numerous friends only learned of his Isandlwana exploit after his death.

Durnford, Anthony William

Durnford was born on 24 May 1830 at Manor Hamilton in the county of Leitrim, Ireland. He was educated in Düsseldorf and entered the Royal Military Academy, Woolwich in July 1846. A member of the Durnford family had served in the Corps of Royal Engineers since 1759, and Durnford's younger brothers, Edward and Arthur, both joined the Corps. Durnford obtained a commission in the Engineers as a 2nd lieutenant in 1848. He served in Chatham and Scotland before being posted to Ceylon in 1851. In 1854 he married Frances Tranchell, but the marriage was not destined to be happy. Although they had a daughter, Frances, to whom Durnford was devoted, they lost several children in infancy and the marriage soured. Durnford took to gambling and the couple later separated but never divorced. Durnford remained in Ceylon until 1856 when he was posted to Malta. In 1858 he returned to England. He was in Gibraltar between 1860 and 1864, when he was sent to China, but he collapsed with heat apoplexy on the way, broke his journey in Ceylon and returned to England. In 1871 he accepted a post at the Cape.

He was briefly employed on the Cape Frontier but was then sent to Natal. He arrived in time to join Theophilus Shepstone's expedition to 'crown' King

Cetshwayo in August 1873. Durnford returned hugely impressed by what he had seen and by the Zulu people. About this time he established a friendly relationship with Bishop Colenso, the Bishop of Natal. Like Colenso he admired and respected the Zulu people, although he was too much a believer in military duty to question British policies in the region. Shortly after his return, Durnford was appointed chief of staff to Lieutenant Colonel Milles, the officer commanding British troops in Natal, who was about to embark on military action against the 'rebellious' *inkosi* Langalibalele kaMthimkhulu of the amaHlubi people. Langalibalele's followers had fallen foul of the colonial authorities because their migrant labourers had received guns as payment from Kimberley diamond-diggers. Langalibalele had been ordered to surrender the arms but procrastinated and, on seeing colonial troops mustering for Cetshwayo's coronation expedition, assumed he was about to be attacked and fled to the Drakensberg mountain passes in the hope of escaping to Basutoland. Durnford was given command of a detachment of colonial troops and ordered, quite literally, to cut Langalibalele off at the pass. Durnford's party got lost; ascending a particularly steep and grassy slope, Durnford's horse Chieftain lost its footing and he fell fifty yards down the slope. When his men reached him they found he had dislocated his left shoulder and badly cut his head. He insisted on continuing, and the party eventually reached the summit of the mountains. Here they rode on until they encountered the amaHlubi working their way up from below. Durnford had been ordered not to fire the first shot if possible. One of the amaHlubi fired a shot and fighting ensued. Three of the colonial troopers were killed and the survivors retreated in disarray; Langalibalele and the majority of the amaHlubi escaped into Basutoland.

The incident left deep physical and psychological scars on Durnford. His left arm did not heal and was useless thereafter; he wore it thrust Napoleon-like into the front of his tunic. Colonial society held him to blame for the deaths of the troopers through his reluctance to open fire; he was mocked as 'Don't Fire Durnford'. Despite his marriage, he formed a relationship with Colenso's daughter Frances.

In 1876 Durnford returned to England but he was back in Natal a year later. In 1878, as the colony's senior Royal Engineer, he served on the Boundary Commission set up by Sir Henry Bulwer to investigate the disputed border between the Transvaal and Zulu kingdom; the commission found largely in favour of the Zulu claims. With the political crisis accelerating, Durnford was asked by Lord Chelmsford to plan the formation of an African auxiliary force to support the British invasion. In November 1878 this became the Natal Native Contingent. Durnford was given command of No. 2 Column, which was composed almost entirely of auxiliary troops. He took unusual pains to secure good calibre officers, who trained his men as efficiently as possible.

Durnford's column was placed on the high escarpment above the Middle Drift overlooking the Thukela River. It was a supporting role, to guard against Zulu attacks on that stretch of the border, or to advance in concert with the main invading columns as needed. On 14 January, three days after the war began, Durnford, acting on local information, decided to take his column down to the Middle Drift, an action that provoked a sharp rebuke from Chelmsford. Probably as a result of this, on the 16th Chelmsford ordered Durnford to move closer to the Centre Column. On the 20th, when Chelmsford moved the Centre Column forward to Isandlwana, Durnford was ordered to Rorke's Drift. When, early on the morning of the 22nd, Chelmsford decided to advance again to reinforce his detachments at Mangeni, he ordered – almost as an afterthought – Durnford forward to Isandlwana.

Durnford's actions at Isandlwana are well known and have remained controversial. Chelmsford's staff openly blamed Durnford for the defeat, stressing that he had failed to take responsibility for the camp and that his movements had prevented a more realistic defensive procedure. When Durnford's body was found on the battlefield on 21 May 1879 the orders found on it from Chelmsford included no explicit instruction to take command of the camp. Durnford's death undoubtedly made him an easy scapegoat for the wider failings of the defeat.

In October 1879 Durnford's body was exhumed at Bishop Colenso's instigation and removed to Pietermaritzburg where it was re-interred in the military cemetery at Fort Napier.

Essex, Edward

Edward Essex was born on 13 November 1847 in Camden Town, London. He entered Sandhurst in February 1866 and passed out third in his class, a position which entitled him to become an ensign without purchase. In March 1867 he was appointed to the 75th Regiment. His early career was spent in peacetime postings in Gibraltar and Hong Kong, where he was appointed Adjutant. In May 1871 he purchased a captain's commission within his regiment – one of the last officers in the British army to do so. Upon completion of a two-year course at the Staff College he was appointed Instructor of Musketry to the Manchester garrison, but volunteered for special duties in the prelude to the Zulu campaign. On 31 October 1878 he sailed for

Natal. On his arrival he was appointed Director of Transport to No. 3 Column.

On 20 January the column moved forward to Isandlwana which left Captain Essex without any particular duties to perform. On the 22nd he was writing letters in his tent when the sound of distant gunfire heralded the approach of the Zulu army; Essex joined the 24th companies deployed on the ridges overlooking the camp and helped direct their fire. After an extended period of firing he returned to the camp to ensure a supply of reserve ammunition was brought forward. He found that his junior, Smith-Dorrien, had already been rebuffed by the Quartermaster in charge of the nearest supply, Bloomfeld of the 2/24th. Bloomfield was concerned about Chelmsford's order that the 2nd Battalion reserve be kept ready for dispatch to Mangeni should it be needed. Essex confirmed that he overruled Bloomfield's objections and sent a considerable quantity of ammunition to the firing lines as the Zulus broke through.

He joined the general rout towards the border and, after a typically fraught escape, crossed the river at Sothondose's Drift. He attempted to rally the survivors on the Natal bank, but most were too exhausted and traumatised to obey him. Instead, they rode together to Helpmekaar, where Essex attempted to place the post on a defensive footing in expectation of a Zulu attack.

Essex left Natal for England with the rank of Brevet Major in early 1880. Between 1883 and 1885 he was Instructor of Musketry and Topography at Sandhurst. In May 1886 he rejoined his regiment with the rank of Brevet Lieutenant Colonel. He retired in June 1892 with the rank of Colonel Commanding the 2nd Battalion Gordon Highlanders. He was to enjoy a long retirement – 'lucky' to the end – and died on 10 September 1939 in Bournemouth at the age of 91.

Gardner, Alan Coulston

Alan Gardner was born in 1846 and entered the army as a cavalry officer, serving first in the 11th and then in the 14th Hussars. He passed out of the Staff College in 1872 and volunteered as a special service officer for the Zulu campaign, where he was a staff officer to Colonel Glyn's No. 3 column. On 22 January he had accompanied Glyn under Lord Chelmsford's command to the hills at the head of the Mangeni Valley, some ten miles from the camp at Isandlwana. After indecisive skirmishing during the morning Chelmsford decided to order the remainder of the column to advance to join him, and Glyn sent Gardner back to Isandlwana with the order. Gardner arrived, however, just as reports reached the camp commander, Lieutenant Colonel Pulleine, that detachments of Durnford's force had discovered the Zulu army beyond the iNyoni heights. At first Pulleine seemed uncertain how to react, until Gardner assured him that Chelmsford knew nothing of these developments. Gardner himself seems to have assisted in directing the movements of some of the mounted men during the battle.

When the British position collapsed he made his escape, crossing the Mzinyathi at Sothondose's Drift, where he met Captain Essex and Lieutenant Cochrane. The three held a brief discussion and Gardner scribbled a hasty note of warning to the garrison at Rorke's Drift, before all three rode to Helpmekaar. Gardner rode on to Dundee to warn Wood's column of the disaster. At Dundee he found a volunteer to take his message to Utrecht. Later, Gardner's actions earned him the appreciation of his senior officers, but an unfounded rumour that he might be rewarded with the Victoria Cross provoked a reaction among his colleagues who composed a ditty satirising his exertions – 'I very much fear, that the Zulus are near, so hang it, I'm off to Dundee'.

When Chelmsford reorganised his forces after Isandlwana, Gardner was transferred as a staff officer to Colonel Wood. Gardner accompanied Buller's detachment during the assault on Hlobane Mountain on 28 March, when Buller mentioned Gardner in dispatches. He survived the disaster and took part in the battle of Khambula the following day, where he was wounded. After the war, Gardner returned to Britain to take up a post as ADC to Lord Cowper, the Lord Lieutenant of Ireland. In 1885 he married Norah Blyth, and the couple had two sons and two daughters. Gardner developed a strong interest in big game hunting, travelling to India, Assam, Africa, North America and Australasia to shoot a representative cross-section of indigenous wildlife; his wife often accompanied him, 'herself shooting many wild animals'.

On retirement from the army, Gardner became a JP and took an interest in politics. In 1895 he contested the East Marylebone constituency on behalf of the Liberals and in 1906 was elected for the Ross Division of Herefordshire. In the winter of 1907 he began to suffer from poor health and took a holiday in Gibraltar to recuperate. There he suddenly succumbed to pneumonia and died in Algeciras on Christmas Day at the age of 62.

Glyn, Richard Thomas
Born 23 December 1831 in Meerut, India, Glyn was the only son of R.C. Glyn, an officer in the Honourable East India Company. On returning to England he became an expert horseman and fanatical fox hunter. Despite his short stature – he was just 5ft 2in – Glyn was physically strong and keen to pursue a military career. When he was nineteen his father purchased him a commission into the

82nd (Prince of Wales's Volunteers) Regiment, later the 2nd South Lancashires. After several years of duty in Ireland, Glyn and his regiment were sent to the Crimea and arrived on 2 September 1855, just six days before the fall of Sebastopol. In 1856 Glyn married Anne Clements, the daughter of the former Colonel of the Royal Canadian Rifles. Their honeymoon was cut short when Glyn's regiment was rushed to India to cope with the crisis of the Mutiny. The 82nd was part of Sir Colin Campbell's force that relieved the besieged city of Lucknow in mid-November 1857 and subsequently suffered in the fighting around Kanpur. Glyn was then promoted to captain and gained experience in the brutal suppression of the Mutiny.

He purchased his majority in 1861 and in 1867 he purchased the lieutenant colonelcy of the 1/24th Regiment, then stationed at Malta. In 1872 the regiment was transferred to Gibraltar, where Glyn was promoted to full colonel. At the end of November 1875 the Glyns and most of the 1/24th embarked on HM Troopship *Simoon* for Cape Town.

In 1876 the 1/24th was ordered to the diamond diggings at Kimberley to counter unrest among the diggers. The march to Kimberley took two months to cover the seven hundred miles. When they arrived, they found that their presence was enough to stifle the rebellion and there was little more to do than march all the way back to the Cape.

With the outbreak of the 9th Cape Frontier War in 1877 the 1/24th were ordered to the Transkei. Glyn was appointed Commander in the Transkei with the rank of Colonel of the Staff and Brevet Brigadier General. He received high praise from both the Duke of Cambridge and Sir Bartle Frere and, in a more tangible sign of gratitude, was made a Companion of the Order of the Bath. In 1878 the 1/24th was ordered to Pietermaritzburg in Natal in preparation for the invasion of Zululand. On 30 November and to the accompaniment of the band, Glyn led his regiment out of Pietermaritzburg towards the desolate post of Helpmekaar to join the No. 3 Column. He was appointed Column commander, although his authority was undermined by Lord Chelmsford's decision to accompany the column in person.

Throughout the campaign, Chelmsford treated Glyn with an air of impatience, although on the 12th Glyn was nominally in command of the successful assault on Sihayo's homestead. Following the encounter with Zulu forces at the head of the Mangeni gorge on the evening of the 21st, Chelmsford decided to advance at once and again offered Glyn nominal command of the force. Yet the main Zulu army was not where Chelmsford anticipated, and Isandlwana camp was meanwhile destroyed; that night, Chelmsford, Glyn and their men returned to the devastated battlefield at

Isandlwana. Glyn, in a state of shock at the loss of his regiment, was left to return to fortify Rorke's Drift.

When the Prince Imperial was killed Glyn was appointed to the Court Martial which tried the surviving officer, Lieutenant J.B. Carey. Glyn was present inside the Ulundi square during the battle on 4 July. For the 24th the war was over, and they began the long march back to Pietermaritzburg, where the Glyns were reunited. Glyn had the pleasant duty of presenting the Victoria Cross to Surgeon Major James Reynolds (Rorke's Drift) and Lieutenant Edward Browne 1/24th (Khambula).

In 1882 Glyn was promoted to Major General and appointed KCB, retiring as a Lieutenant General. In 1898 he was appointed Colonel of the South Wales Borderers. It was in this capacity that he saw off his Regiment as they went to South Africa again, this time to fight the Boers. Within a few months of their departure he died, on 21 November 1900, and was buried in the family grave at Ewell, Surrey.

Griffiths, William

Griffiths was born in Roscommon, Ireland, in 1841 and enlisted in the Army at Warwick on 16 April 1859. In 1867 he was serving in the 2/24th, a party of which had been sent to the Andaman Islands in the Bay of Bengal to investigate the fate of sailors who were feared murdered by islanders. A detachment of soldiers was put ashore and promptly attacked. They were stranded on the beach, and several attempts to evacuate them failed due to the heavy surf. In the end they were saved thanks to the determined effort of a surgeon and four men of the 24th who took a boat through the surf at great personal risk. All five were awarded the Victoria Cross for gallantry (an unusual award since they were not actually engaged with the enemy at the time). Among them was Private Griffiths. He continued to serve with the battalion and was in the camp at Isandlwana on picquet duty when the rest of the battalion marched to Mangeni under Lord Chelmsford. Griffiths was killed during the Zulu attack later that day; no details of his death have survived. His VC was acquired by the regiment at auction in the 1890s, having apparently been found on the battlefield.

Harford, Henry Charles

Harford was born in 1850. His father, Captain Charles Joseph Harford, was a Captain in the 12th Lancers. In 1864 Captain Harford bought a tobacco estate at Pinetown in Natal and the family emigrated to southern Africa. Here Henry Harford spent a happy and adventurous boyhood, learned to ride and shoot, and discovered an interest in the natural world that would last throughout his life.

In 1870 the Harford family began to break up. Henry returned to England to join the Army as an ensign in the 99th Regiment. His early years were spent on garrison duty in Ireland, but in 1877 the Regiment was posted to Chatham, and Harford accepted the post of Adjutant. In late 1878 the War Office requested volunteers for special service posts in Natal in preparation for the invasion of Zululand. Having spent his youth in Natal, and having knowledge of the Zulu language, Harford applied.

His application was accepted, and he arrived in Durban on 2 December 1878, to be given the post of Staff Officer to the 3rd Regiment, Natal Native Contingent, assembling at Sandspruit, near Helpmekaar, on the Mzinyathi border. Harford joined the regiment a few weeks before the invasion began. On 11 January he led the 2nd Battalion across the river border by a previously unknown drift upstream from Rorke's Drift. The following day (12 January 1879) Harford accompanied the 2nd Battalion in the attack on Sihayo's stronghold. Harford noticed that the NNC were suffering heavily from a group of Zulu snipers concealed in a cave further up the slope. He decided to clear them out, climbing up through the boulders and the corpses of Zulus killed in the fighting, a deed which earned him a commendation and the offer of the Victoria Cross – which he declined out of modesty. A similar deed accomplished by two of Evelyn Wood's staff at Hlobane on 28 March resulted in the award of two Victoria Crosses.

At dawn on the 21st Harford accompanied the sweep under Major Dartnell of the Isipezi heights. On the evening of the 22nd the 3rd NNC returned with Chelmsford's force to find the camp at Isandlwana devastated.

The following morning, Chelmsford's command returned to Rorke's Drift. The men of the 3rd NNC were disbanded, but the officers, including Harford, remained at the ruined mission for several months; Harford spent his time between Helpmekaar and Rorke's Drift and he was given custody of both Captain Stephenson and Lieutenant Higginson, who were placed under arrest following desertion on the day of the battle.

On 4 February a group of NNC officers, including Harford and led by Major Wilsone Black, 24th, rode as far as Sothondose's (Fugitives') Drift, and found the lost Colour and bodies of Lieutenants Melvill and Coghill, killed during the rout after Isandlwana. Harford carried the Colour back to Rorke's Drift in triumph.

In April Harford rejoined the 99th Regiment, which, following the relief of Eshowe had returned to the Thukela camp. Harford was present when King

Cetshwayo was captured by Major Marter's patrol, and Harford was given custody of the king during his journey into exile at Capetown.

Harford remained with the 99th Regiment, serving in Malta and India. He rose to the rank of Colonel, and at various times commanded both battalions, but saw no further active service, being deemed by a medical board to be both physically and mentally unfit for active command. In 1907 he was made a Commander of the Order of the Bath. He retired to Sussex and died on 25 March 1937.

Melvill, Teignmouth

Melvill was born in London on 8 September 1842, and educated at Harrow, Cheltenham and Cambridge; he graduated in 1865, the year he joined the Army. He was gazetted as a lieutenant in the 1st Battalion, 24th Regiment in December 1868. He served with the battalion in Ireland, Malta and Gibraltar and, from January 1875, at the Cape. In February 1876 he married Sarah Elizabeth Reed and the couple had two sons. He was appointed adjutant of the battalion and served in the opening stages of the 9th Cape Frontier War. In 1878 he had returned to England to take up a place at the Staff College but, hearing of a fresh outbreak of trouble on the Frontier, offered to return to Africa, where he served throughout the later phase of the Gaika war.

At the end of 1878 the 1st Battalion was attached to the No. 3 or Centre Column which assembled at Helpmekaar on the Biggarsberg heights and crossed into Zululand at Rorke's Drift on 22 January 1879. Melvill was present with the battalion in the camp at Isandlwana when it was attacked on the 22nd; he is known to have ridden about the field delivering orders from the senior officer of the battalion, Colonel Pulleine. Contrary to popular belief, there is no evidence that Melvill was ordered by Pulleine to save the Queen's Colour.

Melvill rode out of the camp with the cased Colour across his saddle. Somewhere on the heights above the Mzinyathi River he met Lieutenant Coghill of the same battalion, and the two attempted to ford the flooded river at Sothondose's (later Fugitives') Drift. Coghill crossed safely but Melvill was unhorsed and, still clutching the Colour, clung to a rock in mid-stream where an NNC officer, Lieutenant Higginson, joined him. Coghill saw their plight and returned to the water; as he did so, his horse was hit by a Zulu bullet. Melvill, Coghill and Higginson succeeded in helping each other across the river, but the Colour was lost in the process. The three officers struggled up the steep slopes on the Natal bank until Higginson left them to look for horses; a few minutes later Melvill and Coghill were overtaken and killed.

173

The 'dash with the Colours' caught the public attention in Britain as being one of the most dramatic and heroic acts from the battle, but both Melvill and Coghill were refused the VC. Melvill's widow, Sarah, and Coghill's father petitioned repeatedly on their behalf, and in 1907 the rules regarding the award of the VC were changed. Among the first batch of posthumous VCs awarded retrospectively were decorations to Melvill and Coghill.

Milne, Archibald Berkeley

Milne was born on 2 June 1855, the second son of Alexander Milne CB who was twice First Sea Lord of the Admiralty. He was educated at Wellington College and followed his father into the Navy. In 1878, serving as a lieutenant on HMS *Active*, he was part of a Naval Brigade put ashore to assist in the invasion of Zululand. Milne was attached to Lord Chelmsford's staff as an ADC, served with the staff throughout the war and was present with Lord Chelmsford during the sweeps through the hills above the Mangeni gorge on 22 January. At one point, shortly after midday, Lord Chelmsford ordered Milne to climb a hillside and look back at the camp at Isandlwana through his powerful naval telescope. Since Chelmsford was at that point between the Magogo and Silutshana hills, Milne climbed the northern flank of Magogo. Looking towards Isandlwana, his view of the iNyoni ridge – from which the Zulu attack developed – was blocked by an intervening shoulder of Silutshana; although he could plainly see the tents, shimmering in the haze, he could see no sign of a battle, and his report reassured Lord Chelmsford that nothing unusual was happening at the camp. At the battle of Ulundi he was slightly wounded by a Zulu bullet while riding beside Chelmsford inside the British square.

Milne later served on the staff of no fewer than four kings, from Edward VII to George VI. In 1905 he was appointed second-in-command of the Atlantic Fleet and in 1912 Commander of the Mediterranean Fleet, with the rank of Admiral. In 1914, on the outbreak of war in Europe, he prevented two German warships, the *Goeben* and *Breslau*, from passing through the Dardanelles en route to Turkey. He died on 5 July 1938 at the age of 83.

Pulleine, Henry Burmester

Pulleine was the eldest son of the Rev. Robert Pulleine, rector of Kirkby Wiske, near Thirsk, Yorkshire, and his wife Susan, née Burmester. He was born at Spennithorne, Yorkshire on 12 December 1838, and was educated at Marlborough College and at the Royal Military College, Sandhurst. On 16 November 1855 he was gazetted to an ensigncy, without purchase, in the 30th

Regiment, in which he served in Ireland. In June 1858 he was appointed as a lieutenant into the 2nd Battalion 24th Regiment (then being raised), and served at Sheffield, at Aldershot, and in Mauritius, where he became a captain by purchase in 1860. In 1866 he married Frances Bell, and the couple had a son and two daughters. He served in Rangoon and Secunderbad and in 1871 transferred into the 1st Battalion as a major by purchase. During his time in the 2nd Battalion he had been highly regarded as an efficient administrator and commissariat officer. He served for three years with the 1st Battalion in Gibraltar and in January 1875 accompanied it to the Cape. In 1877 he was promoted lieutenant colonel.

When the 9th Cape Frontier War broke out, Pulleine was instructed by General Sir Arthur Cunynghame to raise two irregular units, an infantry body known as Pulleine's Rangers and a mounted unit subsequently known as the Frontier Light Horse. He served with the 1/24th in the Transkei for nearly three months, and then, in September 1878, in view of the impending hostilities with the Zulus, returned to embark for Natal; here he was appointed to the command of the city of Durban and then as commandant of Pietermaritzburg. With the invasion imminent, he asked to be allowed to rejoin his regiment and set off in high spirits, riding with his groom and a packhorse, and succeeded on 17 January in reaching the Centre Column, which was then camped on the Zulu river bank at Rorke's Drift. When Chelmsford marched out of the camp at Isandlwana before dawn on 22 January he left Pulleine in charge. When Brevet Colonel Durnford arrived in the camp at about 10.30 that morning he outranked Pulleine, but in the absence of any orders from Chelmsford to the contrary Durnford decided to retain his independence of command. Pulleine was killed during the final stages of the battle.

Russell, Francis Broadfoot

Francis Russell, the eldest son of Lieutenant Colonel F. Russell of the Madras Infantry, was born in India on 4 September 1842. He entered the Royal Military Academy, Woolwich in 1861, graduated in 1865 and took up a commission in the Royal Artillery. He served in Malta, Canada, India and Aden before being promoted Captain in 1877. He was then attached to 11 Battery, 7th Brigade, which was based in Pietermaritzburg. In November 1878 he was promoted Brevet Major. As Lord Chelmsford assembled his forces for the invasion of Zululand, Russell was attached to Colonel Pearson's staff. At short notice, he was ordered to organise a rocket battery that was added to Colonel Durnford's column. Russell's battery – three rocket troughs carried on mules – joined Durnford's command at Middle Drift at the end of December. With the forward movement of the Centre Column, Durnford was ordered to Rorke's Drift in support, and he took with him Russell's battery. On 22 January Durnford was again ordered forward, this time to Isandlwana. On hearing of Zulu movements close to the camp, he decided to continue his advance to ensure that the heights overlooking the camp were clear of Zulus. Russell's battery was intended to accompany them but they were escorted by auxiliaries on foot and soon fell behind. About three miles from the camp they were alerted to the sound of firing out of sight on the high ground. Russell rode up the escarpment to investigate and returned ordering his men to deploy for action. The rocket apparatus was set up on a knoll at the foot of the escarpment. A rocket was fired as the first Zulus appeared over the skyline, but the Zulu attack developed rapidly, the warriors emerging suddenly from a *donga* close by to fire a volley. Russell was killed by the first shots, but there is no report that his body was ever subsequently located or buried.

Wells, Janet
Wells was born in 1859 in Maida Vale, London. In November 1876, aged seventeen, she entered the fledgling profession of nursing and joined the Training School of the Evangelical Protestant Deaconesses' Institution and Training Hospital as a trainee nurse. She was sent to the Balkans to assist the Russian army medical teams in the 1877/8 Balkan War and was decorated with the Imperial Red Cross of Russia. In 1879 she volunteered for service in Zululand and was one of six civilian nurses provided by the Stafford House Committee and sent to Natal to tend the British sick and wounded. She travelled from Durban to Utrecht – over 200 miles – in a post cart. In her first three months at Utrecht she treated over 3,200 patients, both British soldiers and Zulus, including men injured in the battles of Hlobane, Khambula and Ulundi. She performed numerous operations, cared for the sick and wounded and brought an air of discipline, tempered by her charm and femininity, to a chaotic and desperate situation. Towards the end of the war she was sent to Rorke's Drift, where she ministered to the remaining garrison. She walked the battlefields of Rorke's Drift and Isandlwana where she collected flowers for her scrapbooks, which survive to this day. She later visited – and treated – the captive King Cetshwayo in Cape Town. After the war she returned to her home and family in London, just in time for her twentieth birthday. In 1880 she met George King, an up-and-coming young London journalist who was soon to become the distinguished editor of the *Globe* magazine. They married on 6 May 1882 and had two daughters, Elsie and Daisy. Queen Victoria decorated

Janet with the Royal Red Cross, then known as 'the nursing Victoria Cross'. In 1901 she was invited to the Queen's state funeral. She died of cancer at Purley in Surrey on 6 June 1911.

Smith-Dorrien, Horace

Horace Smith-Dorrien rose to the rank of General in the First World War when he commanded the II Corps during their retreat from Mons. He died in a car crash near Bath in 1930.

Hamilton Browne, George

George Hamilton Browne (the name was not hyphenated in early official documents, though it has often been written as such) remains one of the most intriguing and controversial characters to emerge from the Anglo-Zulu War. He was by nature an adventurer, and a garrulous one at that, whose own stories are the principal cause of the confusion that still surrounds his life and career.

He was born on 22 December 1844 in Cheltenham, the son of Major George Browne of the 35th Regiment and his wife Susannah. The Browne family seat was Comber House in Co. Londonderry, and George was one of nine children. He was given a public school education, but by his own account his best efforts were given 'to the play-ground and gymnasium'. He remained athletic in later life and took a keen interest in boxing.

Hamilton Browne's youth was characterised by a romantic penchant for duelling and dramatic entanglements with women that, between them, prevented his gaining entry to the Royal Military College at Woolwich. Instead, he ran away to join the Royal Horse Artillery as a driver, but was discovered by a relative and discharged as under-age. There followed a duel over a lady and a rapid flight across the Channel, which resulted in enlistment in the Papal Zouaves – his first taste of an essentially mercenary lifestyle – and some action in the Italian War of Unification.

In January 1866 Browne arrived in New Zealand, which was at that time coming to the end of several decades of bitter warfare between European settlers and the indigenous Maori over the question of land ownership. He later wrote a book about that period – *With the Lost Legion in New Zealand* (1911).

Browne seems to have left New Zealand about 1870. He probably fought Bushrangers for a spell in Australia – where he was wounded – and might perhaps have served on the American frontier in the Indian wars. A year or two later he was back in New Zealand, serving in the Armed Constabulary until he was discharged at his own request in 1875.

At the beginning of 1878 he arrived in southern Africa. Here he met a number of former acquaintances among the 1/24th Regiment, then serving on the Cape Frontier, and volunteered as an officer in Pulleine's Rangers, an irregular unit formed by Colonel Henry Pulleine, 1/24th. At the end of 1878, with the 24th joining the troops assembling on the Zulu border, Browne again volunteered, this time securing the rank of Major in the 1st Battalion, 3rd Regiment, Natal Native Contingent.

A second book about his experiences, *A Lost Legionary in South Africa* (1913), was originally to be published under a pseudonym – but he wisely decided to use his own name, aware, no doubt, of the controversy his earlier book had caused in New Zealand. Fortunately, his part in the Zulu campaign is well documented and supported by a wide variety of official reports, private diaries and correspondence.

Browne was present at the crossing of the Centre Column into Zululand at Rorke's Drift on 11 January 1879 and he was in the thick of the action at Sihayo's homestead on the 12th. Here he led several companies from his battalion into the centre of the Zulu position among the rocks at the foot of the Ngedla cliffs, only to find that most of his men had fled before they reached the Zulus. On 21 January his battalion was appointed to sweep through the Malakatha and Hlazakazi range. His men were engaged in clearing Zulus from the Magogo and Silutshana hills on the 22nd when they were ordered to return to the camp at Isandlwana to assist in packing up for a general column advance.

Browne's men approached to within three miles of the camp before realising that it was under attack. They then took up a position on a commanding ridge on the left of the road, and Browne's description of the destruction of the British camp remains one of the most chilling accounts to emerge from the war.

In the aftermath of Isandlwana Browne remained at Rorke's Drift, making occasional forays across the border to skirmish there. He then served with Lord Chelmsford's expedition to relieve the besieged garrison at Eshowe, and was present at the battle of Gingindlovu on 2nd April. Sent back to the Cape with a party of irregulars due to be discharged, Browne was badly injured when he was crushed between a mule and its shipboard stall.

He served in the BaSotho 'Gun War' of 1880, and in Sir Charles Warren's Bechuanaland expedition of 1884. In 1885 he was appointed Adjutant of the Diamond Fields Horse. In 1888 he served briefly in Zululand again, during the Dinuzulu rebellion, where he met Robert Baden-Powell.

In 1890 he joined the British South Africa Company's Pioneer expedition to occupy Mashonaland (Zimbabwe), the beginning of several years' involvement in 'Rhodesian' affairs. He served under Major Forbes in the war against the amaNdebele ('Matabele') in 1893 and in 1896 commanded volunteers under Baden-Powell during the Rebellion.

Browne seems to have remained in Rhodesia throughout the Second Boer War, before returning to the Cape. He had apparently lost most of his investments in the epidemics of cattle disease that swept through southern Africa at the end of the nineteenth century. At the Cape, there was worse to come; his wife Dolphina died in May 1904. This ushered in a new period of hardship for Browne, who appealed to the British Government for a pension, but was refused. About this time he seems to have sold his campaign medals, which perhaps explains why of those he wore in later life – now in a private collection – only his BSA Co. was as officially issued. Indeed, the official status of his medals is curious as he was refused the South Africa Campaign Medal for having ordered the slaughter of injured and captive Zulus at Rorke's Drift after the battle. Later reduced to poverty, he sought assistance from the Salvation Army. In 1909 his luck turned when he married Sarah Wilkerson, a lady of independent means.

George Hamilton Browne died in Jamaica in February 1916.

Dartnell, John George
Dartnell was born in 1837 in Ontario, Canada, where his father, George Russell Dartnell, was Inspector-General of Military Hospitals. In 1855 Dartnell purchased a commission as an ensign in the 86th Regiment, and was serving with them in 1857 when the Indian Mutiny broke out. The Regiment was heavily involved in operations in Central India under Sir Hugh Rose, and Dartnell himself was badly wounded in the storming of the rebel stronghold at Jhansi. He was recommended for the Victoria Cross but not awarded it, although he was personally commended by Rose.

After the Mutiny Dartnell remained in India, transferring first to the 16th Regiment and later to the 27th. He also took part in the Bhutan expedition of 1865 as an ADC to the commanding officer. In 1865 he married Clara Steer, daughter of a Judge of the Supreme Court of Calcutta.

In 1869 Dartnell sold his commission and retired from the Army with the rank of Brevet Major. He decided to try his hand at farming in the colonies, and bought a farm in Natal. Following the rebellion of Langalibalele in 1873, the Natal authorities decided to establish a regular force to police the colony, and Dartnell applied for the job. He was appointed largely on the strength of his extensive military experience, and the outcome was the Natal Mounted

Police, which, although not strictly a military body, was then the only full-time professional armed unit maintained by the Natal administration. Dartnell emerged as a popular leader and a prominent voice on military matters within colonial society.

In November 1878 both the Police and various Volunteer corps were mobilised, and Dartnell with them. The Police were attached to the No. 3 Column assembling at Helpmekaar, together with a number of Volunteer units. On 21 January Dartnell was given command of the extended foray through the Malakatha and Hlazakazi hills that heralded Chelmsford's intended forward move from Isandlwana. Once they reached the hills, Dartnell's command divided, the NNC sweeping round the high bastion of Malakatha hill and working up the hot, thorny valleys beyond, towards the Mangeni gorge at the far end of the range. They had not gone far when a line of warriors appeared on a crest above them. Dartnell at once withdrew, as did the Zulus.

It was now late evening, and Dartnell was faced with a dilemma. Chelmsford expected him to return to Isandlwana, but the reconnaissance had so far learned little of the Zulu movements beyond their presence, so word of Dartnell's discovery was sent to Chelmsford with a request for assistance. This was a reasonable decision under the circumstances, but it was to have serious repercussions on the conduct of the Isandlwana campaign. Chelmsford received the report early on the morning of the 22nd and decided to split his force, hurrying out before dawn with a column to reinforce Dartnell in the hope of catching the Zulu army by surprise. While he did so, the main Zulu army fell upon and destroyed the camp at Isandlwana.

With the end of the Anglo-Zulu War, Dartnell returned to his role as Natal's senior military officer. With the outbreak of the BaSotho 'Gun War' in 1880, Dartnell led detachments of Police into the Drakensberg foothills, patrolling the passes – sometimes in atrocious weather – to ensure that the Sotho made no raids into Natal. At the end of the year, with the outbreak of the Boer rebellion in the Transvaal, Dartnell and the Police were attached to the troops assembled by General Sir George Colley in Natal.

In May 1881 Dartnell was appointed a Companion of the Most Distinguished Order of St Michael and St George by Queen Victoria. In 1894 Natal's police forces were reorganised, and Dartnell was appointed Chief Commissioner. With the outbreak of the Second Boer War in 1899, Dartnell's local knowledge was greatly in demand, and he was appointed to the staff of the GOC Natal.

In 1903 Major General Dartnell retired from Natal service. He returned to

England with the intention of enjoying his pension. When the poll tax disturbances in Natal threatened to break into open violence in early 1906, Dartnell again offered his services. Sponsored by a Natal newspaper, he returned to Africa bringing with him a consignment of newly invented Rexer light machine-guns.

Finally, Dartnell again retired to England and settled in Folkestone, where he died on 7 August 1913 at the age of 75.

Nkambule, Simeon

Simeon Nkambule (often spelt Kambule) was the son of Elijah Nkambule, a member of the Edendale Christian community, founded outside Pietermaritzburg by the Methodist minister Rev. James Allison in 1851. Many of the converts originally attracted to this community were Sotho or Swazi speakers (the name Nkambule is Swazi in origin); few were Zulu speakers. In 1873 Durnford was impressed by the performance of his African auxiliaries and, charged with raising an African force to assist in tackling the Zulus in 1879, he again turned to the Edendale community. Fifty-four men responded to the request, and practical command fell to Simeon Nkambule, one of the largest landowners at Edendale. He was given the rank of sergeant major.

The Edendale troop was attached to Durnford's No. 2 Column, and was present at Isandlwana, where it was part of the force led out of the camp by Durnford himself. When Durnford encountered the Zulu left 'horn', he retired to the Nyogane *donga*, where he made a stand. When ammunition ran low, Durnford ordered his men to leave the field. Nkambule kept the Edendale men together but, with the battle lost, the Edendale troop had to force its way through the Zulu right 'horn' into the valley behind Isandlwana, and apparently led the way towards the crossing at Sothondose's Drift. During the retreat Nkambule saved the life of a colonial trooper by taking him up behind his saddle. At the Drift, the men crossed in relatively good order and rallied on the Natal bank, firing several volleys across the river to discourage Zulus from pursuing the survivors.

Later, at the beginning of June, Chelmsford had reached the White Mfolozi River before oNdini. On 3 July a mounted detachment under Lieutenant Colonel Redvers Buller was sent across the river to scout the vicinity of the royal homestead of kwaNodwengu. Here it was drawn into a Zulu ambush and only just extricated itself. Simeon Nkambule again saved the life of a man during the retreat, and this time his gallantry was recognised by the award of the Distinguished Conduct Medal.

Simeon Nkambule returned to play a leading role in the life of the community. During the Second Boer War the Edendale Horse were again called upon, and they took part as scouts during the siege of Ladysmith, again led by Nkambule. At the end of the war, however, the Edendale men were denied the silver campaign medal issued by the British government. After considerable protest, they were issued a cheaper bronze version.

Shepstone, George

George Shepstone was born in June 1849, a few years after his father Theophilus moved the Shepstone family to Natal. George Shepstone grew up fluent in Zulu, a good shot and an excellent horseman. In 1873 he accompanied his father and elder brother Henrique on the expedition to 'crown' King Cetshwayo. Also accompanying the expedition was Major Anthony Durnford RE, and it is likely that he and George first met during this time. Shortly after the expedition's return to Natal, the *inkosi* of the amaHlubi people, Langalibalele ka Mthimkhulu, attempted to cross the Kahlamba Mountains into BaSotholand in an attempt to escape an entanglement with the colonial authorities. Durnford was ordered to block the anticipated escape route, but the mission faltered badly in a skirmish on top of the Bushman's Pass on 4 November 1873; in the aftermath it was Shepstone who collected and buried the colonial dead on the summit.

On the outbreak of war Durnford was given command of No. 2 Column, which consisted largely of auxiliary troops and which was placed on the escarpment overlooking the Middle Drift on the Thukela. George Shepstone was appointed as Durnford's Political Agent, to serve as his adviser on African politics and affairs, a position which effectively made him Durnford's senior staff officer.

Durnford, accompanied by Shepstone, reached the Isandlwana camp at about 10.30 am on the 22nd. A significant enemy presence had been reported on the iNyoni heights nearby, and in the absence of any specific orders from Chelmsford Durnford decided to clear the heights with his own troops. He sent two detachments onto the hills, accompanied by George Shepstone; Durnford himself took the rest of his command along the foot of the hills in what he clearly hoped would be a pincer movement.

The men with Shepstone stumbled across the Zulu army at about noon. The Zulus responded with an immediate attack, and Shepstone rode back to warn the troops in the camp. He arrived somewhat breathless, and Lieutenant Colonel Henry Pulleine seemed at first undecided how best to react to his report. Memorably, Shepstone replied, 'I am not an alarmist, sir, but the enemy are in such black masses over there, such long black lines, that you will have to give us all the assistance you can. They are fast driving our men this way'.

Shepstone apparently rejoined his men, but after the British line began to crumble he was heard to say that he must find Durnford. It is unlikely that he did; the British collapse, when it came, happened quickly, and with the men retiring on the camp, pursued by the Zulus, everything dissolved in confusion.

George Shepstone's body was found on a rocky outcrop below the southern peak of Isandlwana, on a spot which overlooks the approach from the Manzimnyama Valley. It is surrounded today by a cluster of cairns which suggests that a determined stand was made there, perhaps in the hope of holding back the Zulu right 'horn', or of covering the flight of survivors by the road.

Today Shepstone's grave is one of the few which is individually marked on the Isandlwana battlefield.

II Zulu participants

Cetshwayo kaMpande, King

Cetshwayo was born at emLambongwenya, one of the royal homesteads of his father, Prince Mpande kaSenzangakhona, in 1832. The name Cetshwayo ironically means 'the slandered one', and if ever a man's history grew to suit his name it was Cetshwayo's. The reason he was so named is obscure, but is thought to reflect an intrigue within the Zulu royal house, for the kingdom had not yet recovered from the assassination of the legendary King Shaka, only four years before. Shaka had been succeeded by his brother and assassin, Dingane kaSenzangakhona, who eliminated a number of his brothers on various pretexts. Prince Mpande survived, largely by assuming a pose of indolence and lack of ambition. In dismissing the threat posed by Mpande, King Dingane made a serious political error. In 1838 Dingane became embroiled in a brutal war against the Boer Voortrekkers, and Mpande and several thousand of his followers crossed the Thukela River and offered their allegiance to the Boers; this was a decisive split within the royal house, and was remembered as 'the breaking of the rope' which bound the nation together.

Cetshwayo spent much of his youth at another of his father's homesteads, oNdini, which was sited near the coast. About 1850 he was enrolled as a cadet in what would later become the uThulwana *ibutho*. In 1852 the uThulwana were given their first taste of military action. Although not yet formally enrolled, they were attached to an army dispatched by Mpande to raid southern Swaziland. Although the Swazis retired before their advance, taking refuge in natural strongholds, there was considerable skirmishing during which Cetshwayo is said to have killed an enemy warrior. The campaign gave much-needed experience to the king's younger regiments and enhanced Cetshwayo's prestige. Two years later the uThulwana were formally enrolled as a regiment.

By this stage Cetshwayo had begun to accrue considerable support within the country. Worried, however, that he might prove a threat, King Mpande let it be known that Cetshwayo's brother, Mbuyazi, had a claim to kingship by virtue of being an heir to Shaka's estate. In response, Cetshwayo gathered a circle of close supporters who took the name uSuthu, from a drinking boast that they were as plentiful as the Sotho cattle Mpande had plundered during his raiding. Mbuyazi's own followers took the name iziGqoza.

By the middle of 1856 it was clear that Cetshwayo's followers far outnumbered their rivals and, worried for Mbuyazi's safety, Mpande urged him to cross the Thukela into Natal, as Mpande had once done, and secure the support of the whites. Mbuyazi delayed too long, and when he finally gathered his supporters in November 1856, the rains had begun and the rivers were swollen. By the time he reached the Thukela, with 7,000 fighting men and 13,000 dependants, the river was impassable. Mbuyazi could do little beyond appeal to the Natal authorities to intervene – they refused – and await the arrival of the uSuthu.

On 2 December as many as 20,000 uSuthu arrived, commanded by Prince Cetshwayo himself. At first Mbuyazi's warriors tried to make a stand on a ridge above the river but they collapsed under the uSuthu assault and were slaughtered in their thousands; the survivors jumped in panic into the Thukela, where many of them drowned or were taken by crocodiles. Mbuyazi himself was killed, and by this victory Cetshwayo secured the succession.

Cetshwayo took steps to eliminate any further opposition, but it was not until August 1873 that he felt able to proceed with his inauguration. He began the construction of a new royal homestead close to the site of his father's kwaNodwengu. The complex was known as oNdini or Ulundi, from the common root 'undi', meaning a high place. It contained as many as 1,400 huts and was widely regarded as one of the most impressive settlements in the kingdom's history.

King Cetshwayo was now in his forties, in the prime of life and self-confidence, secure at last in his birthright. But throughout 1877 his relationship with colonial Natal was going sour. Cetshwayo was astute enough to recognise the fact but had little idea that the underlying cause was the British decision to adopt the confederation policy. In April the Transvaal Republic was annexed to the Crown, and the Transvaal's boundary dispute with the Zulus now became a British affair. In addressing it, Theophilus Shepstone adopted such a high-handed manner that many influential Zulus were outraged. Cetshwayo eagerly seized upon the suggestion of a boundary commission, but when the findings of the commission were finally presented to the king's representatives on 11 December 1878, tagged on to them were a series of demands, prompted by border incidents, which amounted to an impossible ultimatum. The king could do little more than wait and see whether the British were in earnest; once it became clear in the first week of January that they were massing on his borders, he ordered his army to assemble at oNdini.

Although the king listened attentively to his military advisers – and in particular his commanders-in-chief, *inkosi* Mnyamana kaNqgengelele and Ntshingwayo kaMahole – the final choice of Zulu strategy was his. When news arrived that the British had crossed the border, and that the Centre Column was targeting royal favourites on the Rorke's Drift border, King Cetshwayo decided to dispatch his main striking force to oppose that column. The king allowed his generals full scope, only suggesting that they should be sure the British were in earnest before committing themselves to action. In the event, both armies were engaged on the 22nd when his warriors decisively defeated the Centre Column at Isandlwana. Yet the victory would prove double-edged, for the Zulu losses were staggering and the king had little option but to allow the regiments to disperse once they had undergone their post-combat purification rituals.

With the British again massing on his borders, Cetshwayo reassembled his army, and this time decided to direct it against the northern column commanded by Colonel Wood. When it marched out, the army was accompanied by *inkosi* Mnyamana, a token of the importance the king placed on the expedition. Yet despite Cetshwayo's instructions that it should not attack defensive positions, the army dashed itself to pieces against Wood's fortifications at Khambula on 29 March.

On 3 July Chelmsford probed across the Mfolozi, and on the 4th he crossed it in force, forming some 5,000 men into a large square within sight of oNdini. The *amabutho* gathered for the last time to resist, but they could not penetrate the fearsome curtain of British fire and were driven away.

The king had anticipated the defeat and did not stay to witness it. He fled into the remote Ngome forest. The British dispatched several patrols to capture him and on 28 August he was surprised and taken by Major Marter's patrol of the 1st Dragoon Guards.

The king was brought to the camp of Chelmsford's successor, Wolseley, near the burned-out ruins of his oNdini homestead, where he was officially informed that he was to be exiled from Zululand. He was taken to Cape Town and lodged in apartments in the old Cape Castle. His kingdom was then divided up among British appointees.

In captivity, Cetshwayo increasingly lobbied to be allowed to return to his country, now under British authority. His personal circumstances improved when he was moved from the Castle to a farm known as Oude Moulen on the Cape flats. Finally, in August 1882, he was granted permission to visit London to argue his case. He arrived, smartly dressed in European clothes, to find that he was a celebrity, and crowds gathered curious to see the victor of Isandlwana. He was granted an audience with Queen Victoria at Osborne House on the Isle of Wight and, while the Queen herself was wary of the man who had damaged Lord Chelmsford's reputation and destroyed the 1/24th, she presented him with a large silver mug as a souvenir and ordered her court painter to paint his portrait.

The Colonial Office agreed that the king might be restored to Zululand, but only to part of his old kingdom. Large tracts of the country were to be set aside for those Zulus who had ruled in his absence – and who could not be expected to welcome his return – and he would not be allowed to re-establish the *amabutho* system. Nor was his return announced to his countrymen; he arrived back on Zulu soil on 10 January 1883 to find few Zulus waiting to greet him. He was escorted to his old capital by Sir Theophilus Shepstone, who had come out of retirement for the occasion. Once news of his return spread, his old supporters, *amakhosi*, *izinduna* and commoners alike flocked to renew their allegiance.

King Cetshwayo began rebuilding a new version of oNdini, not far from the complex destroyed in 1879. He found the country deeply divided by several years of friction between his supporters and the appointees set up by the British. His followers bitterly resented the oppression they had suffered at the hands of his erstwhile general, *inkosi* Zibhebhu kaMapitha, and they were keen take revenge. A number of royalist supporters assembled an army in March to attack Zibhebhu. But Zibhebhu was equal to the challenge and on the 30th he routed the royalists in the Msebe Valley and destroyed them utterly.

The attack caused consternation at oNdini. Cetshwayo assembled his most prominent advisers to discuss the crisis and, despite the British ban on the *amabutho*, summoned those who still recognised their old allegiances. Before he could act, Zibhebhu struck first. At dawn on 21 July 1883 a line of warriors silhouetted against the dim sky advanced rapidly. Zibhebhu had made a daring night march with 3,000 men and was advancing to attack oNdini itself. Urged to flee, King Cetshwayo was led away on horseback but was spotted by two young warriors from Zibhebhu's army who hurled spears at him, striking him in the thigh. Even under such circumstances he maintained his composure. 'Do you stab me, Halijana son of Sumfula?' he asked, recognising one of his assailants, 'I am your king!' Awestruck, the young warriors assisted him in dressing the wounds and helped him on his way.

King Cetshwayo escaped the slaughter of his army, and made his way to the territory of *inkosi* Sigananda kaSokufa, head of the Cube people, a staunch loyalist who lived in the rugged country above the Thukela River. Here he hid in a cave at the head of the Mome stream until, in October, he surrendered himself to the British authorities in Eshowe. Then, suddenly, on the morning of 8 February 1884, King Cetshwayo kaMpande collapsed and died. A British doctor examined the body but was refused permission to conduct an autopsy; he officially gave the cause of death as heart failure, but privately suggested Cetshwayo may have been poisoned.

Cetshwayo's remains were taken by waggon back to *inkosi* Sigananda's territory and buried not far from the Mome Gorge. The waggon was left on the spot and allowed to decay; its remains can now be seen in the Zulu Cultural Museum at oNdini.

Dabulamanzi kaMpande, Prince

Prince Dabulamanzi achieved a level of fame among his British enemies in 1879 due largely to his attack on Rorke's Drift. He was born shortly after his father, Prince Mpande, crossed into Natal in October 1839 to secure the support of the Boers in his coup against King Dingane. Dabulamanzi's name commemorated the event; it means 'divider of the waters'. Dabulamanzi and his older brother, Prince Cetshwayo, grew up to be firm friends. Indeed, Dabulamanzi's fortunes were entirely connected with those of his brother. Dabulamanzi supported Cetshwayo without question, and he may have been present at the battle of Ndondakusuka in which his brother's rival Mbuyazi was defeated.

Dabulamanzi spent much of his youth in the coastal districts and became acquainted with the white trader, John Dunn, whom Cetshwayo had set up as an appointed *induna* to supervise European traffic in the region. Dabulamanzi learned to ride, to appreciate fine guns and to shoot, and acquired a fondness for European clothes and alcohol.

King Cetshwayo appointed Dabulamanzi an officer in the eSiqwakeni royal homestead, not far from his eZulwini residence. He was not, however, a commander in the Zulu army, and urged that the king should comply where possible with the British demands of late 1878; but once war became inevitable, he committed himself wholeheartedly to its prosecution. He attended the general muster with his uDloko regiment, and took part in the great advance towards the British camp at Isandlwana. On the morning of 22 January the uDloko were camped in the Ngwebeni Valley together with other *amabutho* associated with the royal homestead at oNdini. When elements of Durnford's force stumbled upon them, they were held back from the general advance by the senior commander, Ntshingwayo kaMahole. They swung wide of the Zulu right 'horn', cutting the British line of retreat by the road to Rorke's Drift before extending in pursuit of routed British troops fleeing towards the Mzinyathi River. One section of the reserve, the iNdluyengwe *ibutho*, apparently under Zibhebhu's command, crossed upstream from the survivors. The rest of the reserve – the uThulwana, iNdlondlo and uDloko – crossed higher still. Although Dabulamanzi held no official command within the reserve, his status as a royal prince and his strong personality led him to assume control, the more so because Zibhebhu abandoned his command at the river.

Once across the river, numbers of Zulus split away to loot deserted homesteads, while the main body, perhaps 3,500 strong and led by Dabulamanzi on horseback, moved towards the supply depot at Rorke's Drift. The Zulu attack on Rorke's Drift showed little tactical sophistication, reflecting the fact that no thought had been given to assaulting it beforehand. Dabulamanzi seems to have accepted the inevitability of defeat at about midnight and began to withdraw his exhausted men. Some of these – including Dabulamanzi himself – were retreating across the Isandlwana road the following morning when Lord Chelmsford passed in the opposite direction, the two forces watching each other go by.

Dabulamanzi's failure at Rorke's Drift earned him general disapproval across Zululand. On 12 July he submitted to the officers of the 1st Division. He was allowed to live in his own area and found himself under the chieftainship of John Dunn, his erstwhile friend, who had defected to the British. Dabulamanzi closely allied himself to the movement to have the exiled King Cetshwayo returned to Zululand and in May 1882 was one of a number of prominent Zulus from Dunn's districts who walked to Pietermaritzburg to appeal against the settlement. When King Cetshwayo was restored in January 1883, Dabulamanzi attended the ceremonies held on the Mthonjaneni heights, and took the opportunity to deliver a stinging rebuke on British policy to Sir Theophilus Shepstone. He remained in attendance upon King Cetshwayo as he rebuilt his oNdini homestead.

Following the Zulu rebellion, on 21 September 1886, Dabulamanzi was arrested with his son Mzingeli by the Boers on a trumped-up charge of cattle rustling and taken under the escort to Vryheid. When they passed through the Nondweni district – which was in British territory – the Prince asked to rest at a homestead and then refused to go on, claiming that the Boers had no jurisdiction there. There was a scuffle which ended with Dabulamanzi being shot. Mortally wounded, he died early next morning. His body was later taken to the site of his eZulwini homestead near Eshowe where it was buried.

Mkhosana kaMvundlana Biyela

Mkhosana kaMvundlana was inkosi of the Biyela people, and played a decisive role in the battle of Isandlwana, where he was killed. The Biyela, whose ancestral lands lay south-east of the middle reaches of the White Mfolozi River, enjoyed a particularly close relationship with the Zulu royal house, with whom they claimed common ancestors.

Mkhosana was born about 1835, and enrolled in the iNdlondlo *ibutho*. Mkhosana seems to have retained King Cetshwayo's friendship, although his youth debarred him from sitting on the king's inner council. Following the usual Zulu practice of appointing older men as senior officers among newly-formed regiments, Mkhosana had, by 1879, been given a high-ranking command among the uKhandempemvu (uMcijo) *ibutho*. He is listed among the three most senior officers of the regiment, although overall command rested with Vumandaba kaNthathi, who was both older and one of King Cetshwayo's most trusted councillors. Nevertheless, Mkhosana was the senior *induna* of kwaKhandempemvu, the royal homestead near oNdini, where the uKhandempemvu were based.

With the outbreak of war in January 1879, Mkhosana accompanied his regiment on the advance towards Isandlwana. It was the uKhandempemvu who, having been discovered at about noon on 22nd January by mounted parties sent out from the British camp, launched the spontaneous attack which precipitated the battle. Mkhosana, along with many senior regimental officers, was apparently attending a command conference with the generals Ntshingwayo kaMahole and Mavumengwana kaNdlela when their *impi* was discovered; he did not rejoin his men but remained with the generals as they followed behind the advancing regiments. The generals took up a commanding position above the iNyoni rocks on the escarpment overlooking Isandlwana, as the Zulu centre – including the uKhandempemvu – descended to the *dongas* below and came under heavy fire from the forward British firing line. The men of the uKhandempemvu took cover among the *dongas* and, with the open ground in front of them swept by fire, their advance stalled. Realising that if the centre failed the whole assault would collapse, Ntshingwayo sent Mkhosana hurrying down the steep escarpment to urge his men on.

When he reached the *dongas*, Mkhosana strode up and down fearlessly in front of his men, oblivious to the British bullets striking rocks all around him, berating the sheltering warriors and urging them to renew the attack. Wearing the full finery of an *inkosi*, he presented such a magnificent spectacle, alone and in the open, that the British were reluctant to shoot him down. Famously, Mkhosana rallied his men by calling out lines from King Cetshwayo's praises – *'uhlamvana ubul'mlilo ubaswe uMantshonga no uNgqelebana kashongo njalo'* ('the little branch of leaves that extinguished the great fire kindled by Mantshonga and Nqgelebana') – a reference to Prince Cetshwayo's victory at the battle of Ndondakusuka in 1856. Stung by this allusion to their royal duty, the uKhandempemvu rose up from the *donga* and rushed forward. Their attack coincided with the British withdrawal towards the camp, and the uKhandempemvu were able to drive between the 24th companies and prevent the British reforming. The moment was a decisive one and precipitated the British collapse.

At the moment of his triumph Mkhosana, aged forty-three, was killed, shot through the head. Like most of the Zulu dead, he was covered over and left on the battlefield.

Mnyamana kaNgqengele Buthelezi
In 1854 King Mpande formed a new *ibutho*, the uThulwana. It consisted of men born in the early 1830s, including a number of Mpande's own sons, Prince Cetshwayo among them. Mpande was particularly fond of this regiment and he appointed Mnyamana Buthelezi as the senior commander of the uThulwana, remarking that he was the only man in the country with the strength of character and the standing to overawe them.

Among Mnyamana's responsibilities as *induna'nkulu* was the overall control of the army. When news came that Lord Chelmsford had crossed the border at Rorke's Drift on 12 January 1879 and attacked *inkosi* Sihayo's followers, Mnyamana played a leading and crucial role in determining the Zulu response, urging that the Zulu army be dispatched to the Rorke's Drift front in response. When on 17 January the army, having been ritually prepared, set out for the border from the kwaNodwengu homestead near oNdini, a number of Mnyamana's sons went with it.

The army, of course, encountered the British column at Isandlwana. Among the Zulus killed was Mnyamana's son Mtumengana. Indeed, so great were the Zulu losses – and so ominous the lessons for future fighting – that Mnyamana urged the king to make peace while he was in a favourable position to do so.

When the army set out again, it did so for the north. This time, *inkosi* Mnyamana accompanied the army in person. It was a measure of the importance Cetshwayo placed on the campaign that he sent with it his most senior and respected councillor to represent his 'eyes and ears' and to personally direct strategy. On 28 March part of the army encountered and drove off the British foray against Hlobane Mountain; on 29 March the whole army attacked Wood's camp at Khambula.

Tactical direction passed to Mnyamana's great friend, Ntshingwayo kaMahole. The difficult ground over which the army was forced to approach, and the eagerness of the younger *amabutho* on either wing, meant that the attack got off to an uncoordinated start, and the Zulus were defeated.

The defeat at Khambula was the turning point in the war, for it was clear that the Zulus had little hope of winning by military means alone. The country was once again filled with mourning; among the dead were two more of Mnyamana's sons. King Cetshwayo tried with increased urgency to open negotiations, but the British were now even less prepared to listen.

On 4 July Chelmsford crossed the Mfolozi River and drew up in formation on the very ground where the Zulus had hoped to trap him. Mnyamana was apparently watching the battle with Cetshwayo's representative, Prince Ziwedu, from a hillside nearby. Sadly, the encircling movements which had proved so destructive at Isandlwana, and which had nearly triumphed at Khambula, were checked by a careful British deployment in square, and again the Zulus were defeated.

Wolseley set about establishing a new regime in the conquered land, setting up thirteen appointees to rule on Britain's behalf. He offered *inkosi* Mnyamana a chieftainship, but Mnyamana refused, partly out of loyalty to Cetshwayo and partly out of uncertainty over the fate of his followers, most of whom were placed under the defector, Prince Hamu kaNzibe.

When Cetshwayo returned to Zululand in 1883, Mnyamana hurried to greet him, and assumed his old role of *induna'nkulu*. But Zululand was in disarray and with the subsequent death of King Cetshwayo the royalist cause was in tatters. *Inkosi* Mnyamana was now in his seventies. He had lived to see the fall of the old Zulu order and the inexorable advance of European encroachment. He died on 29 July 1892.

His great-grandson is Dr Mangosuthu Buthelezi, a prominent politician, founder of the Inkatha Freedom Party and a former Minister of the Interior in the South African government.

Ntshingwayo kaMahole

Ntshingwayo was born about 1810 into the chiefly line of the Khoza people, who lived on the upper reaches of the White Mfolozi, north of Nhlazatshe Mountain.

Little is known about Ntshingwayo's early career. As king, one of Cetshwayo's first acts was to appoint Mnyamana, *inkosi* of the Buthelezi, as his new senior *induna*. Mnyamana and Ntshingwayo were of a similar age and were also personal friends; Ntshingwayo soon found himself enjoying a similar relationship, as a supporter and political ally, with Mnyamana as he had previously with Masiphula. King Cetshwayo appointed Ntshingwayo as commander of the kwaGqikazi royal homestead, and seems to have regarded him as commander-in-chief of the Zulu army.

When, from 1877, the increasingly strained relationship with British Natal seemed likely to spill into open conflict, both Mnyamana and Ntshingwayo advocated a policy of caution. They were fearful of the consequences of going to war with the British, but when the Zulu army left oNdini on 17 January for the border, Ntshingwayo marched with it as senior commander.

On the eve of war Ntshingwayo is described as being about seventy years old, a stocky, powerful man whose grey hairs and paunch belied a physical toughness and commanding presence. Ntshingwayo and his colleague Mavumengwana kaNdlela walked at the head of their men rather than riding horses as many *izinduna* did, setting a comfortable and practical pace which would not exhaust the army.

By 20 January Ntshingwayo had directed the army to move towards the sheltered Ngwebeni Valley. That the move was accomplished on the 21st without discovery by the British was arguably one of the great Zulu masterstrokes of the war.

Ntshingwayo controlled the Zulu advance from the edge of the iNyoni escarpment, overlooking the camp at Isandlwana. His choice of lookout again testifies to his skill and experience; it allowed him a panoramic view of almost the entire battlefield, in contrast to the limited perspective of the British officers at the foot of Isandlwana below. From his position Ntshingwayo recognised danger when he saw the Zulu advance stall; he reacted quickly, sending Mkhosana kaMvundlana to rally the uKhandempemvu and urge them on.

Despite the impromptu nature of the Zulu attack, Isandlwana was very much Ntshingwayo's victory. He had outmanoeuvred Lord Chelmsford, moving his army to within five miles of the British camp without being detected, and his thorough scouting and command briefings laid the basis for the Zulu success

It is a bitter irony that Ntshingwayo, the great Zulu victor of Isandlwana, should have been killed along with more than fifty distinguished men, many of whom had served not only Cetshwayo but King Mpande before him, not by foreign enemies but by his fellow countrymen, in the ensuing civil war which was the logical conclusion of the policy of 'divide and rule' pursued by the British.

Zibhebhu kaMaphitha

Zibhebhu kaMaphitha was one of the most able military commanders to emerge from the 1879 conflict, although, ironically, the full extent of his abilities only became apparent afterwards, to the desperate cost of his countrymen. Zibhebhu was *inkosi* of the Mandlakazi, a section of the Zulu royal house who traced their descent from King Shaka's grandfather, Jama.

Zibhebhu had seen little military action prior to 1879, but his flair soon became apparent. He was commanding the Zulu scouts who, on 21 January, brushed aside a British patrol which very nearly intercepted the movement of the main Zulu army from Siphezi towards Ngwebeni Valley, near Isandlwana. The following day, during the battle of Isandlwana, he commanded the reserve which cut the British line of retreat to Rorke's Drift. He harried the British survivors until they reached the Mzinyathi River, where Zibhebhu abandoned his command and crossed into Natal to plunder cattle on his own account.

Appendix A

The Welsh Question

This question arose following the memorial service for David Rattray at Southwark Cathedral when, during his address to the congregation, Brigadier Aitken stated that many of the names in the regiment today such as Evans, Jones and Williams reflected those from Wales who fought at Rorke's Drift and Isandlwana – as portrayed in the film *Zulu*. However, at the time of the Anglo-Zulu War in 1879, the 24th Regiment was the 2nd Warwickshire Regiment and retained that name until 1881, when it became the South Wales Borderers.

The regiment's depot was established in Brecon in 1873, although few recruits were drawn from that area. The 24th Regimental depot certainly recruited in the counties of Brecknock, Cardigan and Radnor, but for the six years immediately prior to the Anglo-Zulu War it had to look further to neighbouring English counties, especially Monmouth (then an English county), with most of the recruits going to the local 2nd Battalion. The 1st Battalion had seen continuous service in various Mediterranean garrisons for the eight years prior to arriving in South Africa on 4 February 1875. At that point, the 1st Battalion's link with Wales was, at the very best, tenuous; indeed, its Regimental March was *The Warwickshire Lads*, composed for Shakespeare's bicentenary celebrations at Stratford-on-Avon in 1769.

Private Robert Jones VC, 2/24th, born in Monmouthshire, was awarded the Victoria Cross for his part in the defence of Rorke's Drift. To ponder whether he was English or Welsh probably never occurred to him, but he wrote about his experiences:

> On the 22nd January 1879, the Zulus attacked us, we being only a small band of English soldiers. My thought was only to fight as an English soldier ought to for his most gracious Sovereign, Queen Victoria, and for the benefit of old England.

The 2/24th certainly had a handful of Welshmen (born or living in Wales when recruited) serving in its ranks; for example, 'B' Company 2/24th who defend Rorke's Drift contained five Welshmen (see Chapter 1 for details). With regard to the 24th Regiment's Rorke's Drift VCs, Bromhead was born in France (to a Lincolnshire family), Hook was from Gloucestershire, Allen was born in Northumberland (and considered himself a 'Scotchman' by birth), Hitch was a Londoner, William Jones was from Worcestershire, Robert Jones and John Fielding (alias Williams) were from Monmouthshire (then an English county) and Fielding was Irish, although hailing from Abergavenny! Jones, defined by the Oxford Names Dictionary as 'son of John' is, of course, a famously English name too – hence its use for the corporal in *Dad's Army*!

This neatly brings us to the question of Welsh names, or names commonly associated with Wales, and a count of soldiers with these names within the two battalions make interesting reading. Of course, there are numerous problems in using such a rough and completely unscientific method; having a Welsh-sounding name has absolutely nothing necessarily to do with one's origins, for example Private Griffiths VC (killed at Isandlwana) had a Welsh name but was born in Ireland, was attested in Warwick and joined the Regiment at Tamworth. With regard to the 1st Battalion, and to a lesser extent the 2nd, after Isandlwana they were reconstructed with recruits (mainly) from thirteen other regiments, which makes any analysis meaningless.

Medal records are equally ambiguous; many of the 24th recipients of medals, reinforcements after the battle, were posted back to their original units after Isandlwana. They have the South Africa Medal for serving with the 24th, but this would not have been their original unit. Many have no clasp, which appears to indicate that they did not cross into Zululand. Rorke's Drift defenders were a curious exception, since they were all given the clasp yet many did not cross into Zululand. This raises another interesting question: as the 2nd Battalion did not arrive in South Africa until 1878, why did they have 1877-8-9 on their medal bar? So the answer to the original question remains elusive and complex.

Nevertheless, if one considers the Welsh or Welsh-sounding names of casualties at Isandlwana, then a rough indication can be found. I offer the following casualties with Welsh names at Isandlwana (I accept there may well be other Welsh names that I am unaware of):

Davis 4, Edwards 4, Evans 2, Griffiths 1, Hughes 5, Jenkins 3, Jones 6, Lewis 2, Lloyd 1, Morgan 2, Parry 2, Thomas 2, Watkins 1, Williams 10.

The film *Zulu* has much to answer for.

Lieutenant Cochrane's Original Report

(Courtesy of AZWHS Journal 13, unabridged and with
original spelling, grammar and punctuation)

Early on the 20th Colonel Durnford marched to Rorke's Drift, crossing the river by means of the Pont, and establishing himself in a camp about half a mile from the river. Here we remained during the 21st; Captn. George Shepstone rode to Sandhlana [sic] Camp & returned same day. Lieut. Smith-Dorrien rode also to the Camp, & returned with a dispatch on the morning of the 22nd Instant. Colonel Durnford was on the road to the Dutch Farms on the Biggarsberg for the purpose of commandeering the Dutchmen's wagons when the dispatch reached him. I was with Colonel Durnford & he remarked to me "Just what I thought, we are to proceed at once to Sandlwana [sic] . . . There is an Impi about 8 miles from the Camp, which the Colonel moves out to attack at daybreak."

Colonel Durnford returned to Rorke's Drift Camp at once, and marched for Sandlwana at about 7.30 or 8 a.m. My orders were to see all the wagons inspanned, start them all off, and hand them over to Conductor McCarthy & then join Colonel Durnford. I complied with these instructions, and arrived at the Sandlwana Camp, with Colonel Durnford, about 10 or 10.30 a.m. Having made all the necessary arrangements for his Column Col. Durnford took over the command from Colonel Pulleine 1/24th Regt. [When Colonel Durnford reached the camp, he received from Colonel Pulleine all the information he could give, when Colonel Pulleine said, "I'm sorry you have come, as you are senior to me, and will of course take command." Colonel Durnford replied, "I'm not going to interfere with you. I'm not going to remain in camp," or words to that effect. Colonel Pulleine gave over to Colonel Durnford, a verbal state of the troops in camp at the time, and stated the orders he had received, viz., to defend the camp; these words were repeated two or three times in the conversation.]

The news was that a number of Zulus had been seen since an early hour on the top of the adjacent hills, and that an attack had been expected; and in consequence the following disposition of the troops had been made. The Natives of Lonsdale's Contingent were on outpost duty on the hills to the left of the Camp, the guns were in position on the left of the Camp, The Infantry were turned out and formed in Column in the open space in front of the General's tent. The Waggons &c were inspanned. Constant reports came in from the Scouts on the hills to the left, but never anything from the men on the top of the Sandlwana hill that I heard. (1) Some of the reports were: "The Enemy are in force behind the hills on the left" – "The Enemy are in three Columns" – "The Columns are separating, one moving to the left rear & one towards the General" – "The Enemy are retiring in every direction." [The bearer of this was not dressed in any uniform]

Upon this latter report Colonel Durnford said he would go out and prevent the one column from joining the Impi, which was supposed at that time to be engaged with the troops under the General. Colonel Durnford on hearing that one Column of the Enemy was moving towards the left rear, had reinforced the Baggage Guard (which at that time consisted of one Company, Native Contingent) with one troop of mounted Natives; and I understand that Captain George Shepstone was sent back with this part. (2)

[Durnford having decided to take out a force to attack the Zulus who were reported to be retiring in every direction said to Pulleine (3) "I will take out some of my own men if you will let me have a couple of Companies of Infantry to support them." Pulleine replied "I think I can hardly do that. My orders are to defend the Camp and we couldn't spare the men.". Colonel Durnford said, "Very well; perhaps I had better not take them. I will go with my own men."]. Lt. Col. Durnford [said] that the Zulus were retiring and urged in favour of taking the men so that after a while Lt. Col. Pulleine said "Oh very well of course if you order them I'll give you them." Lt. Col. Durnford said "That's all right."

Lt. Col. Pulleine consulted with his Officers and in a few minutes, Lieut. Melville [sic] came up and said "Colonel I really don't think Col. Pulleine would be doing right to send any men out of Camp when his orders are to 'defend the Camp.'" Lt. Col. Durnford replied –"Very well it doesn't much matter we won't take them." His manner was persuasive not peremptory. There were no high words passed. Moreover the manner of the officers to one another was perfectly genial, and the conversation took place over some lunch which Lieut. Col. Pulleine was taking with Lieut. Col. Durnford. Colonel Durnford now sent two troops on the hills to the left under Captain Barton N.N.C. and took with him to the front the remaining two troops, and Russell's Rocket Battery with a Company of the N.N.C. under Captain Nourse as Escort to the Battery. (4) On leaving the camp [he] said to Lt. Col. Pulleine "If you see us in difficulties you must send and support us." (5)

Going at a canter the Rocket Battery & Escort were soon left behind. Having proceeded between 5 and 6 miles, a mounted man came down from the hills on the left, and reported that there was an immense "Impi" behind the hills to our left, and he had scarcely made the report when the Zulus appeared in force in front of us & to our left. They were in skirmishing order but 10 or 12 deep, with supports close behind. They opened fire at us at about 800 yards & advanced very rapidly. We retired some little way, taking up a position in a "Donga" or water course, of which there are several across the plain in front of Sandlwana.

We retired steadily in skirmishing order, keeping up a steady fire for about 2 miles, when we came upon the remains of the Rocket Battery, which had been cut off & broken up. There was a hand to hand engagement going on with those that remained.

The left wing while returning was wheeled up to the right & drove the Zulus back who were not in very large numbers just there at that time. It appears that Captain Russell whilst following up with the Battery, perceived some of the Enemy on his left, he fired three Rockets with some effect; this was followed by a volley from the Zulus, the Native Contingent retired, the mules were frightened & disorder was caused. The Enemy seeing this ran down the hill and attacked the Battery. Captain Russell was killed. As the mounted men retired towards them, the Zulus ran back to their Cover. The retreat was continued until we arrived at a "Donga" about half a mile in front of the Camp. Here a few mounted men, Carbineers, Natal Mounted Police &c – reinforced our right. A stand was made here, but we were eventually driven in, & the Camp was taken from the left. It appears that the mounted men on the left became engaged on the hills about the same time as we were engaged on the flat, and I was informed that they held the Zulus back; but my opinion is that the right of the Enemy were only engaging the troops, and did not intend to advance until their left had worked round; and I believe that Captn. Shepstone (who after the arrival of the baggage, took the troop of mounted natives he had used as escort on the hills to the left) (6) rode down to the Camp & asked in the name of Colonel Durnford for assistance.

This Colonel Pulleine gave him by detaching two Companies of the 24th a little to the left front. These together with the mounted men & Lonsdale's Contingent, fell back into the Camp, & in spite of the Artillery fire and the steady musketry of the Infantry, who were in good position amongst the Stones & Boulders to the left & left centre of the Camp, and who stood their ground most gallantly the Enemy steadily advanced. (7) A general move was made towards the mountain to take up a last position, but it was too late. The Zulus were too quick & fleet of foot; they caught up the men on foot before they could reach the new position, completely overpowering them by numbers & assegaing right and left.

Notes

(1) Cf. Lieutenant Higginson's account.
(2) Cochrane is wrong about Shepstone, who rode out with the two troops mentioned below as being under Captain Barton.
(3) Cochrane is trying to be as precise as possible in this supplementary statement, giving the two officers their formal rank, instead of the informal 'colonel'. He is (incidentally) incorrect in Durnford's case, as that officer had been promoted to brevet colonel in the previous month, although it seems that this was not known in South Africa.
(4) According to the report of Lieutenant Davies, who commanded one of the two troops accompanying Durnford, Durnford with Russell and Nourse left the camp half an hour after Barton.
(5) Cf. the following passage attributable to Cochrane: 'According to the testimony of a special-service officer who was present, and afterwards escaped from the camp, Col. Pulleine went into his tent and brought out his written orders, to which Col. Durnford demurred, so far as to say, "Well, my idea is, that wherever Zulus appear, we ought to attack. I will go alone, but remember, if I get into difficulties I shall rely on you to support me."'. The 'special-service officer' is almost certainly Cochrane.
(6) Shepstone. He picked up Vause's baggage escort on returning to camp to ask for reinforcements.
(7) Up to this time there had been no communication with the camp force, which was about 1000 yards to the left rear, holding the rising ground. Lieutenant Cochrane, observing the Zulus massing at a kraal to the left front, pointed it out to Colonel Durnford, and asked if he should send an orderly to call the attention of the artillery to it. The Colonel said, 'No, they may not attend to him; you had better go yourself.' Cochrane at once rode back to the camp force, but could not find his chief again. One gun was in fact moved in the desired direction, and after firing some shells returned to its previous position.

Appendix C

Colonel Glyn's Report

(A transcript of the original hand-written document signed by
Colonel Glyn using his spelling, grammar and punctuation)

The Deputy Adjutant General
South Africa

Rorke's Drift,
Buffalo River.
February, 21st 1879.

Sir,

I have the honor [sic] to report that on the 22nd January last, when the camp of Isandlwanha [sic] was attacked by the enemy, the Queen's Color [sic] of 1st Battalion 24th Regiment was in the camp – the Headquarters and five companies of the regiment being there also.

From all the information I have been since able to obtain, it would appear that when the enemy had got into the camp, and when there was no longer any hope left of saving it, the Adjutant of the 1/24th Regiment, Lt. Teignmouth Melville [sic], departed from the camp on horseback carrying the Color with him in hope of being able to save it.

The only road to Rorke's Drift being already in possession of the enemy, Lt. Melville and the few others who still remained alive, struck across country for the Buffalo River, which it was necessary to cross to reach a point of safety. In taking this line, the only one possible ground had to be gone over, which, from its ruggedness and precipitous nature, would, under ordinary circumstances, it is reported, be deemed almost utterly impassable for mounted men.

During a distance of about six (6) miles, Lt. Melville and his companions were closely pursued or more properly speaking, accompanied, by a large number of the enemy, who, from their well-known agility in getting over rough ground, were able to keep up with our people though the latter were mounted. So that the enemy kept up a constant fire on them, and sometimes even got close enough to assegai the men and horses.

Lt. Melville reached the bank of the Buffalo and at once plunged in, horse and all. But being encumbered with the Color, which is an awkward thing to carry even on foot, and the river being full and running rapidly, he appears to have got separated from his horse, when he was about half way across. He still however held on resolutely to the Color, and was being carried down stream when he was washed against a large rock in the middle of the river. Lt. Higginson of the Natal Native Contingent, who had also lost his horse in the river, was clinging to this rock, and Lt. Melville called to him to lay hold of the Color. This Lt. Higginson did, but the current was so strong that both officers, with the Color, were again washed away into still water.

In the meantime Lt.Coghill 1/24th Regiment, my Orderly Officer who had been left in camp that morning when the main body of the force moved out, on account of a severe injury to his knee which rendered him unable to move without assistance, had also succeeded in gaining the river's bank in company with Lt. Melville. He too had plunged at once into the river, his horse had carried him safely across but on looking round for Lt. Melville and seeing him struggling to save the Color in the river, he at once turned his horse and rode back into the stream again to Lt. Melville's assistance.

It would appear that now the enemy had assembled in considerable force along their own bank, and had opened a heavy fire on our people directing it more especially on Lt. Melville who wore a red patrol jacket, so that when Lt. Coghill got into the river again his horse was almost immediately killed by a bullet. Lt. Coghill was thus cast loose in the stream also, and notwithstanding the exertions of both these gallant officers, the Color was carried off from them, and they themselves gained the bank in a state of extreme exhaustion.

It would appear that they now attempted to move up the hill from the river bank towards Helpmakaar, but must have been too much exhausted to go on, as they were seen to sit down to rest again. This, I sorely regret to say, was the last time these two most gallant officers were seen alive.

It was not for some days after the 22nd that I could gather any information as to the probable fate of these officers. But immediately I discovered in what direction those who had escaped from Isandlwanha had crossed the Buffalo I sent, under Major Black 2/24 Regt. a mounted party who volunteered for this service, to search for any trace that could be found of them. This search was successful and both bodies were found where they were last seen, as above illustrated. Several dead bodies of the enemy were found about there, so that they must have sold their lives dearly at the last.

As it was considered that the dead weight of the Color would cause it to sink in the river, it was hoped that a diligent search in the locality where the bodies of these officers were found might lead to its recovery. So Major Black again proceeded on the 4th inst. to prosecute this search. His energetic efforts were, I am glad to say, crowned with success, and the Color with the ornaments, case & [sic] belonging to it, were found, though in a different place, in the river bed.

I cannot conclude this report without drawing the attention of H.E., the Lt. General Commanding, in the most impressive manner which words can command, to the noble and heroic conduct of Lt. Adjutant Melville, who did not hesitate to encumber himself with the Color of the Regiment, in his resolve to save it, at a time when the camp was in the hands of the enemy, and its gallant defenders rallied to the last man in its defence, and when there appeared but little prospect that any exertions Lt. Melville would make would enable him to save even his own life. Also later on to the noble perseverance with which when struggling between life and death in the river, his chief thoughts to the last were bent on the saving of the Color.

Similarly would I draw His Excellency's attention to the equally noble and gallant conduct of Lt. Coghill, who did not hesitate for an instant to return, unsolicited, and ride again into the river, under a heavy fire of the enemy, to the assistance of his friend; though at the time he was wholly incapacitated from walking and but too well aware that any accident that might separate him from his horse must be fatal to him.

In conclusion, I would add that both these officers gave up their lives in the truly noble task of endeavouring to save from the enemy's hands the Queen's Color of their Regiment, and greatly though their sad end is to be deplored, their deaths could not have been more noble or more full of honor.

I have the honor to be
Sir
Your obedient Servant
signed R.Glyn Colonel
Commanding 3 Column

Appendix D

Wassall's Escape from Isandlwana

(Private Wassall's story, unabridged and with original spelling, grammar and punctuation)

The only way to escape was by the Buffalo River, six or seven miles away and we had to get cross it into our own territory, Natal. A main road led to the river by the road was cut off by the Zulus and I had to take a road across the veldt, I knew nothing about. But, I was not in the mood to care which way I went so long as it took me away from the enemy, and so I furiously went on, stumbling over the rough rocky ground, expecting every instant that my horse, a Basuto pony would fall. In that case I should not have had a chance for the Zulus would have been upon me before I could have got up again. To this day, I cannot understand how a living soul got away from Isandhlwana [sic], because we were seriously harassed by the savages, shots came after us and clouds of spears, but I did escape from the field of the massacre and reached the Zulu bank of the river, and saw on the other side of the Natal territory, where my only hope of safety lay. I knew how dangerous the river was, there was a current running six or seven mile an hour, no ordinary man could swim it. But, the Zulus had a curious ways of using there elbows which made them able to get across. I drove my horse into the torrent, thankful even to be in that part and was urging him to the other side, when I heard a cry for help and I saw a man of my own Regiment, a Private named Westwood was being carried away. He was struggling, desperately and was drowning. The Zulus were sweeping down to the river bank, which I had just left and there was a terrible temptation to go ahead and just save one's self, but I turned my horse around on the Zulu bank, got him there, dismounted, tied him upto a tree and I never tied him more swiftly. Then I struggled out to Westwood, got hold of him and struggled back to the horse with him. I scrambled up into the saddle, pulled Westwood after me and plunged into the torrent again, and as I did so the Zulus rushed up to the bank and let drive with their firearms and spears, but most mercifully I escaped them all and with a thankful heart urged my gallant horse up the steep bank on the Natal side and then got him to go as hard as he could towards Helpmakaar about fifteen miles from Isandhlwana, where our main camp was. I ought to have gone straight onto Rorke's Drift after escaping from Isandhlwana but the Zulus were already surging on towards the Drift, which was held by a mere handful of men of the 24th, expected to wipe out its defenders as they had wiped out the camp at Isandhlwana. At this time I was very lightly cold, I had thrown my helmet aside and my red tunic off, the British soldiers fought in the good old red in those days and not in khaki, so that I was clothed in just my shirt and trousers with my bandolier over my shirt and so I rode on as hard as I could, with a few of the fugitives from Isandhlwana.

Appendix E

Lieutenant General Lord Chelmsford
to Colonel A.W. Durnford

Hd Qr Camp Zululand near Rorkes Drift
14 January 1879

Unless you carry out the instructions I give you, it will be my unpleasant duty to remove you from your command, and to substitute another officer of No. 2 Column. When a column is acting <u>separately</u> in an <u>enemy's country</u> I am quite ready to give its commander every latitude, and would certainly expect him to disobey any orders he might receive from me, if information which he obtained, showed that it would be injurious to the interests of the column under his command – Your neglecting to obey my instructions in the present instance has no excuse. You have simply received information in a letter from Bishop Schroeder, which may or may not be true and which you have no means of verifying – If movements ordered are to be delayed because report hints at a chance of an invasion of Natal, it will be impossible for me to carry out my plan of campaign – I trust you will understand this plain speaking & not give me any further occasion to write in a style which is distasteful to me.

Appendix F

Chelmsford's Original Battle Orders

(Recovered from Durnford's body. Where words or part-words are unreadable, a possible interpretation is shown in **bold**)

The following Instructions are forwarded for the Consideration of Officers Comdg Col**umns** when entering Zulu**land**.

(1) March as early as possible, so that all the animals may have plenty of time to feed during the day.

(2) Take short marches at first, a slow, steady, advance, will be far better than a quick rush forward.

(3) The first consideration must be how to keep man, & beast, healthy & strong.

(4) The Time is sure to arrive, when it will be necessary, to make a forced march, either to seize a position or to pass over an unhealthy district.

(5) Attention to Rule 3 will enable it to be done in the quickest time possible, and with the le**ast** distress.

(6) Clear and precise orders **will be** issued regarding the order of **march. British** Troops must be prepared to form up for attack, or for defence, in any direction at the shortest possible warning.

(7) The leading Troops must not be allowed to outmarch the Baggage wagons. The latter must be kept together as much as possible, and **should one** break down, or stick fast, those **in** front must not be **allowed to leave** it behind.

(8) British Infantry, should form the advanced, and Rear guards, Mounted men being well to the front, and flanks.

(9) The duty of protecting the flanks, and of helping the wagons, when in difficulties, should as a rule be performed by the Native Contingent.

(10) The ground for encampment (while recognising the necessity of having Wood, & water, at hand) should always be selected, with due regard to the defensive requirements of the situation.

(11) It will be well to establish one Uniform System **of** camping, so that every man always knows his place.

(12) The **camp should** be formed, so that in case of a night attack – every man may fall into his place with the least possible delay, and without confusion.

(13) <u>Every night</u> before the men turn in the Whole Force should be made to assemble quickly, in the position told off to it, in case of **attack** just as is done **in practice** when the Fire bell **is rung.**

(14) Outposts, should **be posted far** in advance of the Camp, and as a rule they should be placed on the ground, best suited for defence. At least one sixth of

the Total Force should be employed on this duty. When thought desirable, a group of six, instead of four, may be placed on the line of sentries. In this case a double, instead of a single sentry – will be required equally in both cases.

(15) In order to obtain the earliest information of a night attack, being intended, a group of British Infantry (six men), and a section of Natives (10 men), under an Officer should be pushed well **forward** to the Front, and to **the rear,** and to, each flank of **the** outposts just before dark. **These** groups of (16) men, should be at least 500 yards in front of the Line of outposts, and should be instructed to fire volleys in case the enemy is discovered to be advancing. Each of the 4 parties should be provided with a Lantern, and Flags, **so that** when having to fall **back to their post** they may not be fired **on by their own** side. They **must also** have the countersign given to them.

(16) The possible tactics of the Zulus are as follows –
a. Avoid the Troops and attack our line of communications.
b. Attack the Column when on the line of march.
c. Attack the camp at night & charge into it with all their numbers.
d. Await attack in position between White, & Black Umvelosi Rivers.

(17) Whatever tactics are adopted, it may be looked upon as a certainty – that when Zulus attack, they will threaten one or both flanks, as well as the front.

(18) The Formation which seems best adapted **to meet** such an attack is as **follows** – British Infantry in Front Line, deployed, or extended, with one or both flank companies thrown back.

Both flank companies thrown back - Native Contingent inline, in echelon [sic] well clear **of each** flank of British **Infantry and** well to the **rear of each** flank. The guns in **the forefront** of British Infantry.

Mounted Infantry in rear of each flank, ready to move round the flanks, and rear, of the enemy.

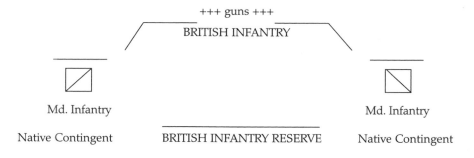

+++ guns +++
BRITISH INFANTRY

Md. Infantry   Md. Infantry

Native Contingent   BRITISH INFANTRY RESERVE   Native Contingent

(19) In an attack by daylight, neither guns nor rockets, - should be allowed to open Fire, until the enemy is within good infantry range, say 600 yards when every available fire arm should be opened upon him.

(20) The British Troops must be told to expect **an** attack upon them by numbers very far in excess of their own and **they must** be cautioned not to **fire until ordered**. A **charge, should it clearly** become necessary, **should** be carried out as **far as possible** without breaking the ranks. This charge might be practised with advantage in presence of the Native Contingent, so that the latter may understand our Tactics, and gain confidence thereby.

(21) In case of attack by day, clear instructions should be given, as to how the wagons & **then other** transport **are** to be placed.

(22) When Halted, Troops should be on the alert at least an hour, before day light.

(23) The more stormy, and wild, the night may be, the more chance there will be of a night attack, if Chaka, and Dingaan's Tactics still hold good.

(signed)   Chelmsford

Lt. Colonel Durnford
Pietermaritzburg
Monday
23.12.78.   Please acknowledge receipt.

[These instructions were addressed and dated as indicated on an envelope]

Colonel Luard to Sir Andrew Clarke on the subject of Colonel Durnford

(Original spelling, grammar and punctuation)

Pietermaritzburg
Natal
22nd January 1885

Dear Sir Andrew Clarke,

Colonel Durnford

Some circumstances of a very remarkable nature in connection with the late Colonel Durnford R.E. one of my predecessors here, have been brought to my notice, & I write to you about them because you are the Head of the Corps, & because you are known as a man who has the power to do whatever you consider should be done.

I have also written to Sir Linton Simmons, who was T.G.F at the time when Colonel Durnford's name was so prominently before the public, & to Sir Gerald Graham, whom I believe to have been a personal friend of Colonel Durnford's, if General C.G. Gordon were in England I would write to him also, as I know he was a personal friend, & that this is a case in which he would take a great interest.

If, after reading this correspondence you will confer with Sir Linton Simmons & Sir Gerald Graham, & will let me know what mode of action it has been decided to adopt in this matter, I shall be much obliged, & I beg that you will understand that whatever trouble it may take, or however unpleasant it may render my position here socially, I as a brother Officer & one of the successors of the late Colonel Durnford, am quite prepared to act, if desired, as a local agent in this matter, & to see that justice is done.

But, after due deliberation I have decided that it is most fit to refer this grave matter in the first instance to officers senior to myself.

I have to go back to this day six year ago, when Colonel Durnford was killed at Isandhlwana [sic]. Dispatches & letters were written, statements & speeches were made & ultimately he was made the scapegoat for the disaster; it is only quite recently that an article by a Military writer appeared in "Blackwood" in which the author was evidently still of opinion that Colonel Durnford was mainly responsible for that disaster to our arms, & this must be assumed to be the general impression both with the general public, & also amongst the great majority of military men, & especially with the latter, as the published official account by the Intelligence Department still conveys that impression.

Prior to the 22nd January 1879 Colonel Durnford received certain orders, & though it was stated soon afterwards & repeated by Lord Chelmsford on the 18th August, & again on the 2nd September 1880 in the House of Lords that Colonel Durnford had received orders to take charge of the camp at Isandhlwana, it subsequently transpired from Colonel Crealock on the 18th May 1882, i.e. nearly three & a half years afterwards by a reference to his note book, that Colonel Durnford had not received orders to take charge of that camp. It must be apparent to any Military man that it never could have been intended that he should have assumed that charge, being at the time in independent command of another column of the army, more especially as not a word appears to have said, either to Colonel Glyn whose camp it was, or to Colonel Pulleine who was left in temporary charge of it, that such a change of command was contemplated! It was also intended to move the camp on up-country as soon as possible.

When Colonel Durnford arrived at the camp, he, as senior officer present seems to have taken cognizance of the state of affairs, so far as it was possible for a man in his position to do, & he stated distinctly that he was not going to remain in camp, an expression of which he certainly would not have made use, had orders been conveyed to him that he was to do so. On the contrary there can be no doubt now that he proceeded on his way to join & help his general in the battle that was supposed to be going on at the front.

However the military authorities refused to allow the question of relative responsibility for the disaster at Isandhlwana to be re opened, & the stigma attached to Colonel Durnford's name never having been publicly removed, will remain till that is done.

But what became of the original order, which was sent to Colonel Durnford? & it is mainly in connection with that subject that I now address you.

For four months the bodies of our slaughtered soldiers laid unburied on the field of Isandhlwana, within eight miles of a British force, & with no one to oppose their burial, but on the 21st May 1879 a cavalry force under General Marshall, composed of the K.D.Gs, the Natal Carbineers, &c., visited the field & buried some of the bodies, including Colonel Durnford's.

In the Natal Witness for the 27th May, & in the supplement of the 7th June, a sentence occurred as follows "after the papers & "maps found on Durnford's person had been removed, a pile of "stones was heaped over the body."

It has been stated to me that this sentence about "the papers "& maps," was originated by a telegram which was received by the Editor of the Witness from a Mr. Dormer, then at Ladysmith, that this gentleman received the information on which his telegram was based directly from the mouth of a Mr. Alfred Davis, one of the proprietors of the Witness newspaper, who was anxious to find the remains of his brother who had fallen at Isandhlwana, that, being at Rorke's Drift in May 1879, & having been a member of the Natal Carbineers Mr. Davis seized the opportunity of one of that Corps being ill to borrow his arms & accoutrements & uniform & accompany the Natal Carbineers, that he found his brother's body & took from the pocket of the jacket his sister's letter, written only a few days before the disaster, which tends to show how little the remains had been disturbed since the battle, that Colonel Durnford's body was found at the same spot & that he Mr. Davis rode post haste to Ladysmith, where he met Mr. Dormer &, being very much fatigued, gave him (Mr. Dormer who was correspondent of another paper) the information for himself, on condition that he would telegraph it to the Witness – which he did.

APPENDIX G

A friend of Colonel Durnford's, on seeing this sentence in the Witness, went & questioned a certain Theophilus Shepstone about it, having been the officer in command of the party of Natal Carbineers who found & buried Colonel Durnford's body, & his reply was that it was quite a mistake, there was no papers of any kind, & could not have been as there was no coat. So the matter was dropped, the questioner having at that time full confidence in the truth of Captain Shepstone's statement.

But on the 22nd May 1879, i.e. the day after the visit to the field of the battle of Isandhlwana, veterinary Surgeon Longhurst K.D.G. writing home to his friends in England, described the burial of Colonel Durnford at which he had been present, & mentioned amongst other articles taken from his body before burial "a letter". When Mr. Longhurst's letter reached its destination a friend of the Durnford family was present, & heard it read aloud, & Colonel E. Durnford about it, who at once wrote out to Natal to request that enquiries might be made. Mr. Longhurst was then in the Transvaal but on his return & before arriving at Pietermaritzburg, he was purposely interviewed by Asst. Comm. General Elmes & he then verbally confirmed what he had previously written home a week afterwards, however during which time he had been in P.M. Burg he declined to answer any questions on the subject.

The K.D.Gs went from Natal to India. Colonel E. Durnford wrote twice, at intervals of six months, to Mr. Longhurst, but these letters were not replied to. A third letter was written & sent to Mr. Longhurst's Commanding Officer, Colonel Master, to be given to Mr. Longhurst, who then, three years having now elapsed since the battle of Isandhlwana, replied, confirming in the most circumstantial way his previous letter. A copy of this letter was sent to Natal to a friend of the late Colonel Durnford, who, anxious that Captain Shepstone would have every chance of proving his innocence or of confessing privately, stipulated that he should be told privately of the contents of Mr. Longhurst's statement.

Captain Shepstone met with a complete denial. But I am informed that he did not merely say "I took no papers", but added, "I could not have taken any because there was no coat on the body."

Captain Shepstone then wrote to Colonel E. Durnford, & sent the names of four persons, viz. Mr. Royston, Mr. Cook, Mr. Macfarlane, & Yabez Mulife, (a Basuto who had been attendant on the late Colonel Durnford), as persons who would support by affidavit the statement that there was no papers & no coat on the body when found.

Captain Shepstone subsequently forwarded affidavits Mr. Royston, Mr. Cook & Yabez Mulife, but not one from Mr. Macfarlane. On these affidavits being forwarded to Natal they were examined by a friend of Colonel Durnford's, & they seemed in several respects so insufficient & unsatisfactory that further reference was made to Captain Shepstone, who caused Mr. Cook to make a second affidavit.

By this time very grave suspicions had arisen in the minds of the late Colonel Durnford's friends that the original orders sent to that officer had been found on his body & concealed, & enquiries were then set on foot with the view of obtaining further information, especially to ascertain whether the body of the late Colonel Durnford had or had not a coat upon it when it was found.

The result of these enquiries seems to establish beyond a doubt the fact that he <u>had</u> a coat on at that time.

209

ISANDLWANA

I must now proceed to explain the position occupied by Captain Shepstone. This gentleman usually known in Natal as "Offy" is the son of Sir Theophilus Shepstone, & is a prominent member of the most powerful & influential family in this Colony. He himself is one of the most astute lawyers in the Colony, & is what is termed a general favorite.

The evidence will be laid before you in extenso presently, but I may say that, when it was far less complete than it is now, the case was submitted to an English Barrister who said it was strong enough to take into any English Court of Justice, i.e. in the Natal Court he seemed to doubt whether justice might be so readily obtained against so powerful & public a man.

It was subsequently submitted privately to a trustworthy lawyer in Natal, who gave it as his private opinion that the case was strong enough to justify any judge in requiring the other side to disprove it, & he has since admitted that if the case were brought into Court. Captain Shepstone must be ruined.

Nevertheless, as an instance of the powerful position held by the Shepstone family in Natal this gentleman whilst giving his private opinion as a friend, refused absolutely to have anything to do with the conduct of the case under any circumstances, as, if he took it up, whether he won or lost it, his position would be rendered so unpleasant that he could scarcely continue to live in the Colony.

I had thought of obtaining an interview with Captain Shepstone, with the view of attempting to get to the bottom of this matter, but I am of opinion that I should not be doing right in taking that step. He has had three chances of clearing himself, & has not availed himself of those chances. In fact it is chiefly due to his attempt to prove too much that the establishment of his guilt has been rendered possible. I do not believe that I am at liberty to render myself individually liable to any legal action which the subtlety of the law might devise, a liability which should be born, if at all, by the Secretary of State for War.

The course which seems the right one to take is that I, as representing the Secretary of State for War, should receive authority to engage the services of a well qualified lawyer, who should be instructed in the first instance to have a private interview with Captain Shepstone, lay before him sufficient evidence to convince him, if he is open to conviction, that his case is one which is sure to go against him if brought into Court, & ask him whether he has anything to urge against a criminal information for theft being laid against him personally.

If he then admits the truth of the charge, & states that he is not alone responsible, & can produce evidence which shall be satisfactory, i.e. if he states – his statement being duly supported; that he took these papers & handed them over to some one else, the prosecution might be diverted to some one even more guilty than himself. If, on the other hand, Captain Shepstone on being interviewed, adhered to his denial, I should have authority to take immediate steps to prosecute him, or take such steps as the law may empower, including the appointment of commissions to take the evidence of those persons in India or elsewhere whose evidence is so important.

I may say that there is one lawyer in Natal in whose ability to conduct such a case & in whose intrepidity to undertake it, regardless of consequences, I should have full confidence, & I should be prepared, if duly authorised, to instruct him accordingly.

210

But as it is possible that, for some reason or other, at present unknown (for I have not communicated with him.) that gentleman may decline to undertake the case, it would be most advisable that a well qualified should be sent from England with full instructions how to proceed, & who should act, if possible, with the lawyer above referred to, who otherwise would be secured by the defendant.

It is, however, for consideration whether, if prosecution has to be undertaken such action should be instituted in our English Court or in a Natal Court, for it must be borne in mind that several of the most important witnesses are colonial gentlemen who are intimately acquainted with, & are in some cases personal friends of Captain Shepstone & the temptation to avoid the consequences of having been instrumental in ruining that gentleman viz the weight of displeasure which could be exerted by members of his powerful family, might have a deterrent effect in obtaining confirmatory of the statements they have made.

This is a point which should be determined beforehand & on which I should receive instructions, but it is manifest that much care would have to be taken to ensure the arrangements being such as will conduce to success & not to failure. But, whatever course it is decided to adopt, I wish it to be clearly understood that it is not in the smallest degree from what is termed a feeling of revenge, that any of these preliminary steps have been undertaken.

All who have been interested in this matter have worked from no other feeling than the earnest desire that a gallant soldier who, whatever others may have done, did his duty nobly & well, shall not be defamed. They have felt as I feel that no conduct is more disgraceful, no act more cowardly, than defamation of the dead.

Captain Shepstone is one whose connection with the case must be considered from an abstract point of view. I am only one of a vast number of people who would regard his conviction as a matter most sad in itself, but justice must take its course, &, if convicted he must take on his own head the full consequence of his crime. Something will at all events been done to show what means were adopted to ruin the reputation of as gallant a soldier as ever breathed.

I am Dear Sir Andrew Clarke
     Yours vy truly
      C E Luard.

Appendix H

Curling's Letter Home

Helpmakaar Feb 2nd
Natal

My dear Mama,

Now things have quieted down again a little, I can tell you more about what has happened. I trust you had no false report: I saw the first man who went into Pietermaritzburg with the news and I hope you may have had no anxiety.

On the morning of the fight, the main body left at 3.30 in the morning, a little before daylight, leaving us with two guns and about 70 men. About 7.30 we were turned out as about 1000 Zulus were seen in some hills about 2 miles from the camp. We did not think anything of it and I was congratulating myself on having an independent command. I had out with my guns only 20 men, the remainder 50 in number stayed in the camp. We remained formed up in front of the camp (it was about 1/2 mile long) until 11 o'clock, when the enemy disappeared behind some hills on our left, we returned to camp. We none of us had the least idea that the Zulus contemplated attacking the camp and, having in the last war often seen equally large bodies of the enemy, never dreamed they would come on. Besides, we had about 600 troops (regulars), two guns, about 100 other white men and at least 1000 armed natives.

About 12, as the men were getting their dinner, the alarm was again given and we turned out at once. Maj. Smith came back from the General's force at this time and took command. This of course relieved me of all responsibility as to the movement of the guns. We, being mounted, moved off before the infantry and took up a position to the left front of the camp where we were able to throw shells into a huge mass of the enemy that remained almost stationary. The 24th Regt. came up and formed in skirmishing order on both our flanks. The Zulus soon split up into a large mass of skirmishers that extended as far round the camp as we would see.

We could form no idea of numbers but the hills were black with them. They advanced steadily in the face of the infantry and our guns but I believe the whole of the natives who defended the rear of the camp soon bolted and left only our side of the camp defended. Very soon bullets began to whistle about our heads and the men to fall.

The Zulus still continued to advance and we began to fire case but the order was given to retire after firing a round or two.

At this time, out of my small detachment, one man had been killed, shot through the head, another wounded, shot through the side and another through the wrist. Maj. Smith was also shot through the arm but was able to do his duty. Of course, no wounded man was attended to, there was no time or men to spare. When we got the order to retire, we limbered up at once but were hardly in time as the Zulus were on us at once and one man was killed (stabbed) as he was mounting in a seat on the gun carriage. Most of the gunners were on foot as there was not time to mount them on the guns.

We trotted off to the camp thinking to take up another position but found it was in possession of the enemy who were killing the men as they ran out of their tents. We went right through them and out the other side, losing nearly all our gunners in doing so and one of the two sergeants. The road to Rorke's Drift that we hoped to retreat by was full of the enemy so, no way being open, we followed a crowd of natives and camp followers who were running down a ravine. The Zulus were all among them, stabbing men as they ran.

The ravine got steeper and steeper and finally the guns stuck and could get no further. In a moment the Zulus closed in and the drivers, who now alone remained, were pulled off their horses and killed. I did not see Maj. Smith at this moment but was with him a minute before.

The guns could not be spiked, there was no time to think of anything and we hoped to save the guns up to the last moment.

As soon as the guns were taken, I galloped off and made off with the crowd. How any of us escaped, I don't know; the Zulus were all around us and I saw men falling all round. We rode for about 5 miles, hotly pursued by the Zulus, when we came to a cliff overhanging the river. We had to climb down the face of the cliff and not more than half those who started from the top got to the bottom. Many fell right down, among others, Maj. Smith and the Zulus caught us here and shot us as we climbed down. I got down safety and came to the river which was very deep and swift. Numbers were swept away as they tried to cross and others shot from above.

My horse, fortunately, swam straight across, though I had three or four men hanging on his tail, stirrup leathers, etc. After crossing the river, we were in comparative safety, though many were killed afterwards who were on foot and unable to keep up. It seems to me like a dream, I cannot realise it at all. The whole affair did not last an hour from beginning to end. Many got away from the camp but were killed in the retreat. No officers or men of the 24th Regt. could escape: they were all on foot and on the other side of the camp. I saw two of them, who were not with their men, near the river but their bodies were found afterwards on our side of the river.

Of the 50 men we left in camp, 8 managed to escape on spare horses we had left in camp. One sergeant only, of my detachment, got away. Altogether, we lost 62 men and 24 horses, just half the battery.

Those who have escaped have not a rag left as they came away in their shirtsleeves. We always sleep at night in the fort or laager, as it is called, and in the open air. It is very unpleasant as it rains nearly every night and is very cold.

We none of us have more than one blanket each, so you can see we are having a rough time. The first few days I was utterly done up but have pulled round all right now.

What is going to happen, no one knows. We have made a strong entrenchment and are pretty safe even should we be attacked. The only thing we are afraid of is sickness. There are 50 sick and wounded already who are all jammed up at night in the fort. The smell is terrible, 800 men cooped up in so small a place. Food, fortunately, is plentiful and we have at least a three months supply. All spys [sic] taken now are shot: we have disposed of three or four already.

Formerly, they were allowed anywhere and our disaster is to a great extent due to their accurate information of the General's movements. What excitement this will cause in England and what indignation.

The troops, of course, were badly placed and the arrangements for defending the camp indifferent but there should have been enough troops and the risk of leaving a small force to be attacked by 10 to 15 times its number should not have been allowed. As you have heard, there were no wounded, all the wounded were killed in a most horrible way. I saw several wounded men during the retreat, all crying out for help, as they knew the terrible fate in store for them. Smith-Dorrien, a young fellow in the 95 Regt., I saw dismount and try to help one. His horse was killed in a minute by a shot and he had to run for his life only escaping by a miracle. You will see all sorts of accounts in the papers and no end of lies. Most of those who escaped were volunteers and native contingent officers who tell any number of lies. We hear the General has telegraphed for 6 Regiments and a cavalry Brigade. Even with these troops, it will take a long time to finish the war. It takes months to accustom troops to the country and in fact they are quite unfit for fighting in the Field as they require such enormous baggage trains. The colonial troops move without anything and always sleep in the open. We shall get no assistance from natives now as they do not believe in us anymore.

Your letters still arrive pretty regularly and are a great treat. I am very sorry to hear about Emmy but trust it is only a mild attack. It is unfortunate, as it will delay your journey very much.

I am very glad Papa continues pretty well. It will be rather a risk crossing the channel and travelling through France if the weather continues so severe. I think I must be promoted by now: I do hope I may get a good fall. It will be depressing indeed if I get out of this safely to be sent to some out of the way part of the world.

All those who escaped have sent in reports, by order, which will probably be published, so you will hear eventually the truth about this sad disaster. The General, poor fellow, seemed quite off his head and so nothing is being done, nor it would seem, has he recovered himself yet.

Give my love to all at home and believe me,

Your most affect. Son
H T Curling

Appendix I

Dogs of the 22nd January 1879

(AZWHS Journal 24, courtesy of Ian Knight)

Soldiers, it seems, love a pet, and certainly the British Army in the 1870s was no different. In a male dominated environment, pets offer a reminder of finer feelings not often displayed in an often harsh existence, reflecting a touch of humanity in contrast to the stresses of campaign life. Hounds were, of course, a feature of the life of the gentry in Victorian times, particularly those with country houses who indulged an interest in field spots, and many officers kept dogs of one sort or another, and often took them to war with them. The Other Ranks were seldom in a position to enjoy such luxuries, but often accumulated strays who were attracted by the smells of the cook-house and who were then seduced away by proffered scraps of food. Certainly the 2/24th had found its fair share of pets during its time on the Eastern Cape Frontier, but to the men's disappointment they were ordered to leave them behind when moving to Natal. Only Col. H.J. Degacher's dog, a Dalmatian named Flip, was excepted.

> Orders were issued that no dogs could be taken, because by this time many had been collected by the men as pets.
> We entrained and left for East London on the new railway, with perhaps forty dogs of all breeds, sizes and colours galloping alongside the train, encouraged by the men shouting, calling and cheering them on, and the dogs all barking and whining at being left behind. The dogs gradually fell out or they became tired, until after a few miles the only one left was Kreli the yellow dog, who continued to keep up with the train 'midst the cheers of the men, the barking of his chum Flip, who was on the train.
> At last the Colonel ordered the train to be stopped for Kreli, and he was helped on to rejoin Flip. The Colonel's kind act was loudly cheered by everyone.
> (1)

Both Flip and Kreli remained with the battalion as it marched to join the Centre Column at Helpmakaar, and no doubt a few others were picked up along the way; and there is no reason to suppose that the 2/24th were any different to any other unit about to go to war. Certainly, Surgeon Reynolds, of Rorke's Drift fame, had his terrier Dick (2) with him, and by the time the Centre Column crossed into Zululand there were many other dogs with it.

The events of 22 January fell harshly on animals as well as men. In the fury of the close-quarter fighting at iSandlwana, the Zulus stabbed at anything that moved and men, oxen, horses, mules and dogs were all killed. At Rorke's Drift later that day, Surgeon Reynolds tended the wounded with Jack barking at his side.

After the fighting, some of the dogs who had been in the camp at iSandlwana managed to make their way back to Rorke's Drift:

> A few hours later Flip came into camp with a rope tied to his neck, and a severe spear wound in the shoulder. Everyone crowded to see and to cheer Flip, the only living thing [sic] to survive the battle where we lost a thousand killed that day. Apparently after being wounded a Zulu led Flip off, and the dog broke away and returned to his master. The yellow dog Kreli was not seen again. In the regiment Kreli was not forgotten, we spoke of him affectionately for many years, this kindly common Kaffir dog that we found in one war and lost in another. (3)

Flip was not the only canine survivor of the battle. The *Graphic* published a picture of 'a splendid animal, who was in the thick of the fight on January 22, and was fortunate enough to escape from the carnage [and] belonged to the late Lieutenant Daly of the 24th Regiment, who was one of the victims of that disaster."Don"is still suffering from two large assegai wounds inflicted by the Zulus, and he will probably carry his honourable scars to the end of his life'. (4)

There is a distinct possibility that'Don' is a mis-transcription of'Lion', the 1/24th's dog, a known survivor of iSandlwana who today has an impressive memorial in County Kilkenny in Ireland. The memorial stone reads:

> This faithful creature followed the fortunes of the battalion throughout the Kaffir and Zulu War of 1877-78-79 and was severely wounded at the battle of Isandlwana. (5)

Other survivors were not so lucky. Many ran away, terrified no doubt by the sound of battle, and returned to iSandlwana to find their masters dead. With no one to feed them, they survived by eating the carrion left on the field. According to Lt. Maxwell of the NNC, their end was a sorry one:

> About half a mile from the camp [Rorke's Drift] I was attacked by a pack of dogs about 20, consisting of various breeds. Newfoundlands, pointers, Setters, terriers etc a few with collars. These were the dogs that had belonged to the camp at Isandhlwana and having lost their masters, and been in the fighting, had become wild and although I tried, by calling them and whistling, could not quiet them, they followed still barking and howling some 3 or 400 yards, when they left me. These were shot at different times with very few exceptions afterwards. (6)

Indeed, the luckless Army dogs were destined to share their masters' fortunes throughout the war. Arriving at the site of the Ntombe disaster on 12 March, Major Tucker of the 80th Regiment noted that in addition to the soldiers the Zulus had'killed all the dogs save one, and that we found with an assegai wound right through its neck'. (7) When the Prince Imperial rode out on his last fatal patrol from the Thelezeni camp on 1 June the party was accompanied by a pet belonging to Bettington's Horse; the dog, too, was killed alongside the Prince in the skirmish later that day. At the battle of

Ulundi on 4 July the regimental mascot of the 17th Lancers, a big cross-breed, distinguished itself at the end of the battle by running around in the long grass, sniffing out wounded Zulus and barking at them, drawing them to the attention of parties of auxiliaries who were killing any who showed signs of life.

Dogs appear in many of the photos of British troops taken on campaign, particularly officer groups. An unnamed dog sits at the feet of a study of officers of HMS *Active*, another beside officers of the 91st Regiment, another nestles on the lap of an officer of the 90th, while no less than three appear in a photograph of D Company of the 1/13th Regiment. Commandant Pieter Raaff was photographed standing beside his horse – and two impressive hounds.

One question about the 'dogs of war' in Zululand remains; who is the dog in the famous photograph of B Company, 2/24th, taken at Pinetown at the end of the war? It has often been identified as Pip, a terrier belonging to Lt. Bromhead's senior officer in B Company, Captain A.G. Godwin-Austen. Godwin-Austen was wounded on the Cape Frontier and when he returned to England apparently left Pip with Bromhead. Yet the dog in the photo appears to be a spaniel, not a terrier, and he sits beside a private soldier, not Bromhead. Pip, indeed, was probably left at the Eastern Cape, when only Flip and the ill-fated Kreli were allowed to accompany the battalion to Natal. Whoever the dog in the photo is, he was probably picked up by the company along the way of its travels after Rorke's Drift.

Notes

(1) Account by Private Buckley of B Co 2/24th c. 1930, *Events Remembered*, Lugg Papers, Killie Campbell Library, KwaZulu Natal

(2) The dog present in the battle at Rorke's Drift belonged to Reynolds, although his name is given variously as Dick or Jack. Since he was a Jack Russell, this may have confused the matter.

(3) *Events Remembered*, Lugg Papers, Killie Campbell Library, KwaZulu Natal

(4) The *Graphic*, 17 May 1879

(5) My thanks to Ian Woodason for drawing attention to this point

(6) *Reminiscences of the Zulu War*, Maxwell,J., University of Cape Town, 1979

(7) Major Charles Tucker, letter to his father dated Luneburg 19 March 1879, reproduced in *The Red Soldier*, Emery, F., Hodder & Stoughton, 1977

Appendix J

Sister Janet Wells at Isandlwana

Following her tour of duty at Utrecht in September 1879, Nurse Wells was sent via Rorke's Drift to Durban for repatriation home to the UK. Whilst at Rorke's Drift she took time to visit Isandlwana, and was probably the very first lady civilian to do so.

She collected a variety of relics, including Zulu spearheads and sticks; she also collected as souvenirs some of the pieces of paper that had been caught in bushes or among the rocky outcrops that studded the area. Some of the papers were especially poignant, such as a frontispiece from Dickens' *Pickwick Papers* and part of a letter signed 'From your own Madgie' and still legible despite being exposed to sun and rain for nearly ten months. She also picked up two pages of Romans and Corinthians torn from a pocket Bible. She found a page ripped from a soldier's pay-book which had belonged to Private Thomas Vedler of 'C' Company 2/24th Regiment, who had perished along with Captain Younghusband.

A full biographical account can be found in *Sister Janet*, Best, B., Pen & Sword Books, 2004.

Bibliography

Books

Ashe, W. and Edgell, E., *The Story of the Zulu Campaign*, Sampson Low, 1880

Atkinson, C., *The South Wales Borderers 24th Foot 1689-1937*, Cambridge University Press, 1937

Clements, W., *The Glamour and Tragedy of the Zulu War*, Bodley Head, 1936

Colenso, F., *History of the Zulu War and its Origins*, Chapman & Hall, 1885

Coupland, R., *Isandhlwana: Zulu Battle Piece*, Collins, 1948

Cunyngham, *My Command in South Africa*, Macmillan, 1879

Droogleever, R., *The Road to Isandhlwana*, Greenhill Books, 1979

Emery, F., *The Red Soldier*, Hodder & Stoughton, 1977

French, G., *Lord Chelmsford and the Zulu War*, Unwin Brothers, 1939

Glover, M., *Rorke's Drift*, Wordsworth Military Library, 1997

Hope, R., *The Zulu War and the 80th Regiment of Foot*, Churnet Valley Books, 1997

Knight, I., *Anatomy of the Zulu Army*, Greenhill Books, 1995

Knight, I., *Reasons of Defeat at Isandlwana 1879*, MI, 1986

Knight, I., *The Sun Turned Black*, Waterman, 1995

Knight, I., *The Zulu War – Then and Now*, Plaistow Press, 1993

Knight, I., *There Will Be an Awful Row at Home About This*, West Valley Books, 1987

Knight, I., *Zulu: Isandlwana & Rorke's Drift, 22-23 January 1879*, Windrow & Greene, 1992

Lock, R., *Blood on the Painted Mountain*, Greenhill Books, London, 1995

Lloyd, Lt., *On Active Service*, Chapman & Hall, 1890

Montague, W., *Campaigning in South Africa*, 1880

Morris, D., *The Washing of the Spears*, Cardinal, 1964

Mossop, G., *Running the Gauntlet*, Nelson, 1937

Norburg, H., *The Naval Brigade in South Africa*, 1880

Norris-Newman, C., *In Zululand with the British in 1879*, W.H. Allen, 1879

Payne & Payne, *The Harford Diaries*, Ultimatum Tree, 2008

Ritter, E., *Shaka Zulu*, Penguin, 1955

Smith-Dorrien, H., *Memories of Forty-Eight Years Service*, Murray, 1925

Stalker, Rev. J. (ed), *The Natal Carbineers 1855-1911*, Davis, 1912

Temple, B., *A Treatise on the British Martini-Henry*, Greenhill Books, 1983

Wood, E., *From Midshipman to Field Marshal*, Methuen, 1906

Worsfold ,W., *Sir Bartle Frere: a Footnote to the History of the British Empire*, Butterworth, 1923

Official Records and Journals

1. *Archives of the Anglo Zulu War 1879*, Archival Publications International, 1999
2. Blue Books Nos. 2222–2505, 1878–1880, AZWHS
3. Journals 1-28, AZWHS

4. Cope, R., 'Political Power within the Zulu Kingdom', *Journal of Natal and Zulu History*, 1985
5. Laband, J. (ed), 'Lord Chelmsford's Zululand Campaign 1878–1879', Army Records Society Vol. 10, 1994
6. *Narrative of the Field Regulations connected with the Zulu War*, War Office, 1880
7. *Précis of the Zulu War*, Intelligence Division War Office, 1879
8. Killlie Campbell Africana Library, Durban
9. *Royal Engineers Journal*, 2 February 1880

Author's practical research
Fifty expeditions over twenty-one years to investigate and walk the (roughly) 200 square miles of the battlefield of Isandlwana.

Index